THE GOSPELS TODAY

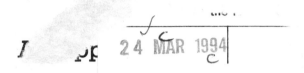

ospels for GCSE

Eileen Bromley

Stanley Thornes (Publishers) Ltd

For Eirlys, whose faith is a continuing inspiration

First published in 1990 by:
Stanley Thornes (Publishers) Ltd
Old Station Drive
Leckhampton
CHELTENHAM GL53 0DN
England

British Library Cataloguing in Publication Data
Bromley, Eileen
    The gospels today.
    1. Bible. N. T. Synoptic Gospels
    I. Title
    226

ISBN 1-871402-33-6

Typeset in 10½/12 pt Palatino by Tech-Set, Gateshead, Tyne & Wear.
Printed and bound in Great Britain at The Bath Press, Avon.

Note: The following abbreviations are used to denote the different versions of the Bible quoted in the text.

GNB	The *Good News Bible*
NEB	*New English Bible*
RSV	*Revised Standard Version*

Contents

Preface

> One very important point to bear in mind . . . is that . . . the texts are not to be studied merely as pieces of ancient history. This has unfortunately been the case in the past and it has robbed them both of their interest and relevance. They are to be seen much more as they are in reality, that is, as authoritative documents which are used to guide and inspire the faithful today.
>
> From Religious Studies GCSE. A Guide for Teachers. *SEC, 1986*

This book is an attempt to consider the Synoptic Gospels in a contemporary as well as in a first-century setting, which, as the above quotation suggests, is a requirement of GCSE Religious Studies. The book provides a comprehensive coverage of the sections of the Synoptic Gospels included in the GCSE syllabuses: there is far more material here than can be used in any one course. The Gospels considered in each Topic are indicated on the contents page, but teachers will need to refer to the biblical index on p. 198 in order to select those sections which are relevant to the syllabus being studied. It will also be necessary for teachers to be selective in the activities they recommend for their pupils; but this is from considerations of time rather than content. Any activities with a restricted application to one or two syllabuses are indicated as such in the text (see, for example, p. 94 Activity 1).

This is not a textbook which provides all the answers. The intention is to stimulate rather than to spoon-feed. The activities are therefore research-based, and stimulus material of various kinds and from various Christian traditions is included to promote thought and discussion. (Details of the sources of quoted material are given in the appendix on p. 196.) It is necessary throughout to refer to the Gospel text being studied. The version used here is the *Good News Bible*, but questions would need little adjustment to be used with other versions. As well as research-based activities, short-answer questions, structured questions, essays and suggestions for coursework are included. Many of the activities, other than those specifically intended as coursework, may be adapted as such. Since requirements for coursework vary with the different boards, the length or nature of the assignments may need to be modified.

The first five Topics provide a general background to the Gospels and introduce pupils to various skills. Topics 6–25 are each divided into three parts: Setting the Scene, To Help You Understand and To Keep You Thinking.

- **Setting the Scene** is relevant to all the Gospels studied in the Topic.

- **To Help You Understand** has sections relevant to all the Gospels and sections relevant to only one or two Gospels. It is not necessary for pupils to read all of these sections. The Gospels concerned are indicated to the left of the text by

  MARK
  LUKE
  MATTHEW

  Follow these 'flags' in order to read the text that is relevant to the particular syllabus concerned. Ignore sections that are not included in the syllabus – for instance, if pupils are studying Mark's Gospel, they should not read sections labelled **LUKE** or **MATTHEW**. Pupils should read all the relevant sections with close reference to the biblical passages.

- The final part of each Topic, **To Keep You Thinking,** hints at issues in the Gospels which are still of vital importance to Christians today and which are also relevant to the 'Christianity' and 'Christian Perspectives' syllabuses of the various boards. These issues are expanded further in the companion volume *Christian Issues in the Gospels*.

It is hoped that teachers will find the two books to be useful tools in encouraging pupils to consider the Gospel texts as 'a living element in the Christian community today' (ibid).

Eileen Bromley, 1990

Notes for Pupils

1 The intention of this book is that you should enjoy your study of the Gospels and understand how Christians find them relevant to life and worship today. The activities encourage you to carry out research, surveys, practical tasks and role-play, and also provide opportunities for discussion and written work. You are much more likely to understand and remember something which you have thought out for yourself, so you are required to be very much involved as you use this book.

2 You will not be able to use all the material in this book. Not all of it is included in your syllabus. You will know which Gospel(s) you are studying, and you may be given a list of set passages. The biblical index on p. 198 indicates where passages from the Gospels are considered in this book.

3 It is essential that every time you open this book you also open and refer to your Bible. You will find that you are unable to answer the questions without referring to your Bible. Remember that your examination is on the text of the Gospels, and not on the contents of a textbook!

Acknowledgements

The author wishes to thank the following for their valuable help in the preparation of the manuscript:

Ron Abbott, Rev Norman Barr, Dr Roger Calvert, Christine Clapinson, Rev David Coombe, Geoff Crowther, Audrey Cull, Rev Fred Dawson, Ken Day, Margaret Fell, Father Keith Frisby, Professor Ken Kitchen, Rev Fred Pritchard, Keith Robinson, Ian Varey, Brenda Whittam, and staff and young people of Kibworth C of E Primary School, Caldecote Junior School, Leicester, and Kibworth Methodist Youth Fellowship.

A particular debt of gratitude is owed to Catherine Hubbard, Mike Rigby, John Pride and Philippa Tomlinson for their encouragement and guidance.

The author and publishers are grateful to the following for permission to reproduce material:

The Associated Press, for material which appeared in the *Daily Telegraph*, p. 112 • Gordon Bailey, for the poem 'Out of Reach' by John Dutton, p. 186 • The Baptist Times, for the headline, p. 79 • Christian Weekly Newspapers Limited for the headline from the Church of England newspaper, 20.1.89, p. 109; and for the extract from the Church of England newspaper, August 1973, p. 23 • Church House Publishing, for material from *The Alternative Service Book 1980* copyright © The Central Board of Finance of the Church of England, p. 48 • William Collins Sons & Co Ltd, for extracts from C S Lewis, *Miracles* © 1947, p. 39; and C S Lewis, *Mere Christianity* © 1955, p. 122 • The Daily Mail, p. 28 • J M Dent & Everyman's Library, for the extract from G L May, *English Religious Verse* © 1937, p. 145 • Timothy Dudley-Smith, for the hymn 'Tell out, my soul' © Timothy Dudley-Smith, reproduced by permission, p. 41 • Ewan MacNaughton Associates, for material which appeared in the *Daily Telegraph*, pp. 28, 76, 79, 146, 150, 152 • Hamish Hamilton Ltd, for the extract from *Personal Mark* by Alec McCowen, 1984, © Alec McCowen. Reproduced by permission of Hamish Hamilton Ltd, p. 66 • The Harborough Mail, pp. 79, 155 • Hodder & Stoughton Ltd/New English Library Ltd for the extract from an article by Fr John Redford in the *Catholic Newspaper* supplement 1987, p. 179 • International Commission on English in the Liturgy, for excerpts from the English translation of *The Roman Missal* © 1973, International Committee on English in the Liturgy, Inc. All rights reserved, p. 124 • Intervarsity Press, for extracts from Dick France, *The Man They Crucified* (republished in 1989 under the new title *Jesus The Radical*), pp. 100, 107 • The Leprosy Mission, Goldhay Way, Orton Goldhay, Peterborough PE2 0GZ, p. 83 • The Methodist Publishing House, (© Methodist Conference Office), p. 130 • The Methodist Recorder, p. 79, and p. 90, quoted from The Reverend John C Trevenna, writing in *The Methodist Recorder* of 25/8/88 • Thomas Nelson and Sons Ltd, p. 109 • The Observer, for material which appeared in the *Observer* newspaper © The Observer, pp. 45, 108 • Oxford University Press, for extracts from H Bettenson (ed), *Documents of the Christian Church*, pp. 22, 23, 30, 32; pp. 71, 80; the quotation from Tertullian in H Bettenson, *The Early*

Christian Fathers, 1956, p. 192 ● The Paternoster Press Ltd, pp. 44, 155, 189 ● Penguin Books Ltd, for the extract from *The Dead Sea Scrolls in English*, G Vermes (Penguin Books, Third Edition, 1987), copyright © G Vermes, 1962, 1965, 1968, 1975, 1987), reproduced by permission of Penguin Books Ltd, p. 82 ● Reuters Limited, for material which appeared in the *Daily Telegraph*, p. 79 ● The Saint Andrew Press, for the extracts from W Barclay, *The Gospel of Mark*, 1964, pp. 68, 91; the extract from W Barclay, *The Gospel of Matthew*, 1965, p. 108 ● SCM Press, for the extract from T W Manson, *The Sayings of Jesus*, SCM Press 1949, p. 106; the extract from A M Hunter, *The Gospel According to St Paul*, SCM Press 1966, p. 195 ● Inter-Schools Christian Fellowship (Scripture Union in Schools), p. 77 ● News Group Newspapers Ltd, for the article which appeared in the *Sun*, p. 28 ● Syndication International (1986) Ltd, for the article which appeared in the *Daily Mirror*, p. 28 ● Viking Penguin for the extract from *The Bible of the World* by Robert O Ballou. Shorter version based on King James Version copyright 1952, renewed copyright © 1980 by Viking Penguin. Reprinted by permission of the publisher, Viking Penguin, a division of Penguin Books USA Inc., p. 115.

Further details of quoted material are given in the Appendix on pp. 196 and 197.

Quotations from the *Good News Bible* are reproduced by permission of The Bible Society.

Quotations from the *New English Bible* are reproduced from New English Bible, second edition © 1970 by permission of Oxford and Cambridge University Presses.

Scripture quotations from the *Revised Standard Version* are reproduced from the Revised Standard Version of the Bible, copyright © 1946, 1952, 1971 by the Division of Christian Education of the National Council of the Churches of Christ in the USA, 475 Riverside Drive, New York, NY 10115. Used by permission.

Every effort has been made to contact copyright holders, and we apologise if any have been overlooked.

The author and publishers are grateful to the following for permission to reproduce copyright photographs and drawings:
Barnaby's Picture Library, pp. 17, 157 ● Bible Society, pp. 61, 127 (Annie Vallotton); 73; 123 (top) (Horace Knowles); 160, 185 ● Bibliotheque Nationale Louvre, p. 189 ● The Bridgeman Art Library, p. 45 (top) ● The British Library, pp. 30 (left), 32 (left), 34 (left) ● Cambridge University Library, p. 115 ● Camera Press, p. 94 ● J. Allan Cash, pp. 11 (right), 24 (right), 93, 132 (bottom), 136 (top), 148, 159 ● The Church Missionary Society, pp. 143, 191 (bottom) ● C J Clapinson, pp. 2 (top right), 16 (left), 141, 151, 164 ● Cliff College, p. 27 ● Coventry Cathedral, pp. 175, 186 ● Geoff Crowther, pp. 29, 72 ● Ken Day, p. 177 ● Dr D R de Lacey, p. 8 ● Dean and Chapter of Westminster, p. 144 ● Derby Evening Telegraph, pp. 113, 156, 191 (top) ● Keith Ellis, pp. 52, 170 ● Margaret Fell, p. 163 ● Fellowship Tours, p. 16 (right) ● Fitzwilliam Museum, Cambridge, pp. 39 (bottom), 55 ● The Flour Advisory Bureau Ltd, p. 75 ● Fotomas Index, p. 155 ● Paul Gatenby, pp. 38, 62, 134, 171 ● Gemeinde Oberammergau, pp. 178, 183 (bottom) ● Glasgow City Art Gallery, p. 184 ● Sonia Halliday, pp. 2 (middle right), 9, 11 (left), 48, 49, 59, 78, 81, 123 (bottom), 128, 130, 136 (bottom), 188 ● Robert Harding Picture Library, p. 60 (top) ● F N Hepper, pp. 104, 119 ● Avi Hirschfeld, p. 19 ● Michael Holford, p. 169 ● Hulton-Deutsch Collection, pp. 2 (bottom left), 84 ● Israel Antiquities Authority, p. 66 ● Israel Colour Slides, p. 76 ● Graham Jeffery (The Barnabas Bible, Wolfe Publishing), pp. 131, 180 ● Frank Lane, p. 194 ● Hugh J McGough, p. 183 (top) ● Magnum/Erich Lessing, p. 121 (top) ● The Mansell Collection, p. 7 ● Middle East Archives, pp. 63, 107, 174 ● MEPhA/Alistair Duncan, pp. 15 (bottom), 142, 162 ● Professor Alan Millard, p. 149 ● The National Gallery, pp. 46 (left), 125 ● The National Trust, p. 111 ● Ny Carlsburg Glypotek, Copenhagen, p. 22 ● Palphot, p. 176 ● Ann & Bury Peerless, p. 14 (bottom) ● Keith Orchard Robinson FRSA, pp. 67, 172 (top) ● The Vicar and PCC of St. Matthew's Church, Northampton, p. 51 ● Ronald Sheridan/Ancient Art & Architecture Collection, pp. 14 (top), 45 (bottom), 99, 138 ● Tear Fund, p. 154 ● The Trustees of The British Museum, p. 165 ● The Trustees of the Roman Catholic Diocese of Middlesbrough, p. 181 ● The trustees of the Wallace Collection, p. 54 ● Woodmansterne, pp. 172 (bottom), 195 ● World Vision of Britain/Eric Mooneyham, p. 135 ● ZEFA, p. 39 (top) ● ZEFA/Neville Kenton, pp. 20, 103 (top) ● ZEFA/W H Müller, p. 60 (bottom) ● ZEFA/T Schneiders, p. 32 (right)
Cover photograph by permission of Jerry Wooldridge and The Regional RE Centre (Midlands).

All other photographs were supplied by the author.

The Land

'A land flowing with milk and honey . . .' (RSV)

It was over 3000 years ago that the Israelites first entered the land which they believed God had promised to them. After their long journey through the Sinai desert it really did seem to them 'a land flowing with milk and honey'.

To a visitor today, the first impression on arrival at Lod airport, near to the first-century village of Lydda, is the sweet scent of orange blossom. We have all enjoyed fruit from this fertile coastal plain near the town of Jaffa (the ancient Joppa). Citrus fruits were not introduced into the Mediterranean area until fairly recently, but the area near the coast has always been 'rich and fertile' (GNB). However, on a journey from the airport to Jerusalem, the land soon becomes very rocky and unproductive, and only 30 miles (48 km) away from the coastal plain is the hot, barren desert of Judaea.

The land of the Israelites, or Palestine, where Jesus lived, is a small area about the size of Wales. It is situated between the Mediterranean Sea and the desert, at the junction of three continents, Europe, Asia and Africa. From ancient times it has been a land bridge across which both merchants and armies have travelled. Its central position made it very important in the ancient world.

ACTIVITIES

1 Two different versions of the Bible have been referred to above. Find as many other versions as you have available. Use them as you continue with the course to compare any biblical passages which you find difficult to understand. Quotations given in this book will normally be taken from the *Good News Bible*.

2 Learn how to use a concordance, if one is available to the group. A concordance lists all the main words used in the Bible and is a very useful tool in biblical studies. You will notice that no references are given for the quotations at the beginning of each Topic. Take it in turns to find them. Look up, in the concordance, each of the key words in the quotation, starting with the most distinctive, e.g. 'land . . . flowing . . . milk . . .', until you discover the reference (book, chapter, verse). Make a note of it.

3 Look up the verse in as many versions of the Bible as you have available. Discuss the differences of translation.

4 If you are not used to finding Bible references, spend some time practising this skill. A member of the group could find and announce a reference, e.g. Joshua 5 (chapter):6 (verse), which the others then find as speedily as possible. You can turn this activity into a game or a competition.

5 Look up the position of Palestine (Israel) in an atlas. Then look up Matthew 28:19. Discuss the significance of the position of Palestine in the early spread of the Christian faith.

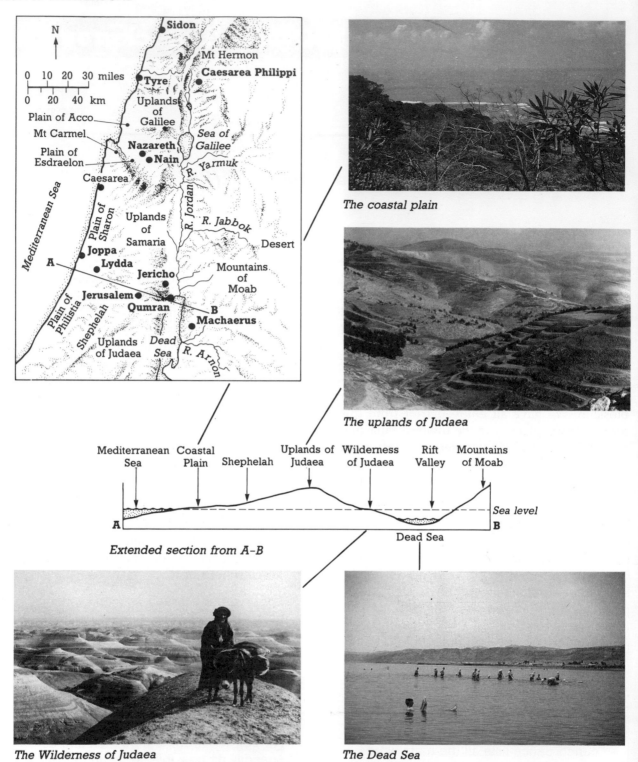

The coastal plain

The uplands of Judaea

Extended section from A–B

The Wilderness of Judaea

The Dead Sea

ACTIVITIES

1 Look at the illustrations in this Topic and elsewhere in the book. Try to identify them with the areas shown on the map on this page.

2 How would you account for the differences in climate between the coastal plain and the Wilderness of Judaea? If you have an atlas of the area, look up a rainfall map and discuss your conclusions.

Although Palestine is so small, it has a great variety of scenery and climate, including high, occasionally snow-capped mountains, tropical valleys, fertile coastal lowlands and scorching hot deserts.

We must now take a closer look at the areas which are important for an understanding of the Gospels:

The Coastal Plain

The coastal plain stretches for over 100 miles (160 km) from Tyre and Sidon in the north to Philistia in the south. At the northern end it is only three miles (5 km) wide, but it broadens to 25 miles (40 km) in the south. It is split into two sections by Mount Carmel. It was to the northern part of this area that Jesus took his disciples to escape from crowds in Galilee, and where he met a Syro-Phoenician woman. (Mark 7:24–30).

View across the plain of Esdraelon

> *Orange groves – gorgeous scent. Barley almost ready for harvest . . . eucalyptus trees . . . enormous cacti . . . fertile red soil . . . bananas. Lemon and palm trees. Brilliant red poppies . . . sandy soil.*
>
> *Extract from the author's diary notes of a visit to Israel made in April*

The Plain of Esdraelon

> *Once a swamp . . . oranges . . . water melons . . . apples and pears. Shepherd leading sheep to fold.*
>
> *Extract from the author's diary*

The plain of Esdraelon is an extension of the coastal plain to the east and separates the hills of Galilee from those of Samaria to the south. This is an area where many battles were fought in the Old Testament period. It is also where the village of Nain is situated, outside which Jesus encountered a funeral procession (Luke 7:11–17).

The Central Uplands

Galilee

> *Up hairpin bends into hills around Nazareth. Goatherd playing pipes . . . fig trees. Boys with mixed flock of sheep and goats present wild flowers. Olive trees . . . very stony ground . . . boulders cleared to edge of field.*
>
> *Extract from the author's diary*

The mountains in the north of Galilee reach nearly 4000 feet (1200 m). There are large areas of chalk and limestone uplands where the main type of farming is the rearing of sheep and goats. Nazareth is situated in a saucer-shaped depression in these hills, overlooking the plain of Esdraelon. This area is where Jesus grew up and spent most of his life.

Goatherd near Nazareth

The Wilderness of Judaea

> *Jerusalem to Jericho . . . black goats on bare yellow hills . . . bedouin on the move with goats and camels. Wadis . . . sea level . . . volcanic rocks . . . amazing colours. Heat!*
>
> *Extract from the author's diary*

The road from Jerusalem to Jericho descends some 3600 feet (1080 m) in 15 miles (24 km). There is very little rainfall here. The Gospels suggest that John the Baptist spent a lot of time in this area and that Jesus was tempted here.

The Jordan Valley

The Jordan Valley is part of the African Rift Valley which extends north into the Lebanon and south for several thousand miles into central Africa.

The Sea of Galilee

> *Views across lake . . . fishermen. Fertile plain of Gennesaret . . . flowers . . . date palms . . . bananas . . . olives . . . wheat . . . figs . . . almonds. Sudden slight storm . . . choppy trip across.*
>
> *Extract from the author's diary*

The Sea of Galilee is also called the sea or lake of Tiberias, Chinnereth (harp-shaped) or Gennesaret. It is surrounded by almost tropical vegetation, being 690 feet (200 m) below sea level. It extends 13 miles (21 km) from north to south and seven miles (11 km) across. In the time of Jesus, this was a busy and populous area, with a number of towns, especially on the western shore. It is where Jesus found his first disciples and carried out his early ministry.

Judaea and Samaria

> *Up into the hills . . . becoming more barren. Terraced vines . . . olives . . . mustard trees . . . carob trees . . . ox and ass yoked together. Camels loaded with crops. First sight of Jerusalem on hills.*
>
> *Extract from the author's diary*

Fertile valleys extend up into the foothills of Judaea (Shephelah). The area becomes more barren towards Jerusalem, situated in a good defensive position on four hills. It is likely that Jesus frequently visited Jerusalem, which was the setting for the events of the last week of his life.

The Sea of Galilee

The Lower Jordan and Dead Sea

> *Lowest spot on earth . . . salt . . . fantastic landforms. Heat . . . 38 °C in shade . . . vultures . . . black tents of bedouin. River a mere trickle . . . Jericho . . . palm trees.*
>
> *Extract from the author's diary*

The Dead Sea, which is 43 miles (69 km) long and nine miles (14 km) wide, is 1200 feet (360 m) below sea level. Little will grow in the area because of salt deposits. Near here is Qumran, where the Essenes had one of their communities. John the Baptist preached by the River Jordan, and Jesus was baptised there.

ACTIVITIES

1 Using both the text and the extracts from the diary, make a list of the incidents in the life and teaching of Jesus mentioned in this Topic. Try to find them in the Gospels. Use any section headings in your Bible, or a concordance, to help you.

2 Use a dictionary to look up any words in the text which you do not understand.

Politics

'It was the fifteenth year of the rule of the Emperor Tiberius; Pontius Pilate was governor of Judaea, Herod was ruler of Galilee . . .'

It may seem strange that a passage in Luke's Gospel, introducing the ministry of John the Baptist in Palestine, should begin with reference to two Roman rulers. At the time of Jesus, as so often throughout its history, Palestine was an occupied country, just a small corner of the powerful Roman Empire. Luke was eager that his readers should see the story in its historical setting.

It was six hundred years since Judah had had complete self-rule; Palestine had been governed by a series of foreign rulers and only for a brief period did the Jews gain their independence.

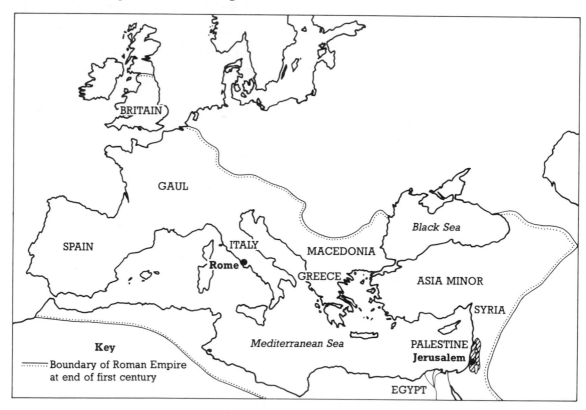

A small corner of the powerful Roman Empire

ACTIVITIES

1 Use a concordance to find the reference of the quotation at the beginning of this Topic.

2 If you have a copy of the *Good News Bible*, look up the Outline Chart of Bible History at the back.

a) Make a list of the foreign powers which ruled Palestine between 600 BC and AD 100.

b) When did the Jews gain their independence during that period?

The Greek Period

Between 333 BC and 63 BC many Greek customs were introduced into Palestine, a process known as Hellenisation. Greek religious practices were introduced by a ruler called Antiochus Epiphanes. This led to revolts by the Jews led by Judas Maccabaeus, who was hailed for a time as the expected Messiah. The Greek language was also introduced and most of the New Testament books were originally written in Greek.

The Roman Period

Throughout the New Testament period, detachments of Roman soldiers, each led by a centurion wearing a plumed helmet, were a common sight in Palestine. An adult could be made to give assistance to these forces (see Matthew 5:41 and Mark 15:21).

Tom Fleming, the actor who played Jesus in a film *Jesus of Nazareth*, tells of seeing tank tracks on the road to Jericho:

> *An army had passed in the night and it reminded me that He [Jesus] lived in a politically explosive countryside. Armies change, politics change, but through the awful tribulations ordinary individual human beings still see great sadness, great ecstasy and joy.*

A poll tax was introduced by the Romans to pay for public services, but this was very unpopular (see Mark 12:13–17).

ACTIVITIES

1 If you can find a copy of the Apocrypha, read 1 Maccabees 1:20–64, which tells the story of Antiochus' persecution of the Jews.

2 Look in the Gospels to find an example of an incident when Jesus came into contact with a Roman army officer.

3 Write down the answers to the following questions:

a) What is the rank of the soldier shown in the picture?

b) What problems did the Roman occupation of Palestine give rise to?

c) What had been the main problems of the Greek period?

d) Imagine you are a Palestinian Jew in either the Greek or the Roman period. What are your feelings about the occupation?

Historical Background

The chart below gives a brief summary of the historical background to the Gospel accounts:

Historical Background (with approximate dates)

333–63 BC	Greeks ruled in Palestine.
63 BC	Roman rule in Palestine began when Pompey, a Roman general, captured Jerusalem.
40 BC	Herod (the Great) nominated as King of Judaea.
27 BC–AD 14	Octavian Augustus Emperor of Rome (Caesar).
7–4 BC?	Birth of Jesus.
4 BC	Death of Herod the Great. Sons ruled: Archelaus (Judaea and Samaria), Antipas (Galilee and Perea), Philip (Iturea and Trachonitis).
AD 6	Archelaus deposed and a Roman procurator (governor) ruled the province of Judaea. Start of the Zealot movement.
AD 14–37	Tiberius Emperor of Rome.
AD 26–36	Pontius Pilate procurator of Judaea.
AD 27–30?	Ministry of Jesus.
AD 29–30?	Crucifixion of Jesus.
AD 34	Death of Philip the Tetrarch.
AD 37–41	Caligula Emperor of Rome.
AD 41–54	Claudius Emperor of Rome.
AD 54–68	Nero Emperor of Rome.
AD 64	Fire of Rome. Persecution of Christians.
AD 66–73	Zealot rebellions against Romans in Palestine.
AD 69–79	Vespasian Emperor of Rome.
AD 70	Siege and destruction of Jerusalem by the Romans.
AD 70–73	Siege and capture of the fortress of Masada by the Romans.

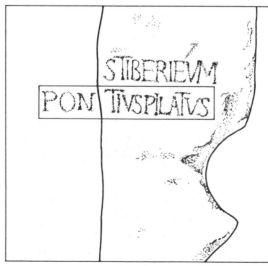

Inscription of Pilate's name, found in the theatre in Caesarea in 1961

ACTIVITIES

1 Read through the historical background summary again, carefully. Do not try to learn all the details!

2 Answer the following questions:

a) When did the Roman Empire take control in Palestine?

b) What was the name of the Roman general who captured Jerusalem?

c) Who was the emperor of Rome at the time of the birth of Jesus?

d) Who was the Roman procurator in Judaea at the time of Jesus' death?

e) What evidence has been discovered in Palestine which would support the biblical statement of the presence of this procurator?

The Herods

Herod the Great 40–4 BC

The Romans allowed a measure of self-government to the Jews and even gave the title 'King of Judaea' to Herod the Great, whose father, Antipater, had earlier been a procurator in the same province. Herod, who was of Idumaean descent (see the map on p. 12) and only half Jewish, was not considered by many Jews to be an acceptable ruler. He tried to please them by building a magnificent new Temple in Jerusalem (see Topic 3). Other building projects included temples to Roman gods, as well as the rebuilding of Samaria, which was renamed Sebaste (the Greek term for the Latin 'Augustus'), and the building of a magnificent harbour and town on the Mediterranean coast which was named Caesarea, also in honour of the Emperor.

> *The city itself was called Caesarea, which was also itself built of fine materials . . . Herod also built therein a theatre of stone; and on the south quarter, behind the port, an amphitheatre also, capable of holding a vast number of men, and conveniently situated for a prospect to the sea.*
>
> *Josephus*, Antiquities of the Jews 15:9.6

So Herod lived up to his title of Herod the Great. However, as the following chart shows, he was also cruel and ruthless (see also Matthew 2:1–22 and Luke 1:5).

Caesarea

Sons of Herod the Great

1 **Antipater** Mother – Doris of Idumaea. Murdered on his father's orders, five days before Herod the Great's own death.

2 **Alexander** Mother – Mariamne the Hasmonaean (later killed on Herod's orders). Murdered on his father's orders.

3 **Aristobulus** Mother – Mariamne the Hasmonaean. Murdered on his father's orders.

4 **Philip** (also known as **Herod** or **'Boethus'**) Mother – Mariamne of Jerusalem. Married Herodias, his niece, the daughter of Aristobulus. Their daughter was Salome.
Mark 6:17; Luke 3:19; Matthew 14:3–4

5 **Archelaus** (Herod the Ethnarch) Mother – Malthace of Samaria. Ruler in Judaea 4 BC–AD 6 (deposed).
Matthew 2:22–3

6 **Antipas** (Herod the Tetrarch) Mother – Malthace of Samaria. Ruler of Galilee and Perea 4 BC–AD 39 (deposed). Married i) the daughter of Aretas IV of Nabataea and ii) Herodias, who had left her husband Philip. Built Sepphoris and Tiberias.
Mark 6:14–28; Luke 3:1, 3:19, 13:31–2 and 23:6–12; Matthew 14:1–10

7 **Philip** (the Tetrarch) Mother – Malthace of Samaria. Ruler of Iturea and Trachonitis 4 BC–AD 34. Founded Caesarea Philippi. Married Salome, the daughter of his brother, Herod Philip.
Luke 3:1

8 **Herod** Mother – Cleopatra of Jerusalem. Some think he should be identified with Philip the Tetrarch (see above).

9 **Pasaelus** Mother – Pallas.

ACTIVITIES

1 Try to construct a family tree, using the information given on the Herods.

2 Read the passages indicated from the Gospels. Make notes on each of the Herods who feature in the Gospel accounts.

3 Look at the map on p. 12 and answer the following questions:

a) Which Herod ruled at the time of Jesus' birth?

b) What information given here suggests that the action of Herod recorded in Matthew 2:16 was in character?

c) Why did Mary and Joseph decide to settle in Galilee, rather than Judaea, on their return from Egypt?

d) Which Herod ruled in Galilee at the time of Jesus' ministry?

e) Why did John the Baptist criticise Herod Antipas?

f) What part did Herod Antipas play in the trials of Jesus?

g) What do the names of the towns built or founded by the various Herods suggest about their relationships with the Romans?

Political Groups

Herodians

A group of Jews known as 'members of Herod's party' supported the Herodian dynasty (ruling family). It has been suggested that some even believed that Herod the Great was the promised Messiah. They were a nationalistic party, distrusting the Roman governors and hoping for more power for the Herods. They tended to be among the wealthiest members of Jewish society. (Mark 3:6 and 12:13)

Zealots

The poll tax referred to on p. 7 was introduced into Judaea in AD 6. Josephus, a Jewish historian writing at the end of the first century, tells us what happened:

> *. . . a certain Galilean, whose name was Judas, prevailed with his countrymen to revolt; and said they were cowards if they would endure to pay a tax to the Romans, and would, after God, submit to mortal men as their lords.*
>
> Josephus, Wars of the Jews 2:8.1

The hilltop fortress of Masada where, from AD 70 to 73, the Zealots withstood a siege by the Romans.

Judas led the Zealot movement, which used terrorist methods against the Roman army. Eventually, in AD 73, they committed mass suicide, rather than be captured by Roman forces. One of Jesus' disciples, Simon, was a Zealot, and Barabbas and possibly Judas Iscariot may have had connections with the movement (Luke 6:15–16).

Tax Collectors

The Romans employed Jews to collect their taxes. Rabbis taught that such people should be avoided and they were treated as outcasts because of their frequent contact with Gentiles (Mark 2:13–17; Luke 3:12–13, 7:34, 15:1, 18:9–14 and 19:1–10; Matthew 5:46, 18:17 and 21:31).

Samaritans

The Samaritans were the descendants of the settlers who had been sent into Israel by the conquering Assyrians at the end of the eighth century BC and who had intermarried with Israelites. As the map on p. 12 shows, Samaria was situated between Judaea and Galilee. A small number of Samaritans still live in the area today. The Samaritans accepted a copy of the first five books of the Old Testament from the Jews, but the Jews did not consider their religion to be orthodox as they offered sacrifice on Mount Gerizim rather than in Jerusalem. As far as Jews were concerned, there were no *good* Samaritans and the two groups tried to avoid travelling in each other's territory (Luke 9:51–5, 10:25–37 and 17:11–19; Matthew 10:5).

A Samaritan with the Pentateuch, the first five books of the Old Testament, still the only part of the scriptures recognised by Samaritans.

ACTIVITIES

1 Read the suggested passages from the Gospels and make notes on the Herodians, the Zealots, tax collectors and the Samaritans.

2 Answer the following questions:

   a) Which tax collectors are mentioned by name in the Gospels?

   b) Why were tax collectors so unpopular with their fellow Jews?

   c) What was Jesus' attitude towards tax collectors?

3 Answer the following questions:

   a) Where was the temple of the Samaritans?

   b) What were the origins of the Samaritans?

   c) Why did Jews travelling from Galilee to Judaea frequently take the route shown on the map below?

   d) What was Jesus' attitude towards Samaritans?

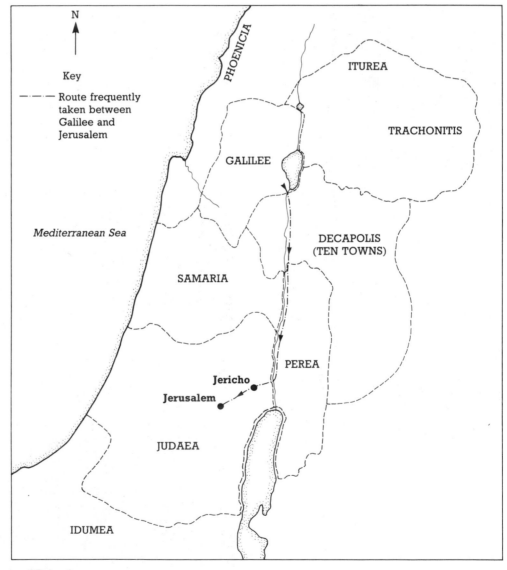

Provinces of Palestine

Faith

'. . . on the Sabbath he [Jesus] went as usual to the synagogue.'

> *Hear, O Israel: The Lord our God is one Lord; and you shall love the Lord your God with all your heart, and with all your soul, and with all your might . . .*
>
> *Deuteronomy 6:4–6 (RSV)*

'S hema Yisrael . . .' (Hear, O Israel . . .) are words which have rung out through the centuries as a statement of Jewish faith. They were used at the time of Jesus and were quoted by him (Mark 12:29–30), and the Shema is still a basic expression of faith for Jews today.

Jesus shared the unique faith of the Jewish world of which he was a part. This faith was in one God (monotheism), a God who had made a covenant or agreement with his people, the Hebrews. A special relationship existed between God and his chosen people, and this brought not only privileges but also responsibilities to the Jews.

Scriptures

The covenant was recorded in the Jewish scriptures (the Old Testament), which had reached its present form by the first century BC, although the order of the books was slightly different. The scriptures were written, and read, in Hebrew, and consisted of three sections:

- **The Law (Torah** or **Pentateuch)**, the first five books of the Old Testament, was, and still is, of prime importance for Jews. It was traditionally believed that the Torah was the teaching of God given to Moses. It was often called the Law of Moses and contained God's laws for living, and so obedience to it was of vital importance.

- **The Prophets (Nevi'im)** included most of the history books and the announcements of the prophets, whom Jews believed to be God's messengers.

- **The Writings (Ketuvim)** was the final section and a number of the books were associated with, and read at, various festivals.

ACTIVITIES

1 Answer the following questions:

   'Hear, O Israel: The Lord our God is one Lord . . .'

   a) What name is given to this statement?

   b) What name is given to the Jewish belief expressed in these words?

   c) In which of the three sections of the Jewish scriptures is the statement found?

   d) In which language were the Jewish scriptures written?

   e) What is meant by the covenant relationship?

   f) Why do you think the Torah has always been so important for Jews?

2 Discover which of the Jewish scriptures are referred to in the first three Gospels. Look at the footnotes in your Bible and make a list of the Old Testament books mentioned. Check in the text of the Gospel that each of the Old Testament books mentioned is quoted from or named. Which of the Gospels includes most Old Testament references?

Herod's Temple

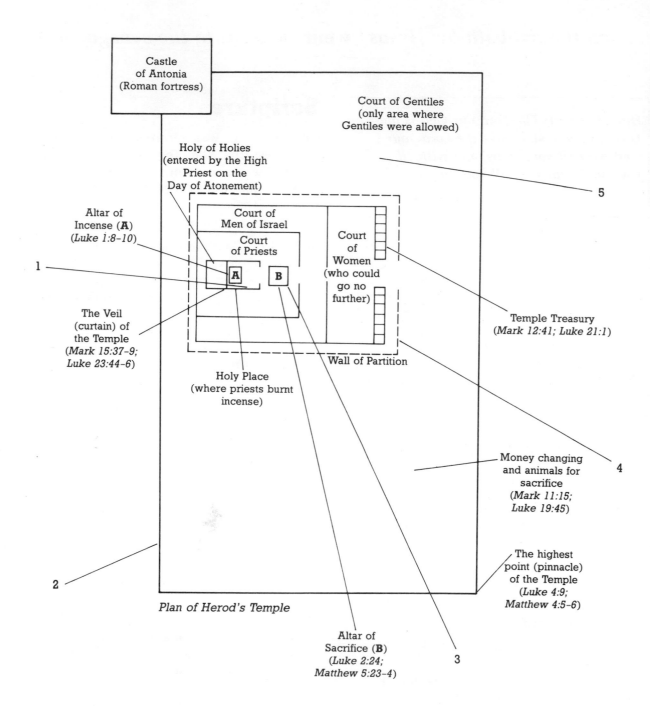

Castle
of Antonia
(Roman fortress)

Court of Gentiles
(only area where
Gentiles were allowed)

5

Holy of Holies
(entered by the High
Priest on the
Day of Atonement)

Altar of
Incense (**A**)
(*Luke 1:8–10*)

Court of
Men of Israel

Court
of Priests

Court
of
Women
(who could
go no
further)

1

A   **B**

The Veil
(curtain) of
the Temple
(*Mark 15:37–9;
Luke 23:44–6*)

Temple Treasury
(*Mark 12:41; Luke 21:1*)

Holy Place
(where priests burnt
incense)

Wall of Partition

Money changing
and animals for
sacrifice
(*Mark 11:15;
Luke 19:45*)

4

2

The highest
point (pinnacle)
of the Temple
(*Luke 4:9;
Matthew 4:5–6*)

Plan of Herod's Temple

Altar of
Sacrifice (**B**)
(*Luke 2:24;
Matthew 5:23–4*)

3

1 *The menorah from the Temple*

5 *Courts of the Temple*

2 *The Wailing Wall – the only remaining section of Herod's Temple*

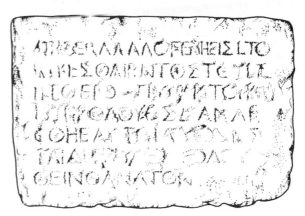

4 *Notice on the Wall of Partition – 'No stranger may enter within the balustrade or embankment round the Temple. Anyone caught doing so will bear the responsibility for his own ensuing death.'*

3 *Possible site of the Altar of Sacrifice*

The Temple

At the time of Jesus' ministry, the magnificent new Temple built by Herod the Great in the north-east quarter of the city dominated Jerusalem. It may not have been entirely completed by the time of Jesus' death, and was destroyed in AD 70 after the siege of Jerusalem by the Romans (Mark 13:2; Luke 21:5–6). A model of Herod's Temple is shown in the photographs on pp. 38, 99 and 164.

The Temple area from the Mount of Olives. Today the Dome of the Rock (a Muslim mosque) stands on the site of the Temple.
Why was this such an important site for Jews?

The Temple area today

ACTIVITIES

1 Look up the references shown on the plan of Herod's Temple.

2 Use the index to find other references to the Temple in the Gospels.

3 Make lists of:
   a) events in the life of Jesus which are set in the Temple,
   b) comments in Jesus' teaching which are connected with the Temple.

4 Answer the following questions:
   a) Who built the Temple in Jerusalem mentioned in the Gospels?
   b) What, according to the Gospels, did Jesus prophesy about the Temple?
   c) Who was the only person to enter the innermost shrine of the Temple and when did this happen?
   d) What happened in the Temple at the time of Jesus' death? What significance do Christians see in this?
   e) What do you think was the purpose of animal sacrifice? What is your opinion of it?

5 Imagine that you are a pilgrim visiting the Temple for one of the festivals during the first century AD. Produce an illustrated description of your visit to show the purpose of the Temple buildings. Include drawings and perhaps a plan.

Synagogues

There was only one Temple in Jerusalem, where sacrifices were carried out and priests officiated. By contrast there were thousands of synagogues throughout Israel and it has been suggested that there were hundreds in Jerusalem alone. It seems that synagogues (from a Greek word meaning 'gathering' or 'meeting') may have had their origins during the exile in Babylon in the sixth century BC, when the Jews were cut off from the Temple in Jerusalem and so were unable to offer sacrifices. The synagogues existed for congregational worship, particularly on the Sabbath, for studying the Law and for the education of children. Worship focused mainly on the Torah, and included prayers and a sermon. Synagogues today still follow a similar pattern of worship. The officials who organised the synagogues were known as 'rulers' and 'elders' (Mark 5:22; Luke 8:41).

Scrolls being removed from the ark during a service in a synagogue.

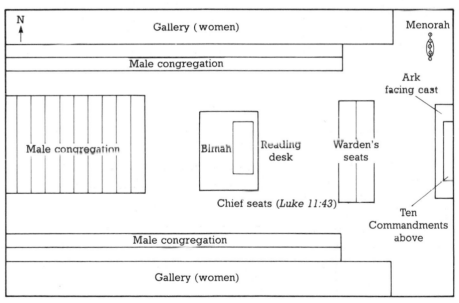

Events:
Mark 1:21–8, 3:1–6 and 6:1–14;

Luke 4:31–7, 6:6–11, 4:16–30 and 13:10–17

Plan of a synagogue

ACTIVITIES

1 Look up the references given on the above plan. Make a list of the events which, according to the Gospels, took place in synagogues.

2 Construct a chart to show the similarities and differences between the Temple and a synagogue.

3 Identify the objects shown in the photograph with the furnishings shown on the plan. If you are able to do so, visit a synagogue for this purpose.

People

Priests

Priests offered sacrifices, burned incense and carried out other duties in the Temple. The High Priest at the time of Jesus' ministry was Caiaphas, but Annas, his predecessor and father-in-law, still had considerable influence.

Levites

Many members of the tribe of Levi were not priests. Some Levites, however, helped the priests in the Temple, and the Temple caretakers, police force and choir also came from this tribe.

Pharisees

> *For there are three philosophical sects among the Jews. The followers of the first of whom are the Pharisees; of the second the Sadducees; and the third sect, who pretends to a severer discipline, are called Essens.*
>
> *Josephus*, Wars of the Jews 2:8.2

In the extract above, Josephus introduces us to the three main sects in Judaism.

The *Pharisees* were the largest and most influential sect, estimated at some *6000* in the first century AD. They may have originated as a group during the period of the *Greek persecutions* (see Topic 2). Their name may be derived from a Hebrew word meaning *'to separate'*. They stressed the importance of all aspects of the *Law*, but also accepted the *Prophets* and the *Writings* as scripture. The Pharisees supported the additional laws (the *oral tradition*) which were intended to prevent people from breaking the Torah. They referred to making a 'hedge about the Law', the 'hedge' being these many additional laws. They believed in the *immortality of the soul* and the *resurrection of the body*, as well as in the existence of *angels*. Josephus (a Pharisee himself) suggests that their moral and spiritual standards were high and that they were *respected* by ordinary people. Jesus was often entertained by them. He criticised the over-emphasis on laws, which led to *hypocrisy*.

Sadducees

The name 'Sadducee' may have been derived from Zadok, a High Priest of the time of David and Solomon, or from a Hebrew word meaning 'uprightness' or 'righteousness'. The Sadducees were a small but influential group, often including the High Priest in their number. They recognised only the Torah as authoritative scripture, rejecting belief in angels and spirits. They emphasised the importance of carrying out the Temple ritual correctly.

Josephus tells us of other ways in which the beliefs of the Sadducees differed from those of the Pharisees:

> *But the doctrine of the Sadducees is this: That souls die with the bodies; nor do they regard the observation of anything besides what the law enjoins them.*
>
> *Josephus*, Antiquities of the Jews 18:1.4

In order to keep their political influence, the Sadducees tended to compromise with the Roman occupying forces.

ACTIVITIES

1 Use the index at the back of the book to find occasions when a) priests and b) Levites are mentioned in the Gospels.

2 Look in the index to check where a) the Pharisees and b) the Sadducees are mentioned in the Gospels.

3 Using the words in *italic* as key words, write your own description of the Pharisees.

4 Write a description of the Sadducees, using the same method as above. Identify key words for yourself and then write your own account.

5 Construct a chart comparing the Pharisees and the Sadducees.

Torah scribe.
What were the two main jobs of a scribe?

Scribes

Scribes, sometimes called lawyers or rabbis (teachers), were experts in understanding the Law and also wrote out copies of the scriptures (Mark 2:16 and 3:22; Luke 11:53, 20:1–2, 20:19, 22:2 and 23:10).

Sanhedrin

The Sanhedrin was the Jewish Council, which met in Jerusalem and consisted of 70 members presided over by the High Priest. It decided religious matters and also acted as a court (Mark 14:53–64; Luke 22:66–71).

Essenes

The Essenes were the third sect or group referred to by Josephus. It seems that one of their communities lived at Qumran, near the Dead Sea, where the Dead Sea scrolls were discovered by a bedouin goatherd in 1947. Most of the scrolls had been hidden in clay pots when

the Romans advanced on the community in AD 68. Some scholars have suggested that there may have been connections between John the Baptist and the Essenes.

Caves where scrolls were discovered at Qumran

ACTIVITIES

1 Read the passages from the Gospels concerning the scribes, and then discuss the following:
   a) What was the attitude of the scribes towards Jesus?
   b) How would you account for this attitude?

2 Read the passages from the Gospels concerning the Sanhedrin. Write a paragraph explaining what you have found out about this Council.

Festivals

There was a weekly day for rest and worship, the Sabbath. This was considered by the Jews to be their most important festival. It was customary for Jews to attend the synagogue on the Sabbath. As we have seen, there are many references to the synagogue in the Gospels.

The three main festivals were known as the pilgrim festivals, as all Jewish men were expected to visit Jerusalem to celebrate them. More details are given in the books of Exodus, Leviticus and Numbers.

All the men of your nation are to come to worship the Lord three times a year at the one place of worship: at Passover, Harvest Festival and the Festival of Shelters. Each man is to bring a gift, as he is able, in proportion to the blessings that the Lord your God has given him.

Deuteronomy 16:16–17

The Gospels refer to two visits to Jerusalem for the Passover celebrations, in Luke 2:41–2 and Mark 14:12. The Passover reminds Jews of the time in their national history when they were saved from slavery in Egypt. As with all festivals, it is seen as an opportunity to teach the children about their religious history. For Jews celebrating Passover today, unleavened bread and wine play a significant part, just as they did for Jesus and his disciples (see Topic 22).

ACTIVITY

Look up Deuteronomy 16:1–8 and make a detailed list of the instructions that were to be followed at Passover.

What kind of questions would a child ask at Passover?

Jesus of Nazareth

TOPIC 4

'The Good News about Jesus Christ . . .'

Our calendar has divided the history of the world into BC (before Christ) and AD (anno Domini = the year of our Lord). A widely accepted modern alternative is BCE (before the common era) and CE (common era).

How is it that Jesus of Nazareth has had such an impact on human history? Records suggest that he was a little-known village carpenter for most of his life, living in a distant corner of the Roman Empire. He gathered followers and, after a short period of preaching and showing his concern for people in practical ways, he was put to death by crucifixion. Yet the new faith that was introduced by Jesus of Nazareth refused to die, and his followers through the centuries have told the world what they consider to be the Good News.

In fact, we know comparatively little about the life of Jesus. The writings about him cover a period of, at most, three years; and unlike some other religious teachers, Jesus did not write any books himself. Why, then, has his life been so influential? (The Activities below will help you explore this question.)

Examining the Evidence

Biblical

The most important evidence concerning Jesus is to be found in the New Testament:

- **The Gospels** The Gospels are the main source of information. We shall consider the first three Gospels in Topic 5.

- **The Epistles** Twenty-one of the New Testament books are letters, most of them written before the Gospels. They contain some vitally important passages, giving facts passed on by those who knew Jesus, e.g. 1 Corinthians 15:1–7.

- **The Acts of the Apostles** This book continues the account of what the apostles did after Jesus' ministry on earth was over. It includes what most scholars consider to be very reliable details of their preaching about Jesus. This preaching is known by the Greek word *Kerygma*. Some important passages are Acts 2:22–39, 3:13–21, 5:29–32 and 10:34–43.

ACTIVITIES

1 Discuss why the life of Jesus has had so much impact on human history.

2 Look out for and make a list of any evidence you can find of the influence of Jesus on society today.
   (*Hints:* Look at buildings, symbols, names, people, the media, the calendar, etc.) After some time, compare your lists.

3 Look in books, magazines, art galleries and so on, and collect details of any 'portraits' of Jesus that you can find. Share your thoughts and feelings about them.

4 Discuss how you would find out about any historical person. Choose someone you may have studied in history, e.g. Elizabeth I or Mahatma Gandhi. Can the same methods be used to find out about Jesus?

ACTIVITIES

1 Look up the passages from 1 Corinthians and Acts. Try to work out what points were made in the early Christians' preaching about Jesus (the *Kerygma*). Make a list of the points in the order in which they were made.

2 Check your list of points against the outline of the *Kerygma* on p. 195.

Early Christian Writings

Possibly the earliest non-biblical Christian writing or inscription was discovered in 1945. Professor E L Sukenik, a Jewish archaeologist, discovered two tomb inscriptions dating between AD 40 and 50. The inscriptions were JESUS, HELP! and JESUS, LET HIM ARISE! These suggest that prayers were being offered to Jesus within a few years of his death.

The writings of a number of Christians survive from the first two centuries. These include writings by Clement of Rome, Justin Martyr and Ignatius of Antioch. The latter wrote *c.*AD 112:

> *. . . Jesus Christ, who was of the family of David, the child of Mary, who was truly born, who ate and drank, who was truly persecuted under Pontius Pilate, was truly crucified and truly died. . . .*

ACTIVITIES

1 Check the points made by Ignatius of Antioch above with those on your list of points made in the *Kerygma*. What similarities are there. What additions?

2 Discuss whether you consider the evidence given so far in this Topic proves the existence of Jesus.

Non-Christian Writings

You might consider the writings of Jesus' followers to be biased. However, there are also documents written by non-Christians concerning Jesus, and these too must be carefully examined. As we might expect, there are only a few of these documents in existence from the first and second centuries; five of these accounts are mentioned below:

Josephus

We have already looked at a number of passages from the works of Josephus in connection with the background to the New Testament period.

Flavius Josephus

Writing *c.*AD 94, Josephus mentions Jesus in two passages. The Greek version of one of these passages (*Antiquities of the Jews* 18:3.3) may have had comments added later by Christians. However, an Arabic version has also been found, which may more accurately reflect the original:

> *At this time there was a wise man who was called Jesus. And his conduct was good and he was known to be virtuous. And many people from among the Jews and from the other nations became his disciples. Pilate condemned him to be crucified and to die. And those who had become his disciples did not abandon his discipleship. They reported that he had appeared to them three days after his crucifixion and that he was alive. Accordingly he was perhaps the Messiah of whom the prophets have recounted wonders.*
>
> Translated from the Arabic by Professor Shlomo Pines

Pliny the Younger

Pliny was a Roman who wrote many letters. In his tenth volume, he asks advice of the Emperor Trajan as to how he should deal with Christians. The date is *c.*AD 110, when Pliny was the Governor of Bithynia.

> *. . . in the case of those brought before me as Christians. I ask them if they are Christians. If they admit it I repeat the question a second and a third time, threatening capital punishment; if they persist I sentence them to death. [He goes on to explain that he discharged any who denied that they were Christians] . . . especially because they cursed Christ, a thing which, it is said, genuine Christians cannot be induced to do.*
>
> Pliny, Epistles *10:96*

Cornelius Tacitus

Tacitus governed Asia during the reign of the Emperor Trajan. In the following extract from his Annals, written *c.*AD 112, he refers to the Emperor Nero:

> *Nero . . . punished . . . a class hated for their abominations, who are commonly called Christians. Christus, from whom their name is derived, was executed at the hands of the procurator Pontius Pilate in the reign of Tiberius.*
>
> Tacitus, Annals *15:44*

Tranquillus Suetonius

Suetonius was a secretary to the Emperor Hadrian. He wrote biographies of 12 emperors. The following extracts were written *c.*AD 112:

> *Since the Jews were continually making disturbances at the instigation of Chrestus, he [Claudius] expelled them from Rome.*
>
> Suetonius, Life of Claudius *25:4*

> *. . . punishment was inflicted on the Christians, a set of men adhering to a novel and mischievous superstition.*
>
> Suetonius, Life of Nero *16*

ACTIVITIES

1 This Topic has dealt only with written evidence for the existence of Jesus. Discuss what other evidence there might be to suggest that he did exist.

2 Make a list of what might be considered to be facts about Jesus which are mentioned by non-Christian writers.

3 Discuss whether you find this evidence about Jesus of Nazareth convincing.

The Expected Messiah

The writer of the quotation at the beginning of this Topic suggests that the Good News is about Jesus *Christ*. We are so familiar with this way of describing Jesus that we tend to think of the word 'Christ' as the second part of the name, much like a surname. In fact, Christ is a title, not a name, so we might understand the significance of the quotation better if we changed it to 'Jesus the Christ'. The Greek word *Christos*, the equivalent of the Hebrew word *Messiah*, means 'anointed one'. The word is used in the Old Testament for someone who is set aside for a special task; for example, both priests and kings were anointed with oil when they started their work, much as monarchs are anointed at a coronation today.

By New Testament times there were several ideas about the kind of Messiah the Jews were expecting:

Prophet

Some Jews were expecting the appearance of a prophet like Moses (see Deuteronomy 18:15 and 18:18). Jesus is sometimes referred to as a prophet, although this does not necessarily imply Messiahship.

Moses, the prophet and law-giver, is shown on the ceiling of the Church of the Transfiguration on Mount Tabor, Israel.
Why is Moses so important in the Jewish faith?

King

Most Jews looked for the coming of a king of the royal line of David who, as a warrior, would lead them against their enemies (Isaiah 7:14, 9:1–7 and 11:1–10; Micah 5:2; Zechariah 9:9–10).

Bethlehem '. . . out of you I will bring a ruler for Israel.'
Which Old Testament ruler came from Bethlehem?

Suffering Servant

There are suggestions in the Gospels that Jesus saw himself as the suffering servant mentioned by Isaiah in his 'Servant Songs' (Isaiah 52:13–53:12).

Divine Being

Some Jews were expecting that God himself would intervene to set up his Kingdom amongst them (Isaiah 35:4 and 52:7–8). Some, therefore, looked for a 'Son of God', others a 'Son of Man' as suggested in Daniel 7:13–14.

ACTIVITIES

1 Make sure that you look up all the Old Testament references in the section on the expected Messiah.

2 Answer the following questions:

a) What is the meaning of the word 'Christ'?

b) Which people were anointed in Old Testament times?

c) Which prophet refers to Bethlehem as the town from which a new ruler will come?

d) What are the 'Servant Songs'?

e) What type of Messiah were most Jews hoping for by the beginning of the New Testament period?

f) Why do you think the idea of an expected Messiah was so important to Jews?

3 Before you begin to study the text of the Gospels, prepare sheets of paper on which you can make notes of the titles used of Jesus. Have a sheet of paper for each of the titles – Prophet, Son of David, Son of Man, Son of God, Messiah (or Christ). Arrange each sheet as shown in the example below. Make notes on each of the titles as you find them in the text you are studying.

MESSIAH (CHRIST)			
Reference	What is stated?	By whom?	Context
Mark 1:1	'... the Good News about Jesus Christ'	Author of Mark's Gospel	Title of Gospel, so part of Mark's purpose is to show that Jesus is the Messiah.

Gospels

'. . . the Good News which I preached to you.'

In Topic 4 we discovered that the source of most of our information about Jesus is the Gospels. There are four of these, but this book is concerned only with the first three, which are commonly called the Synoptic Gospels. Matthew, Mark and Luke are very similar and look at the material about Jesus from the same point of view. So they are called 'synoptic', which indicates that they can be viewed together. The fourth Gospel is very different and, since it looks at the material in a special way, it has sometimes been called a 'spiritual' gospel.

What is a Gospel?

The word 'gospel' is the equivalent of the Greek word *evangelion* and means 'good news'. The Gospels are certainly not biographies of Jesus. Only two of them give any detail at all of his birth; and the only event recorded from his childhood is the visit to Jerusalem with his parents at the age of 12, and that is in only one Gospel. The whole of Mark's Gospel and a large proportion of Matthew and Luke concern only the last one, two or three years of Jesus' life. As you can see from the diagram below, more than a third of Mark and between a quarter and a fifth of both Matthew and Luke are concerned with the last week of Jesus' life. Such an emphasis on the events leading up to an individual's death are not usual in a biography!

We must therefore assume that these events are of particular significance to the writers. They write as believers or, as Hans Küng suggests, they 'see Jesus with the eyes of faith' (*On Being a Christian*. Collins, 1974). So, as with most stories of individuals, the writers wish to show what they believe to be the truth about Jesus.

ACTIVITIES

1 Look up the opening statements of each of the Synoptic Gospels (Mark 1:1, Luke 1:1–4 and Matthew 1:1). What differences of emphasis do you notice?

2 Answer the following questions:
   a) What is the meaning of the word 'gospel'?
   b) Which are the Synoptic Gospels?
   c) What does 'synoptic' mean?
   d) Which two Gospels give accounts of the birth of Jesus?
   e) Which Gospel includes the story of Jesus' visit to Jerusalem at the age of 12?
   f) What statements about Jesus are made in the opening sentence of Mark's Gospel?
   g) What does Matthew say about Jesus in his opening sentence?
   h) What is the difference between a biography and a Gospel?

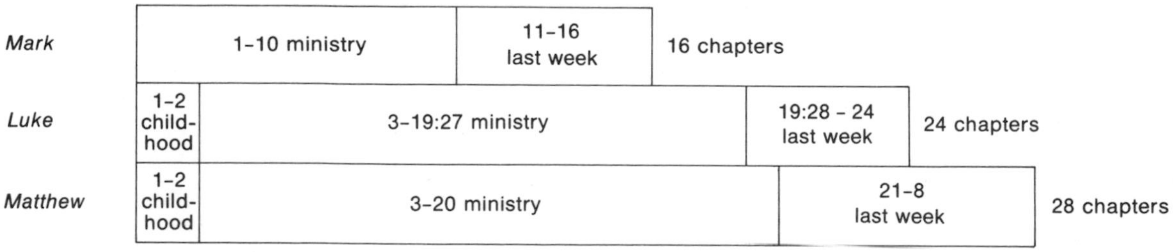

Mark		1–10 ministry	11–16 last week	16 chapters
Luke	1–2 child-hood	3–19:27 ministry	19:28 – 24 last week	24 chapters
Matthew	1–2 child-hood	3–20 ministry	21–8 last week	28 chapters

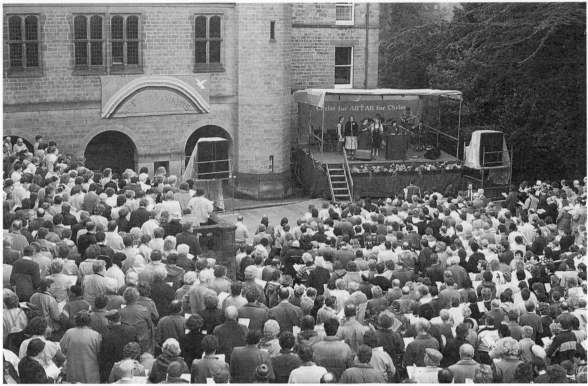

The Good News is preached today in the open air, much as it was by the apostles.

Passing on the Good News

As the quotation at the beginning of this Topic suggests, the Good News was preached long before it was written down. It may have been 30 years or more after the death of Jesus that the first Gospel was written. Since there were few books available, the main emphasis in synagogue schools was on learning by heart. (Your grandparents may have told you that it was the same in their schooldays.) In this way, stories about Jesus would be remembered and passed on very accurately – and so an 'oral tradition' grew up.

The Synoptic 'Problem'

Not only do the first three Gospels see things from the same point of view, there are also more specific similarities. There are many passages which are almost exactly the same in the three Gospels. The Synoptic 'problem' concerns the similarities and differences between the first three Gospels.

ACTIVITY

Look at the account of the healing of the man with leprosy from the three Gospels: Mark 1:40–4, Luke 5:12–14 and Matthew 8:12–14. If one person in the group reads aloud the passage (or 'pericope') from Mark and the rest of the group splits into two, one half following Matthew and the other Luke, you will then be able to discuss the similarities and differences. How would you account for the similarities?

One explanation for the similarities is that two of the writers used the other Gospel when writing. Someone once counted the verses in the Gospels to provide us with the following information:

Mark 661 verses

Matthew 1068 verses: these include 606 of the verses in Mark

Luke 1149 verses: these include 320 of the verses in Mark

27

ACTIVITIES

1 Discuss what conclusions you might draw from the information on p. 27.

2 Look up the story of the healing of the paralysed man: Mark 2:1–12, Luke 5:17–26 and Matthew 9:1–8. Use the same method as with the story of the man with leprosy. Discuss which of the three Gospels might have been written first.

3 Arrange a news-read! Collect together as many different newspapers as you can for a particular day. Consider one news item which they all include. What do you notice about the similarities and differences? How would you account for them? Do you think this has any relevance for a study of the Gospels?

Kids get new hol

PUPILS will be given two extra days' holiday next year — so that teachers can go back to school.

Staff will need the extra time to work on the new national curriculum, Education Secretary Kenneth Baker said yesterday.

Schools will have the choice of taking the extra break before the new time-table starts in September or leaving it until the autumn term.

PUPILS GET EXTRA DAYS OFF

By SUN REPORTER

SCHOOLKIDS will get two extra days' holiday next year. Education Secretary Kenneth Baker announced yesterday.

Britain's 25,000 state schools will shut down so teachers can prepare for the introduction of the new National Curriculum.

The change means that for the first time the country's eight million pupils will have to study key subjects like maths, science and a foreign language throughout their education.

It will ensure that children who change schools at crucial times will get the same lessons.

Extra holiday for schools

PUPILS will get an extra two days' holiday next year while teachers learn how to teach the new national curriculum, Education Secretary Kenneth Baker announced yesterday.

Schools must decide whether they use the days before the new time-table starts next September or in the autumn term, he said in the Commons.

Two-day holiday for pupils

By Our Education Staff

Pupils will enjoy a two-day holiday bonus next year when schools close to allow teachers to prepare for the introduction of the national curriculum, Mr Baker, Education Secretary, announced yesterday.

The 10-subject curriculum will be phased in from next September.

Early Christians considered that Matthew's Gospel was the first to be written, and that is why it appears as the first Gospel in the New Testament.

MARK However, most scholars today believe that Mark's Gospel was the first to be written, and that Matthew and Luke used Mark's account in writing their own.

Q Matthew and Luke share an additional 200 verses, largely sayings of Jesus, which are not found in Mark's Gospel. Did they both use another source of information? For various reasons, it seems that they did not copy from each other. Some scholars believe that they used a document which is now lost and which is referred to as 'Q', indicating *Quelle*, a German word meaning 'source'. Even if this document never existed, the letter Q is used to denote the material that Matthew and Luke have in common.

M In Matthew's Gospel, there is a considerable amount of material that is not found in either Mark or Luke. A quick exercise in mental arithmetic will show that there are about 250 verses which are unique to Matthew. This material is Matthew's special source and is known as 'M'. It may or may not have existed as a written document.

L Luke's Gospel also has material, which is not found in either Mark or Matthew. This unique material makes up half of Luke's Gospel and includes stories of Jesus' birth and a number of parables. The writer of the Gospel tells us in his introduction that he undertook considerable research before writing. The additional material not found in Mark or in Q is known as 'L' – Luke's special source.

If you think of the way you go about writing an essay, you will find it easier to understand how the Gospels may have come about. This can be shown in a diagram:

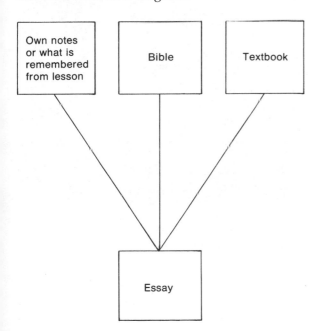

Similarly, we can show how Matthew's Gospel may have been written:

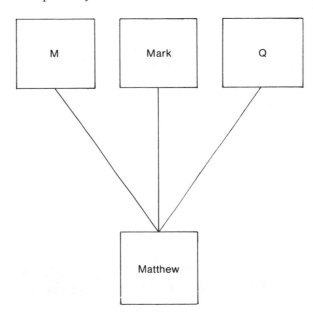

This way of considering how the Gospels may have come about is known as 'source criticism'.

Student using 'sources'

ACTIVITIES

1 Construct a diagram to show the sources which may have been used by Luke in writing his Gospel. Use the diagram of Matthew's Gospel as a pattern.

2 Answer the following questions:

a) What is Q?

b) What is M?

c) What is L?

d) What is 'source criticism'?

The rest of this Topic looks more closely at each of the Synoptic Gospels, Mark, Luke and Matthew.

Mark's Good News

The winged lion is an ancient symbol of Mark the Evangelist. There are a number of theories as to how this came about. It may be because the Gospel starts with John the Baptist, roaring his message in the desert, rather like a lion. Or the lion may indicate the royal line of David, from which Jesus was descended.

The Author

Strictly speaking, the Gospels are anonymous, but we shall examine the traditions associated with each of them.

Writing *c.*AD 130–40, Papias, the Bishop of Hierapolis, who was eager to learn from those who had actually met or heard the apostles, reported what 'the Elder' had told him:

> *Mark became the interpreter of Peter and he wrote down accurately, but not in order, as much as he remembered [or he (Peter) related] of the sayings and doings of Christ.*
>
> *Eusebius*, Ecclesiastical History *3:39*

So, early Church tradition associated this Gospel with a certain Mark, or John Mark, who, it is suggested, obtained his information from the apostle Peter. John Mark is mentioned on a number of occasions in the New Testament. Some have suggested that he may have been the young man of Mark 14:51–2 (verses not included in the other Gospels) and that possibly the Last Supper had been celebrated at the Jerusalem home of his mother, Mary (Acts 12:12).

Tradition identifies the Basilica of San Marco in Venice as the burial place of John Mark. Why does the lion appear in the square?

John Mark was not a prominent member of the early Church, and some scholars have suggested that there is no reason to ascribe this Gospel to him if he was not its author.

Why, When and Where Mark's Gospel was Written

It seems that as the years passed and some of the apostles died, the need for written accounts of the life and teaching of Jesus was realised. It has been suggested that Mark's Gospel was written in Rome, since the author obviously has non-Jewish readers in mind (he translates Aramaic phrases and includes Latin terms). The Gospel may have been written sometime between AD 60 and AD 70, during the persecutions of Nero in which both Peter and Paul were put to death, and before the destruction of Jerusalem. It may be that the reason why the author emphasised Jesus as the 'Crucified Christ' was because he wanted to give encouragement to Christians who were suffering persecution at that time.

ACTIVITIES

1 Look up the following references to John Mark and make notes about what you discover: Acts 12:25, 13:4–5, 13:13 and 15:36–9; Colossians 4:10; Philemon 24; 1 Peter 5:13.

2 Look up the following references to Peter in Mark's Gospel and discuss the conclusions you would draw from them:
   a) 1:16, 1:29, 1:36, 3:16, 5:37, 9:2 and 16:17
   b) 8:29–33, 10:26–31, 11:21–2, 14:27–31, 14:33–42 and 14:66–72

Important Themes

We have already considered the importance of the introduction to Mark's Gospel, which shows something of his purpose in writing. There are also a number of important themes in the Gospel:

- **The humanity of Jesus** An emphasis is placed on the human emotions of Jesus (e.g. 1:43, 3:5, 8:12, 8:33 and 10:14) and the reality of his physical suffering (e.g. 8:31–3, 9:31 and 10:32–4).

- **The authority of Jesus** is shown in passages such as 2:7, 4:41 and 7:37.

- **The divinity of Jesus** is stated at the beginning (1:1) and at the end (14:61–2 and 15:39), but between these passages the writer suggests that anyone hinting at his divinity or Messiahship is told by Jesus to remain silent (e.g. 1:24–5). We shall return to this subject of the 'Messianic secret' in Topic 13.

- **Action** is stressed. This is the briefest of the Gospels; it hurries along with an emphasis on action rather than on teaching. There is no prologue, only a short title to the Gospel (1:1), as if to emphasise the essentials of the Good News.

ACTIVITIES

1 Read through Mark's Gospel, if possible at a single sitting (it is not very long!). Try to spot the emphases noted above.

2 If you have it available, read the introduction to Mark's Gospel from the *Good News Bible*.

3 Head three sheets of paper – 'The Humanity of Jesus', 'The Authority of Jesus' and 'The Divinity of Jesus'. As you read the Gospel, make notes as in the following example:

MARK: THE HUMANITY OF JESUS		
Reference	Quotation	Comment
1:43	'Jesus spoke sternly to him'	Shows human emotion

Luke's Good News

Luke the Evangelist is symbolised by a winged ox. This is possibly because the ox was a sacrificial animal, and Luke's Gospel sees the life of Christ in terms of sacrifice. The opening and closing scenes of the Gospel are set in the Temple.

The Author

The following is a comment made by Irenaeus, the Bishop of Lyons *c.*AD 178, on this Gospel:

> *Luke, the follower of Paul, set down in a book the Gospel preached by his teacher.*
>
> *Irenaeus*, Against Heresy 3:1.1

Another piece of writing survives from the end of the second century, and is known as the Muratorian Canon:

> *The third book of the Gospel is that according to Luke. Luke, the physician, when after the Ascension of Christ Paul had taken him to himself as one studious of right [or 'as travelling companion'] wrote in his own name what he had been told, although he had not himself seen the Lord in the flesh. He set down the events as far as he could ascertain them, and began his story with the birth of John.*
>
> *From Westcott*, Canon of the New Testament

A number of other early Christian writers also identify the author of this Gospel as Luke.

Whoever was writing produced two volumes (see Luke 1:1–4 and Acts 1:1–3), the second of which continues the story of the apostles after the ascension of Jesus. In this second volume it appears that the author includes a travel diary of when he accompanied Paul on some of his journeys (e.g. Acts 16:10–17, where the narrative suddenly changes from 'they' to 'we'). By carrying out some detective work on Paul's travelling companions, we discover that Luke could have been present on these occasions. We further discover from Paul's letter to the Colossians 4:10–14 that Luke was a Gentile and a doctor.

The author of this Gospel undertook a considerable amount of research before writing, as is clear from Luke 1:1–4. The companion of Paul seems to have been in Palestine whilst Paul was in prison in Caesarea, and it has been suggested that Luke met people who had known Jesus and other eye-witnesses to the events during this time.

Why is Rome so important in the history of Christianity?

Why, When and Where Luke's Gospel was Written

The introduction to the Gospel gives one answer to the first of these questions. It seems that here we have a Gentile writing a Gospel for another Gentile – Theophilus. He therefore pictures Jesus as the Universal Saviour. Luke's Gospel, like Mark's Gospel, may also have been written in Rome, possibly between AD 80 and AD 90.

Important Themes

Not only does the author claim to have researched this Gospel carefully, he is also concerned to present the account within its historical setting (1:5 and 3:1–12). It is much more carefully written than Mark's Gospel and the following are among its emphases:

- **Gentiles and Samaritans** The author is eager to show that the mission of Jesus is to all, Gentiles (non-Jews) as well as Jews (e.g. 1:1 and 2:32).

- **The Jewish setting** is also important. We have already noted that this Gospel begins and ends in the Temple (1:8 and 24:53). There are also a number of Old Testament references included.

- **All sections of society** are included. There is a particular emphasis placed on concern for the underprivileged – the poor, outcasts, women and children.

- **The Holy Spirit** There is a marked emphasis on the Spirit of God at work in the world (e.g. 1:15, 1:35 and 1:41).

- **Joy, praise, prayer and worship** are all emphasised. You will notice that four songs of praise are included in the first two chapters.

ACTIVITIES

1 If you are studying the whole of Luke's Gospel, read it through, noticing the emphases mentioned above.

2 Head five sheets of paper – 'Gentiles', 'The Jewish Setting', 'All Sections of Society', 'The Holy Spirit' and 'Joy, Praise, Prayer and Worship'. As you continue with the course, add to your notes as in the example below:

3 If you have it available, read the introduction to this Gospel from the *Good News Bible*.

4 Answer all sections of this essay:
   a) What tradition about the authorship of the third Gospel was present in the early Church?
   b) What can we discover about the author from a study of the Gospel?
   c) What are the emphases of the third Gospel?

LUKE: THE HOLY SPIRIT		
Reference	Quotation	Comment
1:15	'He will be filled with the Holy Spirit'	Comment made to Zechariah about John
1:35	'The Holy Spirit will come upon you'	Comment made to Mary about the conception of her child

Matthew's Good News

The symbol of Matthew the Evangelist is a winged man, possibly indicating that this Gospel sees Jesus as the 'Divine Man', or because it begins with the human genealogy of Jesus.

The Author

There is an even bigger question mark over the authorship of Matthew's Gospel than over either of the other two Synoptic Gospels. The tradition of the early Church was that the Gospel was written by Matthew, the tax collector and apostle.

Some Christian writers of the second century AD comment about a certain 'Matthew'. Papias and Irenaeus (Bishop of Lyons) refer to Matthew as writing 'the oracles' or 'his Gospel'. However, it is by no means certain that 'the oracles' they refer to indicate the Gospel of Matthew. Some scholars think that the author cannot have been Matthew the apostle, who was obviously an eye-witness of the events, as he would not have used Mark's account. But this is by no means certain; if Mark was the interpreter of Peter, who is depicted as being closer to Jesus than Matthew was, there is no reason why Matthew should not have used Mark's account.

Why, When and Where Matthew's Gospel was Written

There is a marked Jewish emphasis in this Gospel, so it seems that the author was a Jew, writing for Jews. The author, perhaps a Jewish/Christian scribe, portrays Jesus as the 'Teaching Messiah'. It is very uncertain where and when the Gospel was written, although somewhere in Syria or Judaea, c. AD 80–90, has been suggested.

Important Themes

- The **Jewish emphasis** is very strong:

  - There are large numbers of references to the Old Testament (e.g. 1:23).

  - Terms such as 'Son of David' and 'Son of Abraham' are frequent (e.g. 1:1).

  - The words 'Kingdom of heaven' are used, rather than 'Kingdom of God' as in Mark and Luke (3:2). This is in order to avoid irreverence for God's name and is an indication of the Gospel's Jewishness.

  - There is an emphasis on the Law and prophets (5:17).

  - Israel is frequently mentioned, sometimes in an exclusive way (10:5–6).

- **Gentiles,** however, are not excluded (see 2:1–12, 8:5–13, 15:21–8 and 28:19–20).

- **Teaching** is emphasised. Three fifths of the Gospel concerns teaching (is didactic). Notice particularly chapters 5–7 and 24.

- There is an emphasis here on **the Church,** which is not found in the other Gospels (16:18 and 18:17).

A Torah scroll. Matthew's Gospel includes many references to the Law. Can you suggest a reason for this?

ACTIVITIES

1 If you have it available, read the introduction to this Gospel from the *Good News Bible*.

2 Look up the following verses in Matthew's Gospel: 7:28, 11:1, 13:53, 19:1 and 26:1. Write a paragraph explaining the significance of these verses and what they show about the possible structure of the Gospel.

3 Head two sheets of paper – 'Jewish Emphasis' and 'Teaching'. Fill them in as you continue with the course as in the following example:

MATTHEW: JEWISH EMPHASIS		
Reference	Quotation	Comment
1:1	'Jesus Christ, a descendant of David'	Jews looked for a Messiah of David's line.
1:1	'a descendant of Abraham'	Jews looked upon Abraham as the founder of their race.

Introducing John the Baptist and Jesus

TOPIC 6

'You will go ahead of the Lord to prepare his road for him.'

Setting the Scene

The only information we have about the birth and early life of John the Baptist is found at the beginning of Luke's Gospel. These accounts are intertwined with stories concerning Jesus' origins, and the first two chapters of Luke's Gospel are often referred to as the 'infancy narratives'. The first two chapters of Matthew's Gospel also concern the early life of Jesus; these are considered in Topic 8.

In the first chapter of his Gospel, Luke is eager to show the relationship between Jesus and John the Baptist, and he returns to this theme later in the Gospel.

> *The Lord Almighty answers, 'I will send my messenger to prepare the way for me. Then the Lord you are looking for will suddenly come to his Temple. The messenger you long to see will come and proclaim my covenant.'*
>
> *Malachi 3:1*

This and a number of other quotations from the Old Testament are referred to in the first two chapters of Luke's Gospel. Although it would appear that the writer is a Gentile, writing for Gentiles, he nevertheless wishes to include the Jewish setting of his story. A number of other themes and characteristics of Luke's Gospel are introduced in these opening chapters, for example:

- Worship – the opening account takes place in the Temple and this has echoes of the above quotation from Malachi. Four poems, which are songs of praise or worship, are also included in these first two chapters.

- The Holy Spirit is frequently mentioned as inspiring and being active in the events.

- There is an emphasis on the poor and underprivileged.

- The central theme of each Gospel is obviously about who Jesus was and why he was so important. This theme is introduced in the first two chapters of Luke's Gospel. Because the writer suggests that Jesus came to bring salvation, the Gospel is sometimes referred to as 'salvation history'.

So the first two chapters of Luke's Gospel form an introduction to the book.

The Infancy Narratives

The accounts of the origins of Jesus given by Luke and Matthew are clearly from their own special sources (see Topic 5), for they contain different material. As you have discovered (p. 22), the early Christians' preaching about Jesus did not mention his birth, but they were convinced that Jesus was the Son of God. Some scholars look upon the infancy narratives as legends which had developed in the Christian community to explain the beliefs about Jesus. Other Christians consider the stories to be so distinctive that Luke's information must have come originally from Mary, and Matthew's from Joseph.

ACTIVITIES

1 Answer the following questions:

   a) What are the 'infancy narratives'?

   b) Where are the stories of the birth of John the Baptist to be found?

   c) In which Gospels are the birth stories of Jesus?

   d) Who prophesied that the Lord would 'come to his Temple'?

   e) How does Luke introduce the theme of worship in the first two chapters of his Gospel?

2 As you study this Topic, remember to include information on your lists of themes from Luke's Gospel (see p. 33).

3 As you continue with your course, be sure to read each passage or pericope from the Gospels very carefully before you read this book. Your examination will test your knowledge, understanding and evaluation of the Gospels, not of this or any other textbook. As you read from the textbook always have your Bible open and refer to it constantly.

To Help You Understand

a) The Birth of John the Baptist Is Announced

Read Luke 1:5-25

LUKE We are introduced here to a priest, Zechariah, and his wife Elizabeth, who was also descended from a priestly family. They were elderly and they had no children, which, for many Jews, would indicate that God was not pleased with them.

Each of the 24 divisions of the priesthood was on duty for one week, twice a year. The division of Abijah was the eighth 'order' or 'course' and would include hundreds of priests. Priests drew lots for the honour of burning incense in the Holy Place of the Temple (see the plan on pp. 14 and 15), and no priest was allowed to offer incense more than once. So, for Zechariah, this would be a once-in-a-lifetime experience.

When we read the word 'angel' we automatically think of a being with wings, a halo and long white robes. However, there is no physical description given in the Bible, and the word in fact means 'messenger'. Zechariah's fear is understandable – he would not expect to see anyone in the Holy Place during the offering of incense. It is impossible to know whether the prayer referred to in verse 13 is intended to suggest a prayer for a child made years before, or a prayer for the coming of the Messiah, or a general prayer for Israel.

Details are given about a son who must be called John, meaning 'the Lord is gracious'. There is an instruction given that he must not drink alcohol. It has been suggested that the intention may have been that he should take Nazirite vows such as are mentioned in Numbers 6, but this is unlikely.

There is also a reference to a further prophecy from Malachi:

> *I will send you the prophet Elijah. He will bring fathers and children together again . . .*
>
> *Malachi 4:5-6*

After the message was given to Zechariah, the 'angel' was identified as Gabriel, a name meaning 'man of God', who is mentioned in the Old Testament. As a result of the shock of this experience and, it is suggested, as a consequence of his lack of faith, Zechariah became dumb until the birth of his child.

A model of first-century Jerusalem has been constructed in the present-day city. This photograph shows a reconstruction of the Temple, the setting for the annunciation to Zechariah.

ACTIVITIES

1 If necessary, look back at Topic 2 to discover when the king mentioned in verse 5 reigned.

2 Make a list of the points made about John in verses 13–17.

3 Consult the diagram on pp. 14 and 15 to find out in which part of the Temple this story is set.

4 Discuss why Luke includes so many references to the Old Testament in the early chapters of his Gospel.

b) The Birth of Jesus Is Announced

Read Luke 1:26–38

LUKE This account is known as the Annunciation, or announcement to Mary concerning her child. The story is linked to the previous one by the dating: in the sixth month of Elizabeth's pregnancy. This time the setting is Nazareth, a small town in Galilee.

As we saw in the discussion about the expected Messiah (Topic 4), the suggested connection with King David is very important. The words of the angel begin with the traditional Jewish greeting, 'Shalom . . .' (Peace).

Mary's reaction was similar to that of Zechariah, but the message to her that follows is very different. The name to be given to her child is Jesus, the New Testament version of the

Hebrew Joshua, which means 'the Lord is salvation'. Mary questioned how this could be possible since she was a virgin, but after being assured that the child would be the Son of God she expressed her willingness to co-operate.

C S Lewis made an interesting suggestion about belief in the Incarnation:

> *The central miracle asserted by Christians is the Incarnation. They say that God became Man. Every other miracle prepares for this, or exhibits this, or results from this.*
>
> From C S Lewis, Miracles

Look up a map and check the position of Nazareth.

ACTIVITY

Look at the illustration of the Annunciation and answer the following questions:

a) Who does the figure on the left represent?

b) Who does the figure on the right represent?

c) What is the meaning of 'Annunciation'?

d) Write down three things stated about the child in the passage you have just read.

e) What was the response to the message?

f) How well do you think this painting interprets the story?

The Annunciation, Domenico Veneziano (c. *1445*)

c) Mary Visits Elizabeth

Read Luke 1:39–45

LUKE In this short section the two earlier accounts in the same chapter are brought together. A further link in the accounts of John and Jesus is the fact that the mothers were related (verse 36). We cannot be sure what the relationship was, but it is suggested that Elizabeth was either the aunt or the cousin of Mary. Similarly, it is impossible to know where Zechariah and Elizabeth lived, but tradition has located the town in the 'hill-country of Judaea' as Ein Karem.

Mary would have many problems to face when she became pregnant and, possibly because she felt that Elizabeth would understand, she decided to make the long journey from Nazareth to visit her relative. Elizabeth believed that a movement of her child within her indicated that Mary's child would be 'the Lord'.

d) Mary's Song of Praise

Read Luke 1:46–56

LUKE This song of praise is known as the Magnificat from the opening word in Latin. It has similarities with Hannah's prayer after the birth of Samuel (1 Samuel 2:1–10).

The Lord has filled my heart with joy: how happy I am because of what he has done!
I laugh at my enemies; how joyful I am because God has helped me.

1 Samuel 2:1

It has been suggested that the writer of Luke's Gospel composed this poem using Hannah's prayer as a pattern. Another view is that Mary had thought about the relevance of this prayer to her own situation before she met Elizabeth, and that it does therefore reflect her thoughts. However it came to be written, the Magnificat has become very important in the Christian Church: it is used, for example, by the Roman Catholic Church at Vespers and in the Anglican service of Evening Prayer.

The Magnificat may be divided into four parts:

- Mary's thankfulness for what God has done for her,
- God's power, holiness and mercy,
- God reverses normal ideas about greatness,
- God's continuing help for his people.

It is suggested that Mary left for Nazareth just before the birth of John.

*Tell out, my soul, the greatness of
the Lord!*
*Unnumbered blessings, give my
spirit voice;*
*Tender to me the promise of his
word;*
*In God my Saviour shall my heart
rejoice.*

*Tell out, my soul, the greatness of
his name!*
*Make known his might, the deeds
his arm has done;*
*His mercy sure, from age to age the
same;*
*His holy name – the Lord, the
Mighty One.*

*Tell out, my soul, the greatness of
his might!*
*Powers and dominions lay their
glory by.*
*Proud hearts and stubborn wills are
put to flight,*
*The hungry fed, the humble lifted
high.*

*Tell out, my soul, the glories of his
word!*
*Firm is his promise, and his mercy
sure.*
*Tell out, my soul, the greatness of
the Lord*
*To children's children and for
evermore!*

Timothy Dudley-Smith

ACTIVITY

Having read the above modern version of the Magnificat, which has become a favourite hymn during this century, answer the following questions:

a) What is the name of the poem on which this hymn is based?

b) Summarise, in your own words, the main theme of each of the four verses.

c) Why do you think Mary was so joyful in this song of praise?

e) The Birth of John the Baptist

Read Luke 1:57–66

LUKE Look up the birth customs mentioned in Genesis 17:1–4, Exodus 13:14, Leviticus 12:6 and Numbers 18:15–16.

It seems that for some Jews it was usual to name the first-born son after his father, but Elizabeth insisted that it should not be so. We have not been told that Zechariah was deaf as well as dumb, but his neighbours insisted on treating him as if he could not hear (verse 62).

Perhaps this reflects attitudes which we can still find today!

f) Zechariah's Prophecy

Read Luke 1:67–80

LUKE This is a second poem, also given a Latin name – the Benedictus – taken from the first word. This poem could well have been based on traditions concerning the thoughts of Zechariah during his nine months of silence.

As with the Magnificat, we can divide the Benedictus into four sections:

- Thanksgiving for a Saviour,

- The promised salvation,

- John's part in the plan,

- God's mercy in providing salvation.

This important prophecy is widely used in the Church; it is recited during morning prayer in Anglican churches, for example. The reference to the desert in verse 80 may mean that John led a secluded life until the start of his public ministry. There may have been a connection with the Essene community (see Topic 3). It is a possibility that John's parents died whilst he was still a child, and it is known that the Essenes brought up orphans.

ACTIVITIES

1 Check that you have added information to the thematic lists for Luke's Gospel, for example, on the subject of the Holy Spirit.

2 Look up the Benedictus and divide it into the four sections shown on p. 41.

3 There are a number of important words used in the Benedictus. Some have already been explained. Look up any of the following that you do not understand and make a note of their meaning:

Holy Spirit   Saviour   covenant   holy   righteous   forgiven   merciful   salvation

4 Look up Luke 1:76–9 and answer the following questions:

 a) Of which poem are these verses a part?

 b) Which child is referred to in verse 76?

 c) What would be the child's job when he grew up?

 d) What is the meaning of the word 'salvation'?

 e) To what is salvation likened in this passage?

5 Discuss how and why the writer of Luke's Gospel weaves together the stories of John and Jesus.

To Keep You Thinking

1 Belief in the Virgin conception
The belief that Jesus was the Son of God rather than the son of Joseph is an important belief for many Christians. Discuss this.

2 The celebration of Advent
Many Christians prepare themselves for Christmas during the preceding month. Find out how.

3 Human rights
Look again at the Magnificat and work out what it suggests about the underprivileged.

The Childhood of Jesus

TOPIC 7

'But when the right time finally came, God sent his own Son. He came as the son of a human mother . . .'

Setting the Scene

What would be your reply to the question: 'When did the birth of Jesus take place?'? The most obvious answer might be 25 December at the end of 1 BC, before the start of AD 1. However, it is unlikely that either the date or the year is correct.

The first Christians did not celebrate the birth of Christ, and it may well be that a considerable length of time passed before they realised its significance. Eventually a date was chosen – 6 January; and the birth of Jesus is still celebrated on this date by the Eastern Orthodox Churches. By the fourth century, 25 December had been chosen by the Western (Roman Catholic) Church, perhaps to replace the Roman festival of Saturnalia. However, if we consider the details of the Gospels, it is very unlikely that shepherds would have been out in the fields overnight in December, when it is quite cold and can be very wet. From this point of view it is much more likely that the event happened sometime between March and October.

The year of Jesus' birth was calculated in the sixth century by a monk, but it is now known that he made a mistake in his calculations. We need to do a considerable amount of detective work in order to find the most likely date. (The details of what follows are not necessary for examination purposes, but the information is given to illustrate that there are still many puzzles remaining in the study of the Gospels, where the evidence needs to be carefully considered.)

- Herod the Great was king in Judaea at the time of Jesus' birth (Matthew 2:1). He died in 4 BC, so the nativity (nativity = birth) must have taken place sometime before that date.

- Luke, who goes to some lengths to give the historical background, mentions that the Emperor Augustus had ordered a census, which took place when someone called Quirinius was governor of Syria. It seems that Quirinius carried out a census in AD 6. Some scholars think that Quirinius may have been in office at an earlier period also, between 10 BC and 7 BC. Roman censuses seem to have taken place every 14 years.

- Matthew tells us about a star which indicated to the magi or wise men that the king of the Jews had been born. Suggestions have been made that:
  – comets appeared in both 5 BC and 4 BC,
  – in 6 BC there was a rare conjunction of the planets Jupiter, Saturn and Venus,
  – a nova (new star) or supernova appeared in 5 BC.

Christmas card with star. In which Gospel is a star mentioned?

- Luke tells us that Jesus was about 30 years old when he began his work (Luke 3:23). He had already suggested that this was in the fifteenth year of the Emperor Tiberius (Luke 3:1). Tiberius began to reign in AD 14, although he had been co-regent from about AD 11. We do not know from which of these dates Luke is calculating the 15 years.

ACTIVITIES

1 Construct a time-line as shown to include the information given above. The first point is inserted to help you:

```
            BC              AD
 8 7 6 5 4 3 2 1 | 1 2 3 4 5 6 7 8
           ↑
      Death of Herod
```

2 Discuss the evidence given here with reference to the date of Jesus' birth. Do you think it is possible to reach any conclusions about the exact date of his birth? Do you agree with the suggestion on p. 8?

3 Some Christian groups do not celebrate Christmas because of the impossibility of knowing the actual date, and because of the many non-Christian customs which are incorporated today. Discuss your opinions about this.

Most people have ideas about the birth stories, which may have been formed by their experience of infant school nativity plays. Often legendary material has been added to the Gospel accounts and conclusions have been drawn from resulting stories which we accept as fact. Where did the birth take place? How many shepherds visited the baby? Did they bring gifts? How many wise men were there? Be very careful to find out exactly what the Gospels say about these and other matters and do not include in your written work fanciful descriptions which are not found in the text.

To Help You Understand

a) The Birth of Jesus
Read Luke 2:1–7

LUKE We have already noted details concerning the census ordered by the Emperor Augustus. A number of interesting documents exist from later Roman censuses. The extract quoted below dates from AD 104:

> *Gaius Vibius, chief prefect of Egypt. Because of the approaching census it is necessary for all those residing for any cause away from their own districts to prepare to return at once to their own governments, in order that they may complete the family administration of the enrolment . . .*
>
> *Translated from the Greek by E M Blaiklock*

Details of census returns have survived in Egypt where the very dry climate helps to preserve papyrus (ancient paper) documents. Details include names, ages and occasionally physical descriptions of those being registered. Sadly, no such records survive from Palestine; they would make interesting reading!

'Welcome to Bethlehem.'
What are the three languages?

The Nativity, *Gerard Van Honthorst*

We know from 1 Samuel 17:12–15 that David came from Bethlehem, and it was necessary for Joseph, a descendant of David, to return there for the census. We are not told how long it was after the arrival that the birth took place, nor that it occurred in a stable! The only association with animals is the reference to a manger or eating trough. Because there was no room in the inn, it may be that the birth took place in either a basement or a cave where animals were sometimes stabled.

Manger found at Megiddo dating from the ninth century BC

Tom Davies, a travel writer, describes a recent visit to Bethlehem on his way from Jerusalem:

Bethlehem is six miles down the road: a sour sight and awash with nastiness. Manger Square is stuffed with souvenir shops and beckoning shop owners. Cheap strings of lights run around the square and there are many soldiers. The Church of Nativity itself even has policemen inside it with hundreds of visitors being herded like so many goats. Move on there please. Move on.

But, away from the square, there are tiny, twisting roads and interlinking houses made from wattle and daub. A goat steps out of one doorway and looks up with crazy bulging eyes. It is difficult to believe the place has changed at all since the time nearly 2000 years ago, when a pregnant woman and her husband journeyed here to give birth.

45

ACTIVITIES

1 Collect reproductions of famous paintings of the nativity, similar to those shown below and on p. 45. Some Christmas cards show these. Display the illustrations with your comments about their interpretation of the Gospel accounts.

2 Begin some coursework which will continue throughout this Topic on the importance of the infancy narratives to Christians today. Include the importance and use of the text in worship, and celebrations which are based on the accounts.

b) The Shepherds and the Angels

Read Luke 2:8–20

The Adoration of the Shepherds, *Guido Reni*

LUKE Although many famous people in Jewish history were shepherds, it seems that by New Testament times the occupation was despised, apparently because shepherds were so busy looking after their animals that they were unable to carry out all the details of the ceremonial law. The references to the incon- veniences of the birth (Luke 2:5 and 2:7) and these first visitors emphasise again Luke's stress on the underprivileged. It was to these representatives of ordinary working people that the news of the birth was first given. Understandably, they greeted the appearance of the angel (messenger) with fear, but were assured that the message was good news. An army of angels is mentioned – announcing peace! The brief song of praise in verse 14 is known as the Gloria in Excelsis; the words are included in some familiar Christmas carols. Notice that we are not told how many shepherds visited the infant, nor that they brought gifts. Notice also that Luke makes no mention of a star.

The area of the Shepherds' Fields, near Bethlehem

ACTIVITIES

1 Complete this front page article, 'Angel Voices!', by writing up the shepherd's description of what happened.

2 A church youth fellowship, including a farm worker, were once discussing the possibility of presenting a realistic nativity play. They eventually decided that the church stewards would not be happy with their proposals! Discuss what might be involved in such an undertaking.

3 Read Luke 2:10–12 and answer the following questions:
   a) Where was 'David's town'?
   b) Mention four things stated by the angel.
   c) What three titles are given to Jesus here? Explain the meaning of each.
   d) Why is it significant that the first people to hear the news of the birth were shepherds?
   e) What was the shepherds' response to what they heard?
   f) What was Mary's eventual response to the events?

Heavenly choir sensation
'STRANGE LIGHT' SAYS SHEPHERD

ANGEL VOICES!
NEWBORN BABY FOUND IN PUB BACK-YARD
From Jochanan ben-Isaac, BETHLEHEM

BETHLEHEM shepherds report that they have seen an angel on the hills outside the town! Not content with that, they also claim to have heard what they call 'the heavenly choir.' This sensational news comes as a climax to the past days of census-taking in which thousands from all over the country have been converging on their family homes to register both themselves and their families.

I spoke to one of the shepherds myself, and questioned the truth of their story. A shy man, he refused to give his name but left me in no doubt that his story was true:

From Eastern Star (a 'newspaper' compiled from biblical and other first-century sources) No. 1

c) Jesus Is Named and Presented in the Temple

Read Luke 2:21–40

LUKE As with John the Baptist, Jesus was circumcised and named on the eighth day after his birth. You considered various customs associated with birth in Topic 6, and here a number of them are illustrated. It is significant that for her purification Mary gave the offering laid down for the poor.

If a woman cannot afford a lamb, she shall bring two doves or two pigeons, one for a burnt-offering and the other for a sin-offering, and the priest shall perform the ritual to take away her impurity, and she will be ritually clean.

Leviticus 12:8 (see also verse 6)

Simeon met the parents and child in the Temple. It is sometimes suggested that Simeon was an elderly priest, but neither of these points is stated in the text. The statement in verse 29 that he was ready to die has been taken to indicate that he was old. We are told that he was devout (earnest in his religious duties) and was waiting for the promised Messiah.

The Song of Simeon (verses 29–32) is the fourth and last of the poems in the early chapters of Luke and again is known by its Latin title – the Nunc Dimittis. Luke includes the statement that a light has come 'to reveal your will to the Gentiles'. Simeon goes on to make prophecies about the child. Again, in the Nunc Dimittis and the prophecies that follow, it is possible to see four themes emerging:

- Salvation will come through the child.

- His mission will be to both Jews and Gentiles.

- There will be varying reactions to Jesus.

- Mary will suffer because of the child.

The Nunc Dimittis is used in some churches as part of Evening Prayer, and may be used as a reading at a Church of England Thanksgiving for the Birth of a Child.

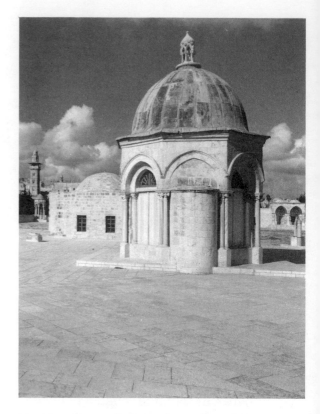

The Temple area in Jerusalem, where Jesus was taken as an infant, is only a short distance from the Church of the Holy Sepulchre which is on a possible site of his crucifixion.

ACTIVITIES

Collect for 2 February:

Almighty Father,
whose Son Jesus Christ was presented
* in the Temple*
and acclaimed the glory of Israel and
* the light of the nations:*
grant that in him we may be
* presented to you*
and in the world may reflect his glory;
through Jesus Christ our Lord.

The Alternative Service Book, 1980

---

1 Answer the following questions:
   a) On which occasion was Jesus presented in the Temple?
   b) Which poem is referred to in the collect (prayer), opposite?
   c) Which themes, found throughout Luke's Gospel, are mentioned in the original poem (Luke 2:29–32)?
   d) What does the collect show about how Christians use the passage from the Gospel in worship?

2 Look again at Luke 2:29–35. Write out the four themes listed above and under each write the words from the passage which illustrate the theme.

3 Make a list of the similarities in the early stories of John the Baptist and Jesus, as they are told by Luke.

d) The Boy Jesus in the Temple
Read Luke 2:41–52

LUKE This passage is the only recorded incident concerning the boyhood of Jesus. Becoming Bar Mitzvah (Son of the Commandments) is an important step in a Jewish boy's education. A Jewish writing, the Mishnah, suggests that preparations for becoming Bar Mitzvah could take place a year or two before the age of 13, and this is probably what is happening in this story.

A Jewish boy celebrates his Bar Mitzvah by the Western Wall of the Temple. Why here?

It has been estimated that the population of Jerusalem increased sixfold at Passover time, and tents and rough shelters would appear everywhere in the surrounding countryside. In such a crowd, it would be easy to lose a child and difficult to find him again. The 'third day' may include the two days' journey. Rabbis taught in the outer courts of the Temple and it was there that Jesus was eventually found. Jesus' reply to Mary's reprimand suggests that he understood his very special relationship with God.

At the end of the account, emphasis is placed on Jesus' obedience and development – physical, intellectual, spiritual and social – and on Mary's reaction to the events.

ACTIVITIES

1 With reference to Luke 2:43–6, answer the following questions:
   a) Which festival is referred to?
   b) Why did Jesus accompany his parents on this occasion?
   c) Where was Jesus eventually found?
   d) What was surprising about what he was doing?
   e) What reply did he give to his mother's reprimand?
   f) Why do you think Mary was surprised by the reply?

2 Make sure that you include all relevant references on your thematic lists.

e) The Ancestors of Jesus
Read Luke 3:23–38

LUKE It is interesting that Luke includes this genealogy immediately following the account of Jesus' baptism, and not before the story of his birth, which is where Matthew includes it. At the baptism, it is recorded that a voice from heaven said, 'You are my own dear Son . . .'. Perhaps the genealogy follows in order to illustrate that statement. Notice that Luke traces the list of names back, beyond Abraham, to 'Seth, the son of Adam, the son of God'. (You will be glad to know that it is not necessary to learn all the names!) Because this genealogy differs from the one given in Matthew's Gospel, it has been suggested that this is Mary's family tree (note that it is made clear in verse 23 that Jesus was not actually the son of Joseph). However, this is by no means certain.

ACTIVITIES

1 Answer the following questions:

'. . . the son of Adam, the son of God.'

a) In which Gospel are the above words to be found?

b) What is a genealogy?

c) Which story precedes this genealogy and why is it significant?

d) Why do you think Luke was concerned to trace Jesus' ancestry back beyond Abraham, the forefather of the Jews?

2 Answer briefly the following questions on the birth stories:

a) What is the most likely date of the birth of Jesus?

b) Who issued a decree for a census?

c) By what Latin name do we know the song of the angels?

d) What sacrifice was brought by Mary to the Temple?

e) When might some Christians use the Nunc Dimittis?

f) Where might Luke have obtained the material for these accounts?

g) What is the meaning of the name Jesus?

h) What were Mary's reactions to the events?

To Keep You Thinking

1 The celebration of Christmas
Discuss how far you think the celebrations of Christmas today are Christian.

2 Family relationships
Consider what can be learned by Christian parents and children today from the account of Jesus in the Temple at the age of 12.

Family Connections

'. . . Jesus Christ, a descendant of David, who was a descendant of Abraham.'

Setting the Scene

Matthew has his own distinctive birth stories, and it is these that we shall consider in this Topic. They are not from the same source as Luke's infancy narratives, and reflect different interests. Matthew's accounts are very Jewish in emphasis and approach the events from Joseph's point of view rather than from that of Mary, as is the case in Luke's Gospel. If you are studying only Matthew's Gospel, look back at the introduction to Topic 7 to find out what is known about when Jesus was born.

To Help You Understand

a) The Ancestors of Jesus Christ

Read Matthew 1:1-17

MATTHEW Notice that Matthew traces the royal descent of Jesus through David, but goes back to Abraham who was considered to be the father of the Jewish nation. It seems that the writer originally arranged this list of names in three groups of 14 (the last group now includes only 13 names). Letters have a numerical value in Hebrew and the Hebrew letters for David add up to 14. Another interesting point about Matthew's list is that it includes four women, which was unusual in a genealogy of those days especially since the ones included are not the best examples of Jewish womanhood!

We learn from verse 16 that this is the genealogy of Joseph; it is therefore the legal family tree of Jesus. At the same time it is worth noting that the verse states that Mary was the mother of Jesus, rather than that Joseph was his father – an idea which is returned to later, in verse 20.

Madonna and Child, *Henry Moore. Discuss your reactions to this sculpture.*

ACTIVITIES

1 Look carefully through the list of names to see which individuals you know about from the Old Testament. (You do not need to *learn* the names!)

2 Look in a concordance or a Bible dictionary to find out about the four women included in the genealogy.

3 If you are also studying Luke's Gospel, look up Luke 3:23–38 and make a note of the similarities and differences between the two accounts.

b) The Birth of Jesus Christ

Read Matthew 1:18–25

MATTHEW Here we are told of Joseph's reaction to the news of Mary's pregnancy. If a woman was unfaithful in the period between her engagement and marriage, this was considered to be adultery and the punishment would be the same as it would be for a married woman.

> *If a man commits adultery with the wife of a fellow-Israelite, both he and the woman shall be put to death.*
>
> *Leviticus 20:10*

When he realised that Mary was pregnant, Joseph decided to break the engagement quietly. Matthew suggests frequently that dreams were used to guide the individuals in these stories. This idea is frequently mentioned in the Old Testament – perhaps you can think of some examples? As in Luke, the significance of the name Jesus is emphasised. The birth stories recorded by Matthew illustrate how Old Testament prophecy has been fulfilled. The verse quoted here is from Isaiah:

> *. . . the Lord himself will give you a sign: a young woman who is pregnant will have a son and will name him 'Immanuel'.*
>
> *Isaiah 7:14*

Some think that Isaiah was referring to a young woman of his time, but Matthew emphasises the meaning of Immanuel and applies the prophecies to Jesus.

Describe what is happening in this scene from the medieval Wakefield plays.

A difference of interpretation is found in verse 25. Roman Catholics believe that Mary and Joseph did not have a sexual relationship at any time, a doctrine which is referred to as the perpetual virginity of Mary. According to this view, the brothers and sisters mentioned in Mark 3:31–2 and named in Mark 6:3 and Matthew 13:55–6 were either stepbrothers and stepsisters (children of Joseph by a previous marriage) or cousins. Most Protestants believe that Mary had other children after the birth of Jesus.

ACTIVITIES

1 As you read the birth stories from Matthew, make a list of the prophecies which he suggests have been fulfilled.

2 Make a note of all the dreams that are mentioned in these stories in Matthew, as you find them.

3 If you are also studying Luke's Gospel, discuss the similarities and differences between the two birth accounts.

c) Visitors from the East

Read Matthew 2:1–12

MATTHEW A similarity to Luke's account is the reference found here to Bethlehem as the place of Jesus' birth. However, it is only in Matthew that we find reference to the wise men and the star. It may seem strange that Matthew, with his Jewish emphasis, should record a story about Gentiles coming to see the child, but notice that they are seeking 'the king of the Jews'.

Which prophet referred to Bethlehem as the place of the Messiah's birth?

There is much extra legendary material which has become associated with this account. Notice that these visitors from the East are not kings but wise men, magi or astrologers. The account does not state that there were three of them, nor are we told their names or which country they came from.

Matthew agrees with Luke that Herod was the king at this time. His actions as recorded in these accounts are in character with what we know of him as a historical figure.

Again, Matthew sees the fulfilment of prophecy, this time in the fact of the birth in Bethlehem.

> *. . . Bethlehem Ephrathah, you are one of the smallest towns in Judah, but out of you I will bring a ruler for Israel, whose family line goes back to ancient times.*
>
> Micah 5:2

In most nativity plays, the entrance of the wise men follows immediately after that of the shepherds; but by the time the wise men arrived, the family were in a house, and up to two years may have passed since the birth (see verses 7 and 16).

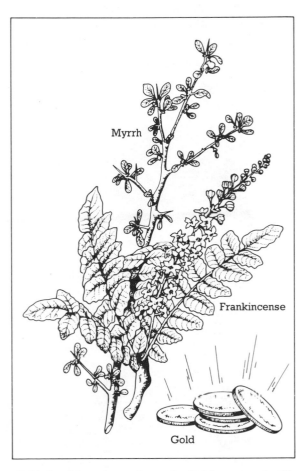

Gold, frankincense and myrrh. Gold was, and still is, a rare and therefore a precious metal. Incense is the hardened resin from the frankincense tree which is still burned in some churches as it was in the Temple. Myrrh is a shrub producing a fragrant gum resin.
How were these gifts appropriate for the child?

Great significance is seen in these very expensive gifts brought by the magi. Gold signified that Jesus was a king, frankincense was used by priests in worship and symbolised prayer being offered to God, and myrrh, which was used at burials, signified Jesus' humanity and death. This last gift was rather like taking a coffin to a newborn baby!

The story ends with the mention of another dream.

53

ACTIVITIES

1 Look back at the information about Herod the Great in Topic 2.

2 Find a carol about this story. Look at it carefully and work out which is a) material taken from the Gospels, b) legend and c) Christian interpretation.

3 Answer the following questions:

a) In which Gospel do we find the story illustrated below?

b) What part did Herod play in the story?

c) What gifts were brought to the child?

d) What symbolism have Christians seen in these gifts?

e) What legends have you heard associated with this story?

f) Do you think it matters that biblical stories and legends are often confused?

Detail from The Adoration of the Magi, *Rubens*

d) Escape to and Return from Egypt

Read Matthew 2:13–23

MATTHEW This sections begins with a dream and a prophecy:

> **The Lord says, 'When Israel was a child I loved him and called him out of Egypt as my son . . .'**
>
> *Hosea 11:1*

You may remember that Moses led Israel out of Egypt. It has been suggested that Matthew wished to show Jesus as a second and greater Moses.

The killing of the children, or the Massacre of the Innocents as the story is sometimes called, demonstrates the cruelty of Herod. Some have seen in it a parallel with the story of Moses in Exodus 1:22 – 2:10. The story ends with a quotation from Jeremiah 31:15, where the prophet thinks of Rachel who died in childbirth centuries before his time, weeping for the Jews who have been taken into exile in Babylon. Now Matthew applies the verse to the women of Bethlehem.

We are not told how long the family remained as refugees in Egypt.

As the result of another dream, Joseph took the family back to Israel after the death of Herod the Great. Archelaus became the ruler of Judaea and became known for his cruelty, like his father before him. After another dream, Joseph decided to settle permanently in Nazareth, in the territory of Herod Antipas. Again, a prophecy ends this section, but there is a mystery here as the verse is not found in this form in the Old Testament.

The Holy Family Asleep, *Rembrandt*

ACTIVITIES

1 Discuss the theme of suffering which is found in the birth accounts.

2 Look up Matthew 2:13–15 and answer the following questions:

   a) Why should Herod want to kill the child?

   b) Which Herod is referred to here?

   c) Who is meant by 'they' in verse 13?

   d) From which event did the family escape?

   e) When did Herod die?

   f) Which prophecy is included here?

   g) Why do you think Matthew includes prophecies in his birth accounts?

3 Discuss the reproduction of works of art which appear in Topics 8–10. Which do you think are most effective in interpreting the Gospel accounts?

4 If you are studying both Gospels, head two columns 'Matthew' and 'Luke'. Then sort the following accounts into the appropriate column and put them into the order in which they appear in the Gospels:

   - The Annunciation
   - The Shepherds
   - The Escape to Egypt
   - Visitors from the East
   - The Presentation in the Temple
   - The Nunc Dimittis
   - The Return from Egypt
   - The Benedictus
   - The Killing of the Children
   - The Magnificat
   - The Birth of Jesus
   - The Birth of John

Matthew's Use of Prophecies

We have noticed that Matthew's Gospel has a Jewish emphasis and includes many references to the Old Testament. All the accounts in this Topic illustrate the fulfilment of Old Testament prophecies. The writer was obviously eager to show that Jesus was the Messiah promised in the Old Testament.

It is possible that early in the history of the Christian Church collections of proof texts or testimonia were gathered together to show that Jesus fulfilled Old Testament prophecies. In Matthew 1:18 – 2:23 we can see the way they were used by Jewish Christian communities.

To Keep You Thinking

1 **Belief in the Incarnation**
   Try to find a Christmas hymn or carol which states the doctrine that God became man in Jesus.

2 **The celebration of Epiphany**
   Discover when, how and why Epiphany is celebrated.

Baptism and Temptation

'God sent his messenger, a man named John, who came to tell people about the light, so that all should hear the message and believe.'

Setting the Scene

When Jews today sit down to their Passover meal, they have a place set for Elijah, who is invited to join them. Look on p. 124 to find out the connection between Elijah and the Messiah.

> *But before the great and terrible day of the Lord comes, I will send you the prophet Elijah.*
>
> *Malachi 4:5*

The sudden appearance of John by the River Jordan was full of drama for the people of his day. It was 400 years since there had been a prophet in Israel, but certain things about John reminded his contemporaries of the prophet Elijah:

> *He [Elijah] was wearing a cloak made of animal skins, tied with a leather belt.*
>
> *2 Kings 1:8*

> *Elijah said . . . 'The Lord has ordered me to go to the River Jordan' . . . fifty of the prophets followed them to the Jordan . . . and Elijah was taken up to heaven by a whirlwind.*
>
> *2 Kings 2:1-16*

ACTIVITIES

1 Look up and discuss the three extracts from the Old Testament.

2 Read Mark 1:4–6 and write down the answers to the following questions:

   a) Where did John the Baptist begin his preaching?

   b) What was there about John that reminded people of the prophet Elijah?

   c) Why do you think the crowds flocked to see and hear John?

Baptism

There is evidence that Jews practised baptism in the first century, so this element of John's ministry would not cause too much surprise. It seems that Gentiles who wished to enter the Jewish faith were baptised. The Essenes (see Topic 3) frequently had ritual baptisms for purification purposes. John's baptism was different from either of these, as it was on the basis of repentance, for Jews as well as Gentiles, and was performed only once for each individual. The method used is not clear. The word 'baptise' means 'dip', and is used for immersing material into dye, for example. So the baptism may have been by immersion, or by pouring or sprinkling water over the head.

57

The Jewish historian, Josephus, writing c.AD 90, made the following comment:

> *John, that was called the Baptist . . . was a good man and commanded the Jews to exercise virtue, both as to righteousness towards one another, and piety towards God, and so to come to baptism.*
>
> Josephus, Antiquities of the Jews 18:15.2

Josephus was not a Christian, and he was writing independently of the New Testament. We shall see later that he gives us more details about John the Baptist.

ACTIVITY

Make a note, in your own words, of what Josephus suggested about who John was and what he said.

Temptation

A Chinese proverb suggests that you cannot prevent birds from flying round your head, but you can stop them making a nest in your hair. This helps us to understand the Christian attitude to temptation; all are tempted but this does not necessarily mean giving in to the temptation. The Gospels suggest that immediately after Jesus' experience at his baptism, when he had confirmation that he was the Son of God, he went into the desert where he was tempted, or tested, by Satan. His experience of dedication to the work God had for him to do was followed by a time of doubt concerning how he could best do it.

It has been suggested that the desert referred to in these accounts was the desert or wilderness of Judaea, which is situated between Jerusalem and the River Jordan (see Topic 1). For many places mentioned in the Gospels, Christian tradition has identified a particular site – in this case a mountain now known as the Mount of the Temptation; there is a monastery precariously situated on its slopes (see the photograph on p. 59).

The desert or wilderness was a place of great danger. Not only was it extremely hot and very difficult to find any food or water, it was also the haunt of wild animals and traditionally considered to be the home of evil spirits. According to Luke, Jesus referred to this tradition in his teaching, 'When an evil spirit goes out of a person, it travels over dry country looking for a place to rest' (Luke 11:24). The accounts in the Gospels of the temptation of Jesus remind us of a number of Old Testament stories. In Genesis 3 there is the story of the temptation and disobedience of Adam and Eve. Before the beginning of his ministry, Jesus was tempted, but he overcame the temptations and was obedient to God's purposes. The writer of a well-known hymn shows the connection between the Old and New Testament stories:

> *O loving wisdom of our God!*
> *When all was sin and shame,*
> *A second Adam to the fight*
> *And to the rescue came.*
>
> *O wisest love! that flesh and blood*
> *Which did in Adam fail,*
> *Should strive afresh against the foe,*
> *Should strive and should prevail.*
>
> From 'Praise to the Holiest in the height',
> J H Newman (1801–90)

Another Old Testament story which took place in a desert and involves a period of 40 days concerns Moses, who it is suggested in the book of Exodus went up Mount Sinai to receive the ten commandments:

> *Moses stayed there with the Lord forty days and nights, eating and drinking nothing.*
>
> Exodus 34:28

We have already discovered connections between Jesus and Moses, especially those made in Matthew's Gospel, and here we discover another parallel. You may remember also that the Israelites were pictured as wandering in the Sinai desert for 40 years; this was obviously a significant number for Jews. Another 40 days is mentioned later in the New Testament – read Acts 1:3.

The Mount of the Temptation

ACTIVITIES

1 Discuss the Chinese proverb mentioned on p. 58. What do you think it means?

2 Try to find a complete copy of the hymn 'Praise to the Holiest in the height'. What sufferings of Jesus, which also involved temptations, are mentioned in the hymn?

3 Answer the following questions, briefly:

a) Which event immediately preceded the temptation of Jesus?

b) Who tempted Jesus?

c) Where may these events have taken place?

d) Why was the desert an appropriate setting for the account of the temptation?

e) Give two examples of the use of the number 40 in the Old Testament.

f) What period of 40 days is referred to later in connection with the story of Jesus?

To Help You Understand

a) The Preaching of John the Baptist

Read Mark 1:1–8, Luke 3:1–20, Matthew 3:1–12

MARK
LUKE
MATTHEW
The ministry of John took place by the River Jordan. The writers of the Gospels see John's work as a fulfilment of prophecies from the Old Testament.

ACTIVITIES

1 If your Bible has footnotes, learn how to use them. Find where the writer of the Gospel quotes verses from Isaiah in the passage you have just read. Look at the note at the bottom of the page to find the reference. Look it up.

2 Discuss why the writer quoted these verses.

As we have seen, John wore similar clothing to Elijah and lived on what he could gather: honey and locusts. The latter may refer to the fruit of the carob tree, called locust beans, or the actual insects, which are still a delicacy for some bedouins, and which Jews were permitted to eat (see Leviticus 11:22).

As one who was preparing the way for the Messiah, John's preaching was rather surprising. He did not denounce the Romans, or preach revolution, but spoke of a personal preparation of repentance (turning around and going in a different direction). He assured those who did repent of their sins (or turn away from them and start afresh) that God would forgive them. We shall see in Topic 10 that Jesus repeated this message. John baptised those who repented as an outward sign of what had happened in their lives. He also ended speculation that he might be the promised Messiah by speaking of a greater one who would come, whose servant he was not fit to be. The one who would come would bring them a more important baptism, which would involve the Spirit of God.

LUKE We have already noticed (in Topic 5) the emphasis in Luke's Gospel on the historical background. Here he dates as precisely as possible the beginning of John's ministry. Luke's quotation from the prophet Isaiah is longer than that of Mark or Matthew, and includes the words 'All mankind will see God's salvation.' Look back at Topic 5 to remind yourself of the significance of this. Luke tells us what was said to each group of people who presented themselves for baptism.

LUKE
MATTHEW
Luke and Matthew have more information about John's preaching concerning judgement than Mark includes. They emphasise that judgement must be faced by all, including Jews, who tended to think that, as God's chosen people, they had special privileges. They speak of the Messiah bringing this judgement, and liken it to fire burning the chaff. Luke and Matthew may have had this information from a common source – turn back to Topic 5 to remind yourselves what it is called and why.

Judgement. How do these two photographs illustrate judgement?

A winnowing fork used to separate grain from chaff

Fire burning stubble

ACTIVITIES

1 Discuss whether you think John's preaching was 'good news'.

2 Answer the following questions:
   a) What was John the Baptist's basic message?

   b) Why did John baptise people?

   c) Why did Luke quote a longer passage from Isaiah than either Mark or Matthew?

   d) What, according to Luke, did John say to i) people in general, ii) tax collectors and iii) soldiers?

   e) Do you find anything surprising about John's message, considering the circumstances in which he preached?

   f) What is the symbolic meaning of the winnowing fork and of fire?

b) The Baptism of Jesus

Read Mark 1:9–11, Luke 3:21–3, Matthew 3:13–17

MARK **LUKE** **MATTHEW** Jesus left Nazareth, realising that it was time to start his ministry. He was baptised by John. After the baptism, Jesus saw 'heaven opening'. This may be a way of telling us that Jesus saw a vision, or it may be a reference to Isaiah 64:1, suggesting that God has come into human history in the person of Jesus. In the Old Testament, the dove was seen as a bringer of good news (see Genesis 8:8–11), and became a symbol of peace. A voice came 'from heaven', by which readers would understand that God was communicating with his Son. The message is a combination of Psalm 2:7 and Isaiah 42:1.

What does the dove symbolise?

MARK Mark's account is very brief and emphasises that events were moving quickly. Notice the phrases 'Not long afterwards' (verse 9) and 'At once' (verse 12).

MATTHEW Matthew tells us that John hesitated to baptise Jesus, and deals with a question which may have occurred to you already. If, as Christians believe, Jesus was sinless, why did he need to be baptised? Matthew's suggestion may indicate that Jesus was showing his obedience to God and dedication to his purposes. It would also seem that Jesus wished to identify himself with the people who were responding to John's preaching.

ACTIVITIES

1 Look up the Old Testament passages referred to above and be sure that you understand their significance.

2 Answer all sections of this essay:
   a) Briefly describe the baptism of Jesus.

   b) What might the 'voice from heaven' signify?

   c) Why do you think Jesus went to be baptised?

c) The Temptation of Jesus

Read Mark 1:12–13, Luke 4:1–13, Matthew 4:1–11

MARK **LUKE** **MATTHEW** It has been suggested that Jesus must have told some if not all of his disciples about his experiences in the desert. As we consider the three temptations we shall discover that each implies that Jesus had powers which we do not possess.

MARK As with the baptism of Jesus, Mark deals with the temptation very briefly. He merely makes six points, the first suggesting that the Holy Spirit (the Spirit of God) compelled Jesus to go into the desert and the last that angels helped him to cope with the situation.

LUKE MATTHEW We shall concentrate on the account given by Luke and then comment briefly on Matthew's version. The two accounts are very similar and it is suggested that they came from the source which they probably shared. Like Mark, Luke introduces the story by stating that Jesus was led by the Holy Spirit into the desert – a suggestion that these experiences were part of God's plan for him.

Each temptation is stated in the form of a conversation between Jesus and the Devil. There is no suggestion that Jesus saw a physical being. Maybe, rather as temptations happen today, the thoughts simply came into his head. Each of the temptations relates to the way in which Jesus would carry out his work as the Messiah.

The desert of Judaea.
How would you describe this landscape?

The first temptation was to turn stone into bread
Having fasted for 40 days, it would seem to be an understatement to say that Jesus was hungry! The idea came into his mind that if he was the Son of God he could provide food for himself miraculously. Jesus' reply to the temptation comes from the Old Testament:

> *. . . man must not depend on bread alone to sustain him, but on everything that the Lord says.*
>
> *Deuteronomy 8:3*

Notice that Luke quotes only the first part of this verse.

We saw in Topic 4 that some Jews were expecting the Messiah to appear as a prophet like Moses. During their desert wanderings, the Israelites had been provided with bread (or manna) by God when Moses was their leader (see Exodus 16:1–16), and perhaps here Jesus was tempted to bring in a Messianic age when he would provide miraculously for the people's needs.

Many different shades of meaning have been seen in this temptation. Some suggestions are that Jesus was being tempted to:

- doubt his divine Sonship,

- use his miraculous power for his own immediate benefit,

- use his miraculous power to provide for his own needs throughout his ministry,

- become a social or relief worker,

- use his miraculous power to convince people that he was the Messiah.

By fasting in the desert, Jesus showed that he believed spiritual matters were more important than food, and by quoting Deuteronomy 8:3 he rejected this temptation.

The second temptation was to worship the Devil in order to gain political power
Many Jews in the first century were looking for a Messiah who would free them from Roman domination, and here Jesus faced the temptation to use political or military means to

achieve his Messiahship. From the summit of the Mount of Temptation (and of other hills in the region), a wide area can be seen, and it has been suggested that this is where the temptation happened. Again, Jesus resisted the temptation by quoting from the book of Deuteronomy:

> *Fear the Lord your God, worship only him . . .*
>
> *Deuteronomy 6:13*

The third temptation was to perform a dramatic stunt to enforce belief

Perhaps, in view of his recent meeting with John the Baptist, Jesus had been thinking of a prophecy in Malachi:

> *The Lord Almighty answers, I will send my messenger to prepare the way for me. Then the Lord you are looking for will suddenly come to his Temple.*
>
> *Malachi 3:1*

A spectacular fulfilment of this prophecy might compel people to accept Jesus as the Messiah.

Either in his imagination or in reality, Jesus was on the highest point or pinnacle of the Temple. This may refer to the south-east corner of the Temple courtyards, which towered some 450 feet (135 m) above the Kidron valley (see the plan on pp. 14 and 15). The tempter suggested that, if Jesus was God's Son, he could throw himself down and come to no harm. Verses from a psalm are referred to:

> *God will put his angels in charge of you to protect you wherever you go.*
> *They will hold you up with their hands to keep you from hurting your feet on the stones.*
>
> *Psalm 91:11–12*

The south-east corner of the Temple area, *possibly* the pinnacle of the Temple

However, a part of this verse was omitted, thus altering the meaning.

This temptation was resisted by reference to another passage from the Old Testament:

> *Do not put the Lord your God to the test.*
>
> *Deuteronomy 6:16*

It is interesting that all three replies to the tempter are taken from a short passage in Deuteronomy, 6:13 – 8:3, which concerns the Israelites before they entered Palestine. It has been suggested that perhaps Jesus was thinking about the experience of the Israelites in the desert during his own stay in the Wilderness.

Luke ends his account with the comment that the Devil left Jesus for a while, which indicates that other temptations were faced later.

MATTHEW This is very similar to Luke's account but there are two important points to notice. In the account of the first temptation, Matthew includes the whole of the quotation from Deuteronomy 8:3. The second and third temptations are reversed in Matthew's account. No satisfactory reason for this has been suggested.

ACTIVITIES

1 List the six points that Mark makes about Jesus' temptation.

2 Discuss the suggested points concerning the meaning of the first temptation.

3 'The end justifies the means.' Either have a discussion on this statement and its connection with the temptations, or organise a debate on the subject.

4 Use the index to discover the other occasions when Jesus was tempted. Make a list of them.

5 Answer the following questions:

a) According to the Gospel accounts, what part did the Holy Spirit play in the temptation of Jesus?

b) 'Man cannot live on bread alone.' What do you think this means?

c) Which temptation was for Jesus to gain political power?

d) How does the misquotation alter the meaning of the verses from Psalm 91?

e) What importance is placed on Old Testament quotations in the temptation accounts?

6 Answer all sections of this essay:

a) Give a brief account of the three temptations of Jesus in the desert.

b) Explain how each temptation was intended to persuade Jesus to do his work as the Messiah in the wrong way.

c) On what later occasions was Jesus tempted?

d) Do you think people are still tempted today? Give examples of what might be considered to be modern temptations.

To Keep You Thinking

1 Morality in society
Find examples of Christians today who speak out against immoral attitudes in society as John the Baptist did.

2 Baptism
Discover which Churches practise infant baptism and which practise adult or believers' baptism, and why.

3 Symbolism
Find out more about the use made by Christians of the symbols mentioned in this Topic – the dove, water and fire.

4 Belief in the Devil
Discuss Christian ideas about the Devil or Satan.

5 The observance of Lent
Find out why and how Christians observe Lent today.

Disciples

TOPIC 10

'They . . . left everything, and followed Jesus.'

Setting the Scene

We do not commonly use the word 'disciple' these days, but from childhood we are in one sense all disciples, for a disciple is one who learns from another.

In first-century Palestine it was common for a person to choose a spiritual teacher, or rabbi, and learn from him, sometimes even staying with him permanently. It was therefore quite usual to find a group consisting of a teacher and his disciples. John the Baptist, for instance, had disciples (Matthew 11:2, Luke 7:18) and the fourth Gospel suggests that some of Jesus' disciples may at one time have attached them-selves to John and met Jesus in Judaea (see John 1:35–42). A difference with Jesus' disciples is that he chose them, and, as we shall see in Topic 17, he even discouraged some whose commitment was doubtful.

Soon after Jesus began his ministry, large crowds would listen to his teaching. Of these we read eventually of 70 people who were sent out to spread the Good News. Jesus decided that he wished to have the company and help of 12 specially chosen men who would be with him, learn from him, and eventually carry on his work of preaching. These men are referred to as apostles, from a Greek word *apostello* which means 'I send'. So the word 'apostle' means someone sent, or a messenger. The choosing of the 12 apostles reminds us of the 12 tribes of Israel, and both Matthew and Luke emphasise the connection (Matthew 19:28, Luke 22:30). It is as if a new Israel is being formed in the Christian Church. Of the 12 apostles, three are sometimes shown in the Gospels as being particularly close to Jesus and with him on important occasions (see, for example, Mark 5:37, 9:2 and 14:33).

The geographical setting suggested in the Gospels for these stories is the west shore of the Sea of Galilee. We read on a number of occasions that Jesus taught from a boat – the shelving shore would form a natural amphi-theatre and water carries sound superbly.

ACTIVITIES

1 Make sure you look up and under-stand the Gospel references given.

2 Answer the following questions:

   a) What is the meaning of 'disciple'?

   b) What is the meaning of 'apostle'?

   c) Name one of Jesus' disciples who may previously have been a disciple of John the Baptist.

   d) Why do you think Jesus chose 12 apostles?

   e) What larger number of disciples were sent out to preach the Good News?

   f) Name the three apostles who were closest to Jesus.

   g) Name two occasions when these three apostles shared an experience with Jesus.

   h) How does the way people became disciples of Jesus differ from the way they might have become disciples of another rabbi?

To Help You Understand

a) Jesus Calls Four Fishermen

Read Mark 1:14–20, Luke 5:1–11,
Matthew 4:18–22

MARK
LUKE
MATTHEW

Mark's Gospel suggests that Jesus' preaching began after John had been imprisoned. His message is described as 'Good News from God'; the time which Jews through the centuries have been waiting for has come. The Kingdom of God (God's kingly rule in people's lives) is announced. So the response required is similar to that suggested by John the Baptist, 'Turn away from your sins and believe the Good News.' An account is then given of the call of the first four disciples.

Alec McCowen, an actor, has been giving a solo recitation of Mark's Gospel, both on stage and on television, over a period of some years. He has written a book of his thoughts on the Gospel. In it, he comments on this story:

> *It is most probable that Simon and Andrew and James and John knew Jesus and had already heard him speak excitingly about the coming kingdom of God, about his ideas to spread the good news, and about his desire that one day they might join him. They must have been ready for the call. I hear Mark interviewing Peter clearly in these verses. 'What happened when he called you?' 'We were casting a net into the sea.' 'And did you complete the catch?' 'No, we forsook our nets and followed him.' 'And was it the same with James and John?' 'No,' – and here is an old man's accurate memory of days long past – 'they were* mending *their nets.' This tiny difference in occupation rings with authenticity.*
>
> From Alec McCowen, Personal Mark

These are, of course, the thoughts of one individual, but they give us interesting insights.

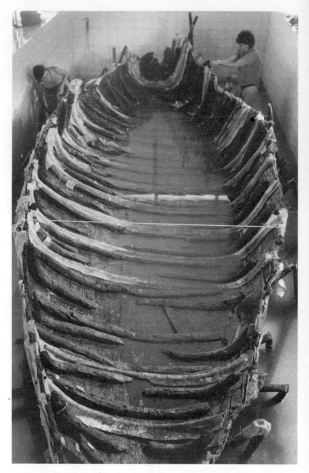

The Kinneret boat.

In 1986, after a two-year drought, timbers of an ancient boat which would have been used for both fishing and transporting goods and people were found in the mud of a newly-exposed beach near to Migdol (Magdala). Excavation and later examination of the boat revealed that it dated from between the first century BC and the first century AD. It has been shown to be of the type used by the fishermen of Galilee in New Testament times. The boat could be both sailed and rowed and is some 26 feet (8 metres) long. It would have belonged to someone reasonably wealthy. It is interesting to note that the family of James and John were sufficiently wealthy to have hired help. As the first ancient boat discovered in the area, it helps in the understanding of the Gospel references to fishing practices on the Sea of Galilee.

The boat is shown here on display at the Kibbutz Ginossar.

As we have already seen, some of these fishermen may previously have had contact with Jesus in Judaea, which would explain their willingness to leave everything in order to be with him. Mark emphasises the authority of Jesus in calling these disciples. The fishermen are told that in future their job will be 'to catch men', or to bring them into the freedom of the Kingdom of God.

LUKE There is much discussion about the relationship of Luke's account of Jesus and the fishermen to that of Mark. Some believe that this is quite a different incident which comes from Luke's special source. There is an account with some similarities at the end of the fourth Gospel, and some scholars see Luke's account as having connections with that story.

We learn from Luke that Simon, James and John were partners (notice that Andrew is not mentioned). After doubts about whether a mere carpenter should be obeyed on a matter about which he and his partners were experts, Simon eventually let down his nets. The amazing catch, after an unfruitful night's fishing, convinced Simon that Jesus was 'Lord', and that he was not fit company for Jesus. Simon was assured that from now on he would be catching men.

MATTHEW The account in Matthew's Gospel is almost identical to Mark's.

'Fishers of Men' – a well-dressing from Wirksworth in Derbyshire. The picture is made by pressing flower petals into soft clay.

ACTIVITIES

1 Discuss why you think the fishermen were willing to leave everything in order to follow Jesus.

2 Look at the picture 'Fishers of Men' and answer the following questions:

   a) Name three fishermen who followed Jesus.

   b) Describe how one of them was called to follow Jesus.

   c) Why do you think the two inscriptions are included in this well-dressing?

   d) What is the meaning of 'Fishers of Men'?

   e) What symbols are included in the picture? Explain the meaning of any two of them.

3 Begin some coursework on the authority of Jesus. Use information from accounts in this Topic and in later ones. Compare the nature of the authority of Jesus with that of other people of his time (e.g. religious and political leaders) and with that of leaders today. Use cuttings from newspapers and magazines in making your comparisons.

b) Jesus Calls Levi

Read Mark 2:13–17, Luke 5:27–32, Matthew 9:9–13

MARK
LUKE
MATTHEW Here we have a very different type of person joining the group of disciples. As a tax collector, Levi would have been very unpopular with his fellow Jews. It is thought that this event took place in Capernaum (Mark 2:1), a frontier town between the area ruled by Antipas and that ruled by Philip, and it has been suggested that import and export duties would need to have been paid here. Or it may be that tolls were collected from travellers. The tax, or tribute, from the area had been assigned to Herod Antipas by the Romans:

> *Now, to him [Antipas] it was that Perea and Galilee paid their tribute, which amounted annually to 200 talents.*
>
> Josephus, Antiquities of the Jews 17:11.4

MARK Mark suggests that a large number of tax collectors and other outcasts (those who were considered not to keep the details of the Law) were already interested in following Jesus, and they were invited to a reception by Levi to meet his new Master. Criticism was made of Jesus for eating with such people – not directly, as you will notice, but to his disciples. Jesus answered by referring to a proverb which suggested that only the sick needed a doctor. Jesus had come for those who knew they had a need.

LUKE Luke's account is very similar to that of Mark but he makes two additional points. He stresses that Levi left everything in order to follow Jesus. He also emphasises that Jesus came to call people to repent, a theme which is found elsewhere in Luke's Gospel.

MATTHEW In this account, the tax collector's name is given as Matthew and the house where the meal took place is identified as his. Otherwise, the account is very similar to Mark's, except that Matthew, typically, adds a reference from the Old Testament:

> *I want your constant love, not your animal sacrifices. I would rather have my people know me than burn offerings to me.*
>
> Hosea 6:6

William Barclay, in his commentary on Mark's Gospel, makes an interesting point about Matthew's discipleship:

> *Of all the disciples Matthew gave up most. He, of all of them, literally left all to follow Jesus. Peter and Andrew, James and John could go back to their boats. There were always fish to catch and always the old trade to which to return; but Matthew burned his boats completely. With one action, in one moment of time, by one swift decision he had put himself out of his job forever, for having left his tax collector's job, he would never get it back again.*
>
> From William Barclay, The Gospel of Mark

ACTIVITIES

1 Discuss the quotation about the sacrifices made by Matthew (or Levi). Can you give examples of people today who have similarly given up things in order to follow Jesus?

2 Check that you understand the information about tax collectors in Topic 2.

3 Start a list for information on discipleship. Begin with listing the information in this Topic, and as you find further teaching on the subject, add it to your list.

c) Jesus Chooses the Twelve Apostles

Read Mark 3:13–19, Luke 6:12–16, Matthew 10:1–4

MARK
LUKE
MATTHEW These accounts suggest that Jesus chose 12 apostles from the larger number of disciples now following him. Hills and mountains are very significant in the Bible and key events take place on them. We have already referred to Moses receiving the ten commandments on Mount Sinai. Can you think of other examples?

MARK We are told why Jesus chose apostles:

- to be with Jesus and learn from him,
- to go out and share the preaching of the Good News,
- to have authority to cast out demons.

LUKE Luke tells us that Jesus spent a whole night praying before choosing his apostles. Elsewhere in the Gospel we are told of occasions when Jesus prayed before taking action, for example, Luke 9:18, 9:28 and 11:1. Look out for others as you study Luke's Gospel.

MATTHEW Matthew concentrates on the apostles' authority to cast out evil spirits and to heal. He identifies Matthew as the tax collector.

The Twelve Apostles

Additional references
Mark 1:30

Simon also known as **Peter** or **Cephas** = the Rock. Married

Andrew [Disciple of John the Baptist]

Brothers, sons of John

Matthew 16:17–18

Fishermen, partners, lived in Capernaum

Mark 1:21 ff.
Luke 9:54
Mark 9:38, 10:35–44

James

Brothers, sons of Zebedee.
Nickname **Boanerges** = sons of thunder

John

Philip [Lived in Bethsaida]

Bartholomew surname [Possibly to be identified with Nathanael]

Matthew or **Levi** Son of Alphaeus. A tax collector

Thomas the twin

James Son of Alphaeus. Some have suggested he was the brother of Matthew or is to be identified with him.

Thaddaeus Probably the same as **Judas,** son of James .

Simon The Patriot or Zealot – this may refer to his political allegiance or his character

Judas Iscariot This may mean 'Man of Kerioth', a town in Judaea, or 'Dagger-man', i.e. a bandit. The traitor

Mark 14:10–11, Luke 22:3–6

Information bracketed [] is from the fourth Gospel.

ACTIVITIES

1 Use information from the chart ('The 12 Apostles') to answer the following questions:

a) Name two sets of brothers who were apostles of Jesus.

b) Name two occupations represented among the group of 12.

c) Which apostle is given a different name in Luke's Gospel from that given by Mark and Matthew?

d) What is the meaning of: i) Peter, ii) Boanerges and iii) Iscariot?

e) Who is the only apostle who probably came from an area other than Galilee?

f) Give an example of the appropriateness of the nickname 'Boanerges'.

2 Discuss the problems which could have arisen within the group of apostles because of differences of personality, occupation or political views.

d) Women Who Accompanied Jesus

Read Luke 8:1–3

LUKE It is interesting that only Luke tells us that a number of women went with Jesus on his preaching missions. Rabbis normally refused to teach women, and so it was revolutionary for Jesus to do so. However, it was not unusual for wealthy women to support rabbis financially, which is what apparently happened here also.

Mary Magdalene (probably indicating that she came from Magdala) is stated to have been an extreme case of demon possession (we shall discuss this in Topic 13). Joanna is also mentioned by Luke as visiting Jesus' tomb (Luke 24:10), and Susanna may have been amongst that group of women also.

Discipleship is sometimes described as an uphill journey or pilgrimage. Why do you think this is so?

To Keep You Thinking

1 Women in the Church
Jesus had women followers. There is much controversy about women taking an active role in the Church today. Share your views.

2 Concern for 'outcasts'
Discuss ways in which Christians today can show their concern for outcasts in our society.

3 Discipleship today
What similarities and differences might there be between the demands made on Christian disciples now and in the first century?

4 Symbolism
Discover what you can of the use made today of the Christian symbol of the fish.

Parables of the Kingdom

'He would not speak to them without using parables, but when he was alone with his disciples, he would explain everything to them.'

Setting the Scene

A British passport states that the holder is a 'citizen of the United Kingdom and Colonies'. It is easy to understand the word 'kingdom' when it applies to a geographical area in this way.

The Old Testament spoke of the Kingdom of God, and a prayer used in the synagogue in New Testament times was, 'May he establish his Kingdom in your lifetime and in your days.' The first recorded preaching of Jesus was '. . . the Kingdom of God is near! Turn away from your sins and believe the Good News!' (Mark 1:15, Matthew 4:17).

What did Jesus mean by the phrase 'the Kingdom of God'? The Greek word used in the Gospels is *basileia*, which emphasises the activity of the king rather than the area over which he rules. The Kingdom of God is God's kingly rule or reign, or the situation in which God is King.

A dictionary definition includes the following:

---

kingdom n 1. organized community headed by king or queen; MIDDLE Kingdom; UNITED Kingdom 2. territory subject to king; spiritual reign of God, sphere of this (the kingdom of heaven; thy kingdom come)

The Concise Oxford Dictionary

Most, but not all, of Jesus' teaching about the Kingdom of God was in the form of parables. We read parables in the Old Testament, and rabbis would often use them in their teaching. There are over 40 recorded in the Synoptic Gospels, so it is important to understand exactly what a parable is. Basically, it is an extended simile, a 'like' saying or a comparison. For instance, Matthew records '. . . the Kingdom of heaven is like this. A man is looking for fine pearls, and when he finds one that is unusually fine, he goes and sells everything he has, and buys that pearl' (Matthew 13:45). Often the simile is expanded to form a story; perhaps the best known of these are the Good Samaritan (Luke 10:25–37) and the Prodigal, or Lost, Son (Luke 15:11–32). Most parables make one main point, although three recorded in the Gospels also include an explanation (Mark 4:13–20, Matthew 13:36–43 and 47–50), of which two make comparisons of a number of points in the story. This kind of comparison is called an allegory. For instance, the Parable of the Weeds (Matthew 13:36–43) suggests:

> sower = Son of Man
> field = world
> good seed = members of the Kingdom
> weeds = those who belong to the Devil
> enemy = the Devil
> harvest = the end of the age
> workers = angels

It has been suggested that these allegories were added by the early Christians to the parables as told by Jesus, although some scholars believe that the allegories are part of the original teaching of Jesus.

Do you remember stories you were told as a child?

Why did Jesus use parables in his teaching? Many reasons have been suggested, and include the following:

- Stories are much more interesting than abstract teaching.

- Jesus' parables reflect everyday events in the home or in society, people at work, or their relationships, and the world of nature. They would therefore be of particular interest to those who heard them.

- The Old Testament includes parables, and rabbis also used them, so people were familiar with this form of teaching.

- People could merely listen to the stories or, if they were sufficiently interested, they could try to work out the spiritual meaning.

- The parables encouraged people to go away and think about Jesus' teaching. Their response to it would therefore be made after consideration.

- Matthew suggests that Jesus used parables as a fulfilment of prophecy (Matthew 13:35).

Fourteen parables will be considered in this Topic. We shall look at others later. You will notice that less comment is given on the parables as the Topic proceeds. Get used to reading each parable carefully, thinking about it, and then working out the main point.

ACTIVITIES

1 Discuss the definitions of 'kingdom' given in *The Concise Oxford Dictionary*.

2 Answer the following questions:

a) What phrase is used by Matthew as an alternative to the Kingdom of God?

b) Why does Matthew use a different phrase?

c) What is meant by 'the Kingdom of God'?

d) What is a simile?

e) What is a parable?

f) What is an allegory?

g) Name two parables which have been given an allegorical interpretation in the Gospels.

h) Write a paragraph explaining why Jesus used parables in his teaching.

3 Head a sheet of paper 'The Kingdom of God' (or 'The Kingdom of Heaven' if you are studying Matthew). As you find teaching about the Kingdom, add it to your list, together with a brief note about the context and meaning and whether it is suggested as having been present in the ministry of Jesus, or future to it:

THE KINGDOM OF GOD				
Reference	Quotation	Context	Meaning	Present/ Future
Mark 1:14 or Matthew 4:17	'the Kingdom of God is near'	When Jesus started preaching	The Kingdom is about to appear.	P

To Help You Understand

a) The Parable of the Sower

*Read Mark 4:1–20, Luke 8:4–15,
Matthew 13:1–23*

MARK
LUKE
MATTHEW In Luke 5:3 it is stated that Jesus used a boat as a pulpit, and this is what happened on this occasion. It has been suggested that the sight of a farmer sowing his seed on a nearby hillside may have prompted this story. Sowers threw the seed skilfully as they walked up and down the field, but some seeds would inevitably fall where conditions were not ideal for growth. The soil is very stony in most parts of Palestine and it is still a common practice to clear the larger boulders and rocks from the centre to the edge of the field; this also helps to make a boundary. Very prickly thorns or thistles will often grow near the 'rocky ground'; but only where the soil is deeper and can more easily be ploughed will a harvest be produced, and then with differing yields, depending on the fertility of the soil.

Which types of ground mentioned in the parable are illustrated here?

This parable is not stated to be about the Kingdom, but it emphasises growth, which is a characteristic of a number of other parables of the Kingdom in this Topic. The comment following the parable, 'Listen, then, if you have ears!' is frequently used by Jesus to encourage people to work out the message.

MARK In verses 10–12, Mark suggests that Jesus was asked by some disciples to explain the parables and in his reply quoted Isaiah 6:9–10. On the surface it seems that Jesus was deliberately trying to mystify all but the disciples; but from other teaching of Jesus it is clear that this was not so. It would seem that here we are told what happened when Jesus used parables, rather than why he used them. The secret of the kingdom is revealed to those who genuinely seek it, but hidden from the casual listener.

Mark's Gospel then records a rebuke of the disciples (verse 13). The allegorical interpretation of the parable follows, which gives the spiritual significance of each detail.

How is this Bible Society logo appropriate?

LUKE Luke shortens Mark's version of the parable and includes only a few different details. He suggests that the seed which fell on the path was stepped on before the birds ate it. Luke's section on the purpose of parables is much briefer and does not include the quotation from Isaiah. With his emphasis on salvation, Luke includes a comment about belief resulting in salvation at the end of verse 12.

MATTHEW Matthew extends the section on the purpose of the parables and includes a saying of Jesus in verse 12 which suggests that spiritual interest means growth, but spiritual apathy (indifference) means atrophy (wasting away). Matthew goes on to stress that Jesus emphasised the privileges enjoyed by the disciples (verses 16–17).

ACTIVITIES

1 Make a list similar to that on p. 71 to illustrate the allegorical meaning given to the Parable of the Sower.

2 Answer all sections of this essay:

a) What do you think was the main point made in the Parable of the Sower?

b) Explain carefully the allegorical meaning of this parable.

c) Suggest attitudes that people have today which correspond with those illustrated in this parable.

b) A Lamp under a Bowl

Read Mark 4:21–5, Luke 8:16–18

MARK This passage includes a number of **LUKE** sayings of Jesus (usually short sentences, often in the form of brief parables which can be easily remembered).

Oil lamps were the main source of light within a home and it would be very foolish to put one under a bowl or under a bed! Instead it would be placed on a stand in order to give maximum light.

An oil lamp.
What does the design represent?

ACTIVITY

'What we do not use we lose.'
Discuss this comment on Mark 4:25, Luke 8:18 or Matthew 13:12.

c) The Parable of the Growing Seed

Read Mark 4:26–9

MARK This is another parable of the Kingdom which concerns growth. It is found only in Mark's Gospel. The farmer sows his seed and then can do nothing about it until the harvest – the growth is not the work of the farmer and he cannot explain it. Perhaps the suggestion is that although the spiritual growth of the Kingdom was not visible, it was surely happening.

d) The Parable of the Mustard Seed

Read Mark 4:30–4, Luke 13:18–19, Matthew 13:31–2

MARK Here we have another parable **LUKE** that suggests that the Kingdom **MATTHEW** is present and growing. 'Small as a grain of mustard seed' is a Jewish proverb – the tree, however, grows to a height of 8–10 feet (2.4–3 m).

'Every kind of bird' is a phrase used by the prophet Ezekiel to represent 'the nations' (Ezekiel 31:6). It would seem that this parable indicates that the Kingdom, which had tiny beginnings in the ministry of Jesus, would grow and spread worldwide. Luke and Matthew both shorten Mark's version.

A mustard tree. The photographer waited for half an hour for some nearby birds to settle on it, without success!

74

ACTIVITIES

1 Add information from these parables and the Parable of the Yeast (below) to your list about the Kingdom of God.

2 Begin to make a chart to include all the parables you read. First list the reference and title of the parable, then the main point it seems to you to be making. Then add information from the key as appropriate.

K   parable of the Kingdom
G   Kingdom present and growing
F   Kingdom future
A   allegory
J   concerns judgement
P   concerns prayer
W   concerns wealth and possessions
For concerns forgiveness
R   concerns race
RJ concerns the return of Jesus (*Parousia*)
C   criticism of Jewish leaders implied

Begin your chart like this:

PARABLES			
Reference	*Parable*	*Main point*	*Significance*
Mark 4: 1-20 or Luke 8: 4-15 or Matthew 13: 1-23	Sower	Growth of Kingdom	G A
Mark 4: 21-5 or Luke 8: 16-18	Lamp under a bed	Spread the message	

e) The Parable of the Yeast

Read Luke 13:20-1, Matthew 13:33-5

LUKE MATTHEW This brief parable is found in Luke and Matthew, but not in Mark. This is another parable concerning growth. If you have ever made bread you will know that, with the addition of yeast and after the rising time, the dough is transformed. As the yeast works quietly and unseen, so does the kingly rule of God transform those who accept it.

The transforming effect of yeast.

f) The Parable of the Weeds

Read Matthew 13:24-30, 13:34-43

MATTHEW Here we begin to consider some parables of the Kingdom found only in Matthew's Gospel.

Young people today may spend part of their summer holiday working for farmers, pulling out the wild oats from fields of corn! Similarly, there were weeds (darnel or tares) growing amongst the wheat in this parable, but here the workers were told not to remove the weeds for fear of damaging the crop.

The explanation of the parable develops it into an allegory. It has been suggested that verses 36–43 is an interpretation of the parable added by the early Church. The explanation suggests that the powers of evil will do everything possible to resist the growth of the Kingdom and that members of the Kingdom and those who reject it will live side by side until the judgement. The 'fiery furnace' is a reference to beliefs about hell as a place of fires and torment (see Topic 18).

g) The Parable of the Hidden Treasure

Read Matthew 13:44

MATTHEW This and the next parable are both very brief and concern the privilege of entering the Kingdom.

It was common to hide treasure in clay pots buried in a field in order to keep it safe. You will remember the scrolls of the Essene community hidden in clay jars in caves at Qumran (see Topic 3). The man in this story found the treasure accidentally, but he sold everything he had in order to buy the field and so gain the treasure.

h) The Parable of the Pearl

Read Matthew 13:45–6

MATTHEW This is the twin of the parable above. The man here is actually looking for fine pearls and similarly gives up everything in order to buy a particularly beautiful one.

i) The Parable of the Net

Read Matthew 13:47–52

MATTHEW This is another parable concerning a future judgement. The picture here may be of a drag net drawn between two fishing boats. Jews were forbidden to eat fish which had no fins or scales (Leviticus 11:10) and other fish were probably inedible, so there had to be a sorting of the catch. The interpretation given is similar to that for the Parable of the Weeds.

This parable is followed by a saying in verse 52 which suggests that scribes who became followers of Jesus would bring to their discipleship all the teaching of the Law, as well as accepting the new teaching of Jesus.

ACTIVITIES

1 Answer the following questions:
   a) Name two parables which suggest there will be a judgement before the setting up of the Kingdom.
   b) How did the first disciples become members of the Kingdom?
   c) What is the central message of the parables of the Hidden Treasure and the Pearl?
   d) What is the difference between these two parables?
   e) Choose one parable from this Topic which is also an allegory and explain the allegorical meaning.

2 Interview a number of Christians concerning what they believe about a judgement. Explain that you are studying the parables and say why you are interested to know their views. Make up two or three appropriate questions. List the different views that emerge.

---

j) The Parable of the Unforgiving Servant

Read Matthew 18:21–35

MATTHEW We now turn to a group of parables in the later chapters of Matthew's Gospel, most of them about people. The first two concern employment. The first parable was told in answer to a question. Seven is a Jewish symbol for completeness and scribes suggested that people should be willing to forgive to that extent. Jesus suggested that forgiveness should be unlimited. The vivid parable implies that Christians have been forgiven so much themselves that they must never be unwilling to forgive others.

Forgive killers, soldier's note tells parents

k) The Workers in the Vineyard

Read Matthew 20:1–16

MATTHEW This parable is another very vivid story and this time concerns rewards in the Kingdom. Some think that the parable should be understood in the light of Matthew 19:30. Rewards are due to God's generosity and not based on human merit.

The parable is not intended as guidance on industrial wages or employer–worker relationships, but at least one Christian Trades Union leader has found points of interest here. Len Murray, a former General Secretary of the TUC, was asked if the parable was acceptable to him as a Trades Union leader. He replied:

> *Yes – because it looks from the parable as though it was a time of great unemployment, and men were idle with no work to do. In times like this men and their families must be supported even up to the level of a full wage.*
>
> From an article 'People matter more than things' in Viewpoint, 43

ACTIVITIES

1 The parables had a meaning for the people who first heard them and for Christians at the time the Gospels were written. Most Christians believe that they also speak to people today. Discuss what meaning Christians today might find in:

   a) the Parable of the Unforgiving Servant,

   b) the Parable of the Workers in the Vineyard.

2 Make sure you know the details of the parables that you have read. Write a summary of each.

l) The Parable of the Ten Girls

Read Matthew 25:1–13

MATTHEW A wedding is the setting of this parable. The girls would be bridesmaids waiting to escort the bride to the home of the bridegroom. In Topic 19 we shall look at Jesus' teaching about the future. One of the points that he made was that he would return to the world at some future point. Theologians call this the *Parousia* (a Greek word meaning 'arrival') or the Second Coming. Some members of the early Church believed that it would happen very soon after Jesus' ascension. When the return was delayed, parables such as this assumed a new importance. Perhaps this parable is suggesting that it is important to be watchful and to be prepared for the *Parousia*.

m) The Parable of the Three Servants

Read Matthew 25:14–30

MATTHEW This parable also concerns the *Parousia;* we are told of a man who goes on a journey and later returns. The servants mentioned here would probably be slaves, since slaves often managed their master's business affairs. You will notice that faithfulness resulted in new responsibilities. The third slave had not been worthy of his master's trust and lost everything. Compare verse 29 with Matthew 13:12 (p. 73).

ACTIVITIES

1 Discuss the main points of the Parable of the Ten Girls and the Parable of the Three Servants.

2 The *Parousia* is believed by many Christians to be still in the future. If possible, ask a visiting speaker, perhaps a clergyman, to speak to you on the subject.

n) The Final Judgement

Read Matthew 25:31–46

MATTHEW Unlike many of the longer parables, this is an illustration and not a story. The parable concerns the *Parousia,* and identifies the Son of Man as a future King who will act as judge. As in two earlier parables, there is a separation; this time of sheep from goats. Mixed flocks are quite usual and the animals are separated before being penned for the night.

Remember that a parable normally has one main point – there is no suggestion here that goats are inferior to sheep! The message is rather that the righteous (those in a right relationship with God) have shown their belief in Jesus by their practical attitude to people in need; while those who are condemned are judged because of their failure to do good, rather than because of wrong-doing.

Sheep and goats.
Which other parables are about a separation or sorting out?

ACTIVITIES

1 Check that you have filled in all the appropriate information on your list about the Kingdom of God or the Kingdom of heaven.

2 Check that you have included all the parables you are studying on your list of parables.

3 Write a modern parable based on any of those that you have read in this Topic. Form groups, choose the best of the parables and read, act or mime them. Discuss the main point of each parable.

4 Answer the following questions:
   a) Name two parables that suggest that the Kingdom was present and growing during Jesus' ministry.
   b) What do you consider to be the main point of the Parable of the Mustard Seed?
   c) Name three parables which concern the *Parousia.*
   d) Which two parables suggest that it is worth giving up everything to become a citizen of the Kingdom of heaven?
   e) Which parable is about trustworthiness?
   f) What do you consider to be the main point of the Parable of the Unforgiving Servant?

To Keep You Thinking

Practical Christianity

Look again at Matthew 25:31–46 and try to find examples of how Christians follow the teaching of Jesus in caring for the needy.

Power over Disease and Death

TOPIC 12

'. . . the blind can see, the lame can walk, those who suffer from dreaded skin-diseases are made clean, the deaf can hear, the dead are raised to life, and the Good News is preached to the poor . . .'

Setting the Scene

A HARBOROUGH man had a miracle escape when he walked away from a 'fireball crash' on Tuesday night.

Miracle man is home

MIRACLE man Andy Spalding is today back home just 11 weeks after doctors feared he could die following a horror car smash.

And now Mr Spalding (35), of Lovelace Way, Fleckney, is looking forward to returning to full fitness and getting back to gliding.

Battling Mr Spalding suffered multiple injuries including two broken arms, two broken legs, a broken pelvis and a broken cheekbone in the car crash at Dingley in August.

And minutes after he was dragged clear from the wreckage of the head-on crash his car burst into flames.

"It is a miracle. I find it difficult to believe how I got out." said Mr Spalding, who was on his way home from his job as a community facilities officer with Corby Council when the accident happened.

65th miracle cure

Delizia Cirolli. a Sicilian woman whose malignant tumour vanished after she visited the French shrine of Lourdes in 1976. is the 65th person to be accepted by the Catholic Church as miraculously cured, an official said yesterday. — Reuter

Discussing miracles

MIRACLES are a subject of continuing interest to Christians. For some they are a vital support for faith, while others see them as a stumbling block.

Miracle bank for the poor women of Bangladesh

Doubts raised on 'miracle' survival of six in quake ruins

I have seen a miracle

Saved by 'economic miracle'

The word 'miracle' is often used today, as the press cuttings on p. 79 illustrate. But very different meanings are given to this word. Think about the following definitions and comments:

Marvellous event due to some supernatural agency; remarkable occurrence.

The Concise Oxford Dictionary

Miracles are not contrary to nature but only contrary to what we know about nature.

Augustine, fourth century

An event contrary to the known laws of nature

An event that cannot be satisfactorily explained

Various words are used in the Gospels, all translated by the word 'miracle'. One is the Greek word *semeion,* meaning 'sign', an event that points to something of greater significance. This word is frequently used in the fourth Gospel. The most commonly used term for miracle in the Synoptic Gospels is 'mighty work', from the Greek word *dynamis,* meaning 'power', and from which we get our word 'dynamite'. So a miracle or 'mighty work' is an event or action through which the power of God is shown.

Jews of the time of Jesus had a strong belief that God was the Creator and Sustainer of the world, and still active within it. For them, the idea of the laws of nature would not have been as meaningful as the belief in the power of God at work in the world.

There are a number of references in Greek, Roman and Jewish writings to the working of miracles by people in the first century. They were usually accompanied by magical formulas or rituals, and were often exorcisms (the driving out of evil spirits). There is an example of some Jewish exorcists in Acts 19:13–16.

So the inclusion of miracles in the Gospels would not appear to be as unusual to readers at the end of the first century as it may appear to us in the present century. The writers of the Gospels show that the first Christians believed that Jesus taught by 'mighty works' as well as by parables. According to the Gospels, even Jesus' enemies accepted that he worked miracles, but they suggested that he did so through the power of the Devil (see Mark 3:22).

ACTIVITIES

1 Discuss the newspaper cuttings at the beginning of this Topic. What are the different meanings of the word 'miracle' as it is used there? Do you believe miracles happen today?

2 Discuss the various definitions of miracles given earlier. Turn also to p. 39 and discuss C S Lewis' comment given there.

3 Look through the Gospel you are studying and find examples of miracles which fit into the five categories suggested in the quotation at the beginning of this Topic. For example:

MIRACLES ILLUSTRATING LUKE 7:22/ MATTHEW 11:4		
Category	*Reference*	*Miracle*
'the blind can see'	Mark 8: 22–6	Jesus heals a blind man at Bethsaida.

There is a reference to Jesus as a 'doer of wonderful works' in the writings of Josephus:

> *Now, there was about this time, Jesus, a wise man, . . . he was a doer of wonderful works, a teacher of such men as receive the truth with pleasure.*
>
> *Josephus*, Antiquities of the Jews *18:3.3*

In another Jewish writing, the Babylonian Talmud, there is the more typical suggestion that Jesus practised sorcery.

The miracles of Jesus as recorded in the Gospels present difficulties for some readers today. Many ideas have been suggested about the miracles, of which the following are just a few:

• Some scholars consider that the miracle accounts are myths composed by the early Christians to state their belief in the divinity of Jesus. However, Mark's Gospel, for instance, was written within 30 or 40 years of Jesus' resurrection – this would scarcely have given time for the development of such myths, since individuals who had known Jesus would still be alive.

• Those who consider that the miracles of Jesus are contrary to the laws of nature, and therefore could not have happened, have suggested various explanations for the events, for instance:

– Some of the illnesses cured by Jesus, such as certain types of paralysis, may have had a psychosomatic origin (influence of the mind upon the body). In this event, by helping with a mental problem, Jesus may have brought about a cure.

– Those who were 'raised from the dead' may have been unconscious rather than actually dead.

– The miracles involving the multiplying of food may be suggesting that, through the example of Jesus or others, people were willing to share what they had.

Many other explanations have been suggested, some of which we will discuss later.

• Some Christians believe that the miracles were supernatural events, 'mighty works' which show that God was active in the ministry of Jesus.

Capernaum, the setting for many of Jesus' early miracles. Excavations of the first-century village were started in the nineteenth century, and archaeologists now have an accurate knowledge of the type of house of the period.

Whatever attitude is taken to the miracles of Jesus, it is important to realise that although a number are recorded in the Gospels, they are certainly not given prominence over the teaching and other activities of Jesus. As you study the miracles, keep the following points in mind:

- At the time of his temptation, and on other occasions (e.g. Mark 8:11–13), Jesus refused to perform signs to draw attention to himself or to prove who he was.

- The Gospels frequently state that Jesus healed and helped needy people because he was 'filled with pity' (e.g. Mark 1:41 and 8:2). If he had had the power to heal, it would have been amazing if he had not used it when he encountered people in need. So the suggestion is that he 'made whole' those who were considered outcasts. By contrast, the Essenes who lived at Qumran (see Topic 3) would not accept people who were incapacitated in any way:

No madman, or lunatic, or simpleton, or fool, no blind man, or lame, or deaf man, and no minor shall enter into the Community.

Translated by G Vermes in The Dead Sea Scrolls in English

- The miracles were obviously not the main events of Jesus' ministry, for on a number of occasions he instructed those who had been healed to tell no one about it (e.g. Mark 1:44 and 5:43).

- The 'mighty works' were not performed to compel people to believe in the power of God. On the contrary, it was in response to this faith that the healings took place (Mark 5:34 and 10:52; Luke 17:19). We are told on one occasion that because faith was not present, Jesus could not heal many people in his home town of Nazareth (Mark 6:1–6).

- Unlike most recorded miracles performed by other healers of the day, the 'mighty works' of Jesus had no connection with magic or sorcery. No ritual formula or manipulation was used. Sometimes there was a touch, but more often only a word of command.

- The 'mighty works' cannot be separated from Jesus' teaching. Often the miracle stories are constructed in such a way that they make an important point, for example about Jesus' authority over the powers of evil (Mark 1:23–7) or about forgiveness (Mark 2:5–7).

- The quotation at the beginning of this Topic is very important. In both Luke (7:18–23) and Matthew (11:2–6) we read of John the Baptist sending messengers to ask whether Jesus was in fact the Messiah. In reply, Jesus quoted words from Isaiah and added to them, suggesting that the miracles indicated that the Messianic age had come.

- The miracles can be divided into four types: healing, raising the dead, exorcisms and nature miracles. We shall consider the first two types in this Topic, and exorcisms and nature miracles in Topic 13.

ACTIVITIES

1 Discuss the three attitudes suggested concerning the miracles of Jesus. What is your opinion about these? Can you suggest any others?

2 Answer the following questions:

a) What is the meaning of *dynamis*?

b) What is an exorcism?

c) Mention one occasion when Jesus refused to perform a miracle.

d) Where was Jesus unable to perform a miracle?

e) Mention one occasion when someone was told to keep quiet about a healing.

f) Mention one miracle where faith was stated to be important.

g) Which healing is used to teach something about forgiveness?

h) In what way were miracles 'mighty works'?

3 Collect examples from newspapers, magazines and so on of what might be considered to be modern miracles. Pass them around and discuss them.

To Help You Understand

a) Jesus Heals Many People (Simon Peter's Mother-in-Law)

Read Mark 1:29–34, Luke 4:38–41, Matthew 8:14–17

MARK We understand from this passage
LUKE that Simon Peter and Andrew
MATTHEW lived in Capernaum. Simon's mother-in-law may have been suffering from a bout of 'flu, or from malaria. The vivid descriptions of Jesus taking her by the hand, and later of the crowd, would suggest that the information came from an eye-witness, possibly Peter. The statement that the woman 'began to wait on them' emphasises the completeness of her cure.

As we shall see later (Topic 14), no work was allowed on the Sabbath. Giving medical aid and carrying loads were considered to be work and therefore unlawful (see Jeremiah 17:24). So when the Sabbath ended, at sunset, the people of Capernaum, having witnessed the healing in the synagogue earlier, felt free to bring their sick friends for healing. We shall examine the suggestion that 'demons' were silenced in the next Topic.

LUKE Luke's version is very similar to that of Mark, but an interesting point is that Luke, probably a doctor, specifies that the woman had a 'high fever'.

MATTHEW Matthew's account follows Mark's but, as often happens, Matthew adds a fulfilled prophecy (Isaiah 53:4).

b) Jesus Preaches in Galilee

Read Mark 1:35–9, Luke 4:42–4

MARK Here is an example of Jesus getting
LUKE away from people in order to pray. It is interesting that Mark and Luke both insert this brief passage after suggesting that crowds seeking healing had thronged Jesus. Jesus' comment to those who find him suggests that his priority is preaching.

c) Jesus Heals a Man (The Man with a Skin Disease)

Read Mark 1:40–5, Luke 5:12–16, Matthew 8:1–4

MARK Various skin diseases, including
LUKE leprosy, were very common in
MATTHEW ancient Israel, and strict instructions were given in the book of Leviticus to prevent the spread of diseases which were considered to be highly contagious:

> *Any person who has a dreaded skin-disease must wear torn clothes, leave his hair uncombed, cover the lower part of his face, and call out 'Unclean, unclean!' He remains unclean as long as he has the disease, and he must live outside the camp, away from others.*
>
> *Leviticus 13:45–6*

We now know that one of these skin diseases, leprosy, is not easily caught from other people, unless there is prolonged contact. The man referred to in this passage showed great faith, and Jesus' compassion in touching him is emphasised. He is told to keep silent about his cure, other than reporting to a priest for the necessary medical examination. We can easily understand how the man wanted to tell everyone about what had happened!

LUKE Luke and Matthew both shorten
MATTHEW Mark's account, but otherwise follow it closely.

WHAT IS LEPROSY? Caused by a bacillus, leprosy is a mildly infectious disease otherwise known as 'Hansen's Disease'.

It affects mainly the nerves, skin, eyes and nose. If left untreated, the extremities may become anaesthetic. It is this loss of feeling – not the disease itself – which can lead to deformity.

ACTIVITIES

1 Look up Leviticus 13:1–46 and 14:1–32. Look through the passages quickly. Discuss why such detail should be given in the Law about these matters.

2 Summarise each of the miracles of Jesus as you read them. Try to pick out the key words, and write your summary around these words. (Look back to the work you did in Topic 3 on the Pharisees.)

3 You may like to see a film about the work done by Christians to help leprosy sufferers today. Your teacher can contact The Leprosy Mission, Goldhay Way, Orton Goldhay, Peterborough PE2 0GZ.

4 Begin a chart to include all the miracles you read in your course. Include the reference, title, method used, words spoken (if any), and the following key:

H	Healing
RD	Raising the dead
E	Exorcism
N	Nature miracle
S	Sabbath
Sy	Synagogue
F	Faith important
D	Distance (Jesus was not present)
C	Criticism of Jesus involved
G	Gentile
FS	Forgiveness of sins mentioned
Com	Compassion of Jesus mentioned
Sil	Instruction to tell no one
P	Performed in private

Start in this way:

MIRACLES				
Reference	Title	Method	Words spoken?	Key
Mark 1: 29–34 or Luke 4: 38–41 or Matthew 8: 14–17	Peter's mother-in-law	Touch		H S
Mark 1: 40–45 or Luke 5: 12–16 or Matthew 8: 1–4	Man with skin disease	Touch and command	'Be clean!'	H F C Sil Com

d) Jesus Heals a Paralysed Man

Read Mark 2:1–12, Luke 5:17–26, Matthew 9:1–8

MARK LUKE MATTHEW Mark here begins a sequence of stories with the theme of conflict between Jesus and religious leaders. This account includes controversy about the forgiveness of sins.

According to Mark, the event took place in Capernaum where Jesus is described as being 'at home'. This might mean that he was again in Peter's home. The four friends of the paralysed man would gain access to the flat roof via an outside staircase and would be able to remove part of the earth-covered or tiled roof.

The faith of the man's friends is commented on, followed by the statement of Jesus that the man's sins were forgiven. It was a general belief of the time that suffering was a result of sin, although the writer of the fourth Gospel points out that Jesus did not share this view (John 9:1–3). Perhaps Jesus' words were intended to

A flat-roofed house

assure the man that any guilt he felt was forgiven. Even so, to the Jewish mind, it would be unthinkable that any human being, even the Messiah, should forgive sins – only God could do that. So to them, Jesus' statement was blasphemous.

Jesus commented that it was, from one point of view, easier to say that sins are forgiven (a statement which could not be proved or disproved) than to pronounce healing (the proof or otherwise would be immediately obvious in this case). Jesus then went on to heal the man physically, and so showed that he had power to bring about spiritual wholeness too.

Notice the reaction of the onlookers at the end of the account. Notice, too, that Jesus uses the term 'Son of Man' of himself.

LUKE Luke tells us that the teachers of the Law had gathered, not only from Galilee, but also from Jerusalem.

MATTHEW Again, Matthew's account is a shortened version of Mark's.

Ruins of a second-century synagogue at Capernaum, possibly built on the site of and with materials from a first-century building. Notice the Graeco-Roman architectural style.

e) Jesus Heals a Roman Officer's Servant (The Centurion's Servant)

Read Luke 7:1–10, Matthew 8:5–13

LUKE
MATTHEW Once again, this story is set in Capernaum, and is from the source common to Luke and Matthew. The Gentile officer was probably a centurion – originally a commander of 100 men, although later the number varied. He may have been a 'God-fearer', who was interested in the Jewish faith, and it is suggested that he had built the local synagogue.

LUKE A message was brought to Jesus, possibly to avoid the embarrassment of asking a Jew to enter a Gentile's home. The Roman understood all about giving orders and recognised Jesus' authority to do so. Jesus commented that he had never before found such faith, even among Jews. This is the first recorded miracle which took place without Jesus being present with the sick person.

MATTHEW Matthew suggests that the centurion came to Jesus in person, and includes a section about a banquet in the Kingdom of heaven, a very Jewish theme.

ACTIVITIES

1 Fill in the appropriate information on your sheet headed 'Son of Man' (see Topic 4).

2 Add information from the healing of the Roman officer's servant to the work you started on the authority of Jesus (see Topic 10).

3 Begin some coursework on forgiveness. As you continue with the course, make notes of anything stated on the subject. Look for information about both divine forgiveness and human forgiveness, including material from Topic 11 j). Collect information from newspapers and magazines to illustrate your work.

f) The Woman Who Touched Jesus' Cloak (The Woman with a Haemorrhage)

Read Mark 5:25–34, Luke 8:43–8, Matthew 9:20–2

MARK
LUKE
MATTHEW This event occurred as Jesus was on his way to help the dying daughter of a synagogue official. The nature of the woman's haemorrhage, a continuous menstrual flow, would make her 'unclean', and she would be unable to mix freely with others. Her decision to touch the fringe of Jesus' clothes showed not only her embarrassment at speaking about her problem, but also her tremendous faith. The cost of healing to Jesus is pointed out. The woman was encouraged to speak about what had happened, and Jesus commended her faith.

LUKE It is of interest to note that Luke, the doctor, avoids including Mark's comment that doctors had been unable to help this woman.

MATTHEW Again, Matthew's account is much briefer than those of Mark or Luke.

g) Jesus Heals a Deaf-Mute (The Deaf and Dumb Man)

Read Mark 7:31–7

MARK This event is recorded after a visit to the coast to the north–west of Israel. The particular route mentioned in verse 31 was probably taken in order to avoid the territory of Herod Antipas (see map).

Deafness from birth causes great difficulty with speech, since we learn to speak by imitating others. The touching of the man's ears and tongue is interesting, as obviously the man would not hear words of command. Saliva was believed to have healing properties (think what most people do instinctively if they cut a finger!) and was sometimes used in folk medicine. *Ephphatha* is an Aramaic word. Again, all concerned are asked to keep quiet about the event.

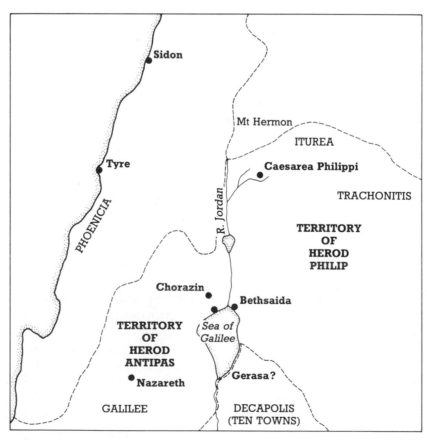

Map of northern Israel

h) Jesus Heals a Blind Man at Bethsaida

Read Mark 8:22–6

MARK This 'mighty work' has a number of points in common with the previous miracle. Bethsaida was in the territory of Herod Philip (see the map on p. 86). Blindness was very common, as it still is today in many tropical and sub-tropical countries. As in the previous account, the man is taken aside and the miracle is performed privately, saliva again being used.

ACTIVITIES

1 Construct a chart to show the similarities between the above two miracles.

2 Be sure to include on your list of miracles all the miracles you have read.

---

i) Jesus Heals a Sick Man (The Man with Dropsy)

Read Luke 14:1–6

LUKE This event occurs on a Sabbath day in the home of a leading Pharisee. We often read of Jesus being entertained by Pharisees. The man mentioned here may well have been suffering from dropsy, a disease which causes limbs to swell and which is a sign of heart failure. Whether he had been invited deliberately in order to set a trap for Jesus is not certain. There was nothing in the Torah (Law of Moses) which would prevent healing on the Sabbath, but the regulations introduced by the scribes and rabbis would not allow medical aid to be given on the Sabbath unless life was in danger. Jesus saw this as hypocritical when even animals could be rescued on the Sabbath.

j) Jesus Heals Ten Men

Read Luke 17:11–19

LUKE This story has some similarities with the account in Luke 5:12–16. The suggestion that Jews and a Samaritan were prepared to mix together shows the desperate situation they were in as fellow-sufferers. It is significant that the Samaritan is referred to as a foreigner, and that his faith is commended.

k) Jesus Heals Blind Bartimaeus

Read Mark 10:46–52, Luke 18:35–43

MARK This story is found in all three
LUKE Synoptic Gospels, but only Mark tells us the man's name. Notice the title he gives to Jesus, 'Son of David', indicating that he believed Jesus to be the Messiah. According to Mark, this story took place before the beginning of Jesus' last week in Jerusalem. It is significant that, by this point, Jesus did not rebuke him or ask him to keep quiet about his belief. The man's faith was commended and he became a disciple.

A blind beggar in a Nazareth street – blind beggars can still be seen sitting by the roadside in the Middle East today.

ACTIVITY

Answer all sections of this essay:

a) Mention a miracle where the faith of the sick person's friends is referred to.

b) Describe, briefly, a miracle in which the faith of the person healed is commended.

c) Explain carefully why faith is stated to be important in the accounts of these miracles.

d) Do you think a person's attitude is important in recovery from illness today?

l) Jairus' Daughter

Read Mark 5:21–4 and 35–43, Luke 8:40–2 and 49–56, Matthew 9:18–26

MARK The next two miracles concern
LUKE the raising of the dead.
MATTHEW Jairus' function would probably have been to arrange the services of worship in the synagogue. Synagogue officials were frequently in conflict with Jesus, so Jairus was obviously desperate to seek his help. Notice that we are told the age of the girl.

The incident concerning the woman who touched Jesus' cloak would clearly cause delay, but despite the sad news from Jairus' home, Jesus encouraged him to believe that something could still be done. Professional mourners had already gathered, and Jesus' words to them indicate that he thought of death as a sleep (although some suggest that this should be taken literally, and that Jesus realised that the girl was only unconscious).

Some Christians still refer to death as a sleep, as this 'In Memoriam' notice suggests:

Treasured memories of a dear grandmother, fell asleep February 2, 1964, also a dear brother, fell asleep January 28, 1985.

Notice that only three disciples and the girl's parents were present when Jesus took her by the hand and spoke the Aramaic words which her mother would use to waken her each morning. Jesus gave strict instructions that they should tell no one of what had happened, and then suggested that the girl needed food.

A stained-glass window in a village church illustrates the story of Jairus' daughter.

LUKE Luke adds the detail that the girl was Jairus' only daughter.

MATTHEW As usual, Matthew shortens the account considerably and has Jairus himself announcing to Jesus that his daughter has died. Only Matthew mentions the flute-players who would accompany the wailing women.

m) Jesus Raises a Widow's Son (The Widow of Nain's Son)

Read Luke 7:11–17

LUKE Only Luke records this particularly sad event. For a widow to lose her only son would mean that she was without any means of support. The event took place outside Nain, six miles (10 km) south–east of Nazareth, and the 'coffin' was probably an open bier. The statement that Jesus touched the coffin is significant, as this would make him 'unclean'. The reaction of the crowd is also important; they saw this as an indication that God was at work amongst them to bring salvation.

ACTIVITIES

1 From which sources do the following accounts come?

a) Jesus heals a paralysed man

b) The centurion's servant

c) Jesus heals ten men

Look back to Topic 5 if you do not remember the details.

2 Discuss the comment that Jesus taught by both parable and miracle. What do you think Jesus was teaching when he did the following?

a) heal the paralysed man,

b) raise Jairus' daughter.

3 Answer the following questions:

a) Why did the people of Capernaum bring their sick friends to Jesus 'after the sun had set'?

b) Why do you think it is suggested that Jesus got up early and left Capernaum?

c) What, according to both Mark and Luke, was the main reason for Jesus' ministry?

d) What instructions did Jesus give to the man healed of the skin disease, and why did he give them?

e) Why do you think the paralysed man was told that his sins were forgiven before he was healed?

f) When and why did Jesus ask the question 'Who touched my clothes?'?

To Keep You Thinking

1 **Prejudice**
Jesus commended the faith of non-Jews. Discuss ways in which Christians can follow the example of Jesus in today's multiracial society.

2 **Healing**
Jesus said, 'Heal the sick' (Luke 10:9). In what different ways do Christians carry out this teaching today?

Power over Spiritual and Natural Forces

'. . . it is by means of God's power that I drive out demons, and this proves that the Kingdom of God has already come to you.'

Setting the Scene

It was a common belief in both Old Testament and New Testament times that people could be possessed or taken over by evil spirits, unclean spirits or demons. Josephus, writing at the end of the first century, referred to the practice of driving out demons in his own day, and a thousand years earlier. He writes about King Solomon:

> *And he left behind him the manner of using exorcisms, by which they drive away demons, so that they never return, and this method of cure is of great force unto this day; for I have seen a certain man of my own country whose name was Eleazar, releasing people that were demoniacal . . .*
>
> Josephus, Antiquities of the Jews 8:2.5

So it is not surprising that the Gospels frequently record that Jesus released people from the power of evil spirits. Some of the conditions described in the Gospels can be identified with certain types of mental illness, but this is not necessarily the complete explanation. It has often been said that because it was impossible to explain mental illnesses at the time of Jesus, they were seen as the result of the activity of demons. This may be so, but modern interest in various occult practices and films about exorcisms might suggest that we have not exactly outgrown belief in demonic powers even in the present day. Some branches of the Christian Church still recognise the need for exorcism and practise it.

In an article in a weekly Church newspaper dealing with this 'deliverance ministry', the following comments appear:

> *Clearly Jesus believed in the existence of a personal devil, not the caricature with horns, a tail and pitchfork, but a real spiritual being, created as a high angelic being and fallen by pride — see Ezek 28:12–19 and Isaiah 14:12–14, particularly in the Authorised Version, where the references are very clear. He also clearly believed that people could be afflicted by evil spirits, often called "unclean" spirits or "demons" in the New Testament. The New Testament word "diamonidzomai" (afflicted or affected by a demon or evil spirit) is probably better translated by the English "demonised" rather than "possessed".*
>
> *Jesus also commissioned his followers to share in this ministry (Mark 3:15, Matt 10:8 et al), as well as to preach the Gospel and heal the sick.*
>
> From 'The place of deliverance ministry', J. and E. Trevenna

Luke tells us that on one occasion Jesus was accused of practising black magic in order to cure people who were demon-possessed (Luke 11:14–20). In his reply Jesus said that it was illogical to suggest that he used the power of the devil to cast out devils. As the quotation at the beginning of this Topic states, the driving out of demons proved the presence of the Kingdom of God. Jesus' power over evil spiritual forces demonstrated God's victory over Satan.

The 'nature' miracles often prove difficult for modern readers and various explanations have been offered. Villagers of Myvatn, Iceland, believed they had experienced a miracle when the church in which they had taken refuge was encircled but not destroyed by a lava flow.

Myvatn, Iceland – a modern church stands on the site of the one saved from an eruption.

The Gospels suggest that the disciples were puzzled by certain events (Mark 4:41 and 8:14–21), yet having experienced the mighty works of Jesus they became convinced that these miracles were signs of the presence of God's kingly rule among them.

ACTIVITIES

1 Share what you know about the occult or exorcism today.

2 Discuss the 'miracle' at Myvatn. Have you heard of any similar 'miraculous' events?

3 Answer the following questions:
   a) Give two other terms used for demons.
   b) What is meant by a 'deliverance ministry'?
   c) What explanation was given by Jesus' enemies for his ability to cast out demons?
   d) According to Luke, what explanation did Jesus give for this ability?
   e) Can you suggest any explanations that have been put forward to account for the nature miracles?

To Help You Understand

a) A Man with an Evil Spirit (The Madman in the Synagogue)

Read Mark 1:21–8, Luke 4:31–7

MARK LUKE It was common practice to invite visitors to preach in the synagogue. We are not told the subject of the address on this occasion, but those who listened were amazed at the authority of Jesus. Speaking in the plural, 'What do you want with us . . .', the man recognised who Jesus was – we shall notice this in similar stories later. Professor Barclay makes the following comment:

> *When a man believed himself to be possessed he was 'conscious of himself and also of another being who constrains and controls him from within'. That explains why the demon-possessed in Palestine so often cried out when they met Jesus. They knew that Jesus was believed by some at least to be the Messiah; they knew that the reign of the Messiah was the end of the demons; and the man who believed himself to be possessed by a demon spoke as a demon when he came into the presence of Jesus.*
>
> From William Barclay, *The Gospel of Mark*

With a word of command, and after a convulsion, the man was healed. The crowd was amazed, and commented on the authority of Jesus in being able to give orders to demons!

This story follows the typical form of miracle accounts. First the illness is described, then the healing takes place and then comments are made about the reaction of the onlookers.

b) Jesus Heals a Man with Evil Spirits (The Madman of Gerasa)

Read Mark 5:1–20, Luke 8:26–39

MARK LUKE The arrangement of the various stories in this part of Mark's Gospel is significant. This account follows immediately the story of the calming of the storm, and

91

Cliffs of Gerasa?
Why do you think this area has become associated with this event?

balances that account, for here a storm within an individual is calmed.

The exact location of Gerasa is difficult to be sure about, but an area on the south-east shore of the Sea of Galilee would fit the description given (see the map on p. 86). The story is set in Decapolis, a Gentile area. Notice that pigs were kept here; pigs were unclean for Jews. The man described was so violently ill that all attempts to bind him for his own good had failed. Evil spirits were believed to live among tombs. The cave tombs were probably the only shelter the man could find.

The man recognised Jesus as 'Son of the Most High God'. He stated that his name was 'Mob' or 'Legion'. A Roman legion consisted of up to 6000 troops. Perhaps the man, feeling that he had been taken over by so many demons, had given himself this nickname, which he may have thought appropriate to his depersonalised state.

The destruction of the herd of pigs has presented problems, some people feeling that cruelty to animals is involved. The following suggestions have been made:

- The general disturbance caused by the man's shouting and violent behaviour scared the pigs into their stampede.

- The man had been so desperately ill that he needed some proof that he was cured. It was believed that evil spirits could enter animals, so the man requested that they should enter the pigs.

- Jesus allowed the evil spirits to enter the pigs – but only on the request of the sick man.

Perhaps the truth lies in a combination of these suggestions.

Jesus, seen as a threat to people's possessions, was asked to leave the area. The man, now cured, was asked to remain as a missionary. This is in marked contrast to other stories where people are told to keep quiet about cures.

ACTIVITIES

1   Consider carefully the threefold form of the miracle accounts suggested on p. 91. Look back at the miracles you studied in Topic 12 and make a note of those which fit into this pattern.

2   You have discovered that people cured were often told to keep quiet about what had happened and demons were frequently silenced (see also Mark 1:34). Discuss why this should have been so.

3   Refer to Mark 1:21–8 or Luke 4:31–7 and answer the following questions:
   a)   Where did this miracle take place?
   b)   What title did the man give to Jesus?
   c)   Give two reasons why people in the synagogue were amazed.
   d)   In what ways did Jesus show his authority?
   e)   Why do you think Jesus silenced those possessed by demons?
   f)   Why do you think there was no criticism of Jesus' action on this occasion?

c) A Woman's Faith (The Syro-Phoenician Woman's Daughter)

Read Mark 7:24–30, Matthew 15:21–8

MARK Jesus went to a Gentile area, the
MATTHEW coast of Phoenicia near to Tyre
(see the map on p. 86). He may have gone to this
area to escape from the crowds, or to avoid
being in the territory of Herod Antipas. Perhaps
Jesus was having a meal when the woman arrived
– which could account for the conversation
which followed. Jesus tested the woman's faith
by suggesting that he had come first for the Jews
('the children'). The woman persisted by saying
that even dogs would eat left-overs (pieces of
bread were sometimes used to wipe the fingers
after a meal and then thrown to the pets). The
normal word for a dog was used as a term of
abuse for Gentiles, but Jesus here used a more
affectionate term meaning puppy or pet. The
woman obviously did not take offence. Notice
that Jesus is not present with the person
healed.

MATTHEW Matthew's account is much
more Jewish in emphasis than Mark's. He refers
to this woman as a 'Canaanite' woman and tells
us that she addressed Jesus as 'Son of David'. A
comment is also included about the disciples'
attitude and Jesus' words about his mission to
the Jews.

d) Jesus Heals a Boy with an Evil Spirit (The Epileptic Boy)

Read Mark 9:14–29, Luke 9:37–43

MARK This event is placed immediately
LUKE after the Transfiguration of Jesus (see
Topic 16), when the three disciples who accompanied him were much impressed. The other
disciples had been unable to cure a sick boy.
They were later told that this was because they
did not have enough faith in the power of God –
shown by their lack of prayer.

The description of the boy's illness corresponds closely to the symptoms of severe
epilepsy, a condition which is still common
today. Notice that the boy's father did have faith,

but he was sufficiently honest to admit to doubts
also.

LUKE Luke's account is a shortened version
of Mark's.

e) Jesus Heals a Crippled Woman on the Sabbath

Read Luke 13:10–17

LUKE Strictly speaking, this is a healing
miracle, but it is included in this Topic because
the woman is said to have had an evil spirit, and
later the comment is made that Satan had bound
up the woman. (Be sure to indicate on your list
of miracles that this is both a healing and an
exorcism.) It is also one of the conflict stories
which will be considered in more detail in the
next Topic.

The woman's condition may have been due
to spinal curvature, or an arthritic illness.
Criticism was made by the synagogue official,
and in his reply, Jesus again made reference to
the fact that work was done for animals on the
Sabbath, in order to justify the help he had given
to this Jewess (descendant of Abraham). Notice
the reaction of the people in the synagogue.

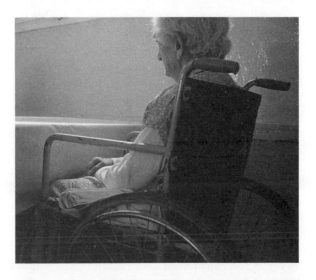

*Why would crippling conditions be more common
in the first century than they are today?*

ACTIVITIES

1 If you are studying Luke's Gospel, look back to Topic 12 i) and compare that miracle with Luke 13:10–17. Make a note of the similarities and differences between the two.

2 Talk about what you know of epilepsy.

3 Refer to Mark 9:14–29 or Luke 9:37–43 and answer the following questions:

   a) What event preceded this story?

   b) Which of the disciples would not have been trying to cast out the evil spirit?

   c) What symptoms of severe epilepsy did this boy have?

   d) How does this account bring out the importance of faith?

Lord God Almighty, none is as mighty as you;
in all things you are faithful, O Lord.
You rule over the powerful sea;
you calm its angry waves.

Psalm 89:8–9

Throughout the centuries, Christians have given this story a devotional interpretation. During the eighteenth century, John Newton (the writer of the hymn 'Amazing grace . . .'), who was at that time the captain of a slave-trading ship, became a Christian after praying for help in a terrible storm at sea. He later became a Church of England clergyman, and wrote a number of hymns, one of which begins:

Begone, unbelief; my Saviour is near,
And for my relief will surely appear:
By prayer let me wrestle, and He will perform;
With Christ in the vessel, I smile at the storm.

John Newton (1725–1807)

---

f) Jesus Calms a Storm

Read Mark 4:35–41, Luke 8:22–5, Matthew 8:23–7

MARK LUKE MATTHEW Sudden storms are very common on the Sea of Galilee, where winds are funnelled between the hills. This storm must have been unusually severe, for there were Galilean fishermen among the panicking disciples.

The account in Mark appears to have come from an eye-witness, with its vivid description of the storm and Jesus asleep in the stern of the boat with his head on a pillow. The Kinneret boat (see p. 66) appears to have a raised platform in the stern. A contrast is drawn between the calmness of Jesus and the confusion of the storm – and of the disciples.

The command of Jesus – 'Be still!' – is similar to that given to the evil spirit (Mark 1:25) and it has been suggested that this points to a belief that storms were caused by evil spirits. The reaction of the disciples is emphasised: 'Who is this man?' A number of Old Testament passages state that God has control over the sea, for instance, Psalms 89 and 107:23–30.

LUKE MATTHEW Luke and Matthew both avoid using the implied rebuke of Jesus which Mark includes: 'Teacher, don't you care that we are about to die?'

How do we know that the storm was particularly severe?

g) Jesus Feeds Five Thousand Men

Read Mark 6:30–44, Luke 9:10–17,
Matthew 14:13–21

MARK
LUKE
MATTHEW This is the only miracle recorded in all four Gospels. Mark suggests that, after returning from a tiring mission, the disciples were taken away from the crowds by Jesus in order that they might rest. The crowds followed them, however, and as he was sorry for them, Jesus first taught them and then fed them with five small barley loaves and two dried or salted fishes.

An Israeli kibbutz produces 'real Lake of Galilee fish caught and canned by Galilee fishermen' with a photograph of a mosaic from the church at Tabgha and the story of the feeding of the 5000 on the box!

Many suggestions have been made concerning this miracle:

- Perhaps there has been an exaggeration of the number of people involved.

- The fourth Gospel suggests that a lad offered his picnic to Jesus. Perhaps there were others who had also brought food and were willing to share it.

- Perhaps this story suggests the banquet which Jews believed would take place with the coming of the Messiah.

- Perhaps this story is based on that in 2 Kings 4, where, in a time of famine, 20 loaves were given to the prophet Elisha:

> *Elisha told his servant to feed the group of prophets with this, but he answered, 'Do you think this is enough for a hundred men?' Elisha replied, 'Give it to them to eat, because the Lord says that they will eat and still have some left over.' So the servant set the food before them, and, as the Lord had said, they all ate and there was still some left over.*
>
> *2 Kings 4:42–4*

- Perhaps, since it is stated that Jesus 'gave thanks to God', a phrase connected with the word Eucharist, we are meant to see this in connection with the Last Supper and the Christian celebration of Holy Communion. So the miracle is seen as a sign that Jesus provided spiritual as well as physical food. The 12 baskets of left-overs may suggest that the apostles continued to distribute spiritual food.

- Perhaps the miracle should be seen as a sign of a different kind, pointing to who Jesus is, in view of a passage from Exodus:

> *Then Moses said, 'It is the Lord who will give you meat to eat in the evening and as much bread as you want in the morning'.*
>
> *Exodus 16:8*

LUKE Luke tells us that this happened near to Bethsaida (see the map on p. 86).

MATTHEW Matthew suggests that there were more than 5000 people, for that number did not include women and children.

h) Jesus Walks on the Water

Read Mark 6:45–56, Matthew 14:22–33

MARK **MATTHEW** The fourth gospel suggests that after the feeding of the 5000, the people tried to make Jesus their king. So he went away from them to pray, sending the disciples ahead in a boat. Again, various suggestions have been made to explain the walking on the water, for instance that Jesus was actually walking on the sea-shore or on a sand-bank. Neither of these explanations would account for the terror of the disciples. Mark suggests that this event, and the feeding of the 5000, may have a deeper meaning (verse 52). Knowing their Old Testament very well, perhaps the disciples would later remember verses from a psalm:

> *When the waters saw you, O God, they*
> *were afraid . . .*
> *You walked through the waves;*
> *you crossed the deep sea,*
> *but your footprints could not be seen.*
>
> *Psalm 77:16, 19*

MATTHEW Matthew adds the details that Peter attempted to walk on the water to Jesus.

i) Jesus Feeds Four Thousand People

Read Mark 8:1–13, Matthew 15:32–9

MARK **MATTHEW** Because there are similarities, this account is sometimes seen as a duplicate of the story of the feeding of the 5000. Mark believed that there had been two distinct events (see also Mark 8:14–21). The differences in the two accounts have led to the suggestion that the feeding of the 5000 was a sign for Jews, whereas the feeding of the 4000, which may have been set in Decapolis, was a sign for Gentiles.

ACTIVITIES

1 Look up the psalms mentioned in section f). Discuss their significance in connection with this miracle.

2 Discuss the six suggestions concerning the interpretation of the story of the feeding of the 5000. What is your opinion?

3 Make a chart to show the similarities and differences between the accounts of the feeding of the 5000 and the feeding of the 4000.

4 Discuss in what ways the nature miracles can be interpreted as signs.

5 Answer the following questions:
   a) Where did the calming of the storm take place?
   b) What evidence is there in the story of the calming of the storm that Mark may have received the information from an eye-witness?
   c) What is significant about the command 'Be still!'?
   d) Why did Jesus leave the 5000 after feeding them?
   e) Why do you think Jesus fed crowds of people when he had earlier overcome the temptation to turn stones into bread?

6 Answer all sections of this essay:
   a) Name two miracles where the power of Jesus over spiritual forces is shown.
   b) Describe briefly one miracle where the power of Jesus over natural forces is shown.
   c) Describe in detail any two suggestions that have been made to explain the account of the feeding of the 5000.
   d) What do you think is the meaning of the suggestion that the accounts of the miracles of Jesus are 'deep stories' rather than 'tall stories'?

The Messianic Secret in Mark's Gospel

Mark's Gospel begins with a statement that Jesus is the Messiah (Mark 1:1) and suggests that Jesus acknowledged this title at the time of his trial (Mark 14:61–2). However, throughout most of the Gospel, Mark suggests that the Messiahship of Jesus was to be kept a secret. It is not important to understand all the theories about this at this stage. We have noticed that on a number of occasions, Jesus asked people who had been healed not to tell anyone about it. He also silenced demons who recognised him as the Son of God or Messiah. In Topic 16 you will see that while admitting to the disciples that he was the Messiah, Jesus also asked them to keep this a secret for a time.

One idea about the Messianic secret concerns the Messianic 'cross-purpose'. Jesus' understanding of his work as the Messiah was rather different from what the Jews were expecting the Messiah to do. So perhaps it is under-standable that he wished to avoid publicity about his Messiahship in the early part of his ministry.

ACTIVITIES

1 Head a sheet of paper 'The Messianic Secret in Mark's Gospel'. Divide the page into four horizontal sections and head them:
   - Acknowledgements of Messiahship
   - Secrecy after cures
   - Silencing of evil spirits
   - Warnings to the disciples

   Fill in examples that you have already discovered in Topics 12 and 13 (the index at the back of the book might help to jog your memory). Complete the list as you continue with the course.

2 Write a short paragraph in your own words to explain what is meant by the 'Messianic secret'.

To Keep You Thinking

World hunger
Find out in which parts of the world people suffer from malnutrition. What is the relevance of Mark 6:37 to this problem?

Opposition and Rejection

TOPIC 14

'. . . they were filled with rage and began to discuss among themselves what they could do to Jesus . . .'

Setting the Scene

Jesus' popularity continued to grow as crowds flocked to listen to his teaching and to benefit from his healing. At the same time, however, there was increasing conflict between Jesus and the religious leaders. The Pharisees and scribes (see Topic 3) were the groups with whom Jesus most frequently found himself in conflict; although it must also be remembered that Jesus often accepted the hospitality of Pharisees, and the fourth Gospel suggests that some were amongst his followers.

Jesus was a Jew and he accepted many of the religious beliefs and practices of his day, so that he had much in common with the scribes and Pharisees:

- He shared their reverence for the scriptures. Jesus frequently quoted from the Law, the Prophets and the Writings (especially the Psalms) and insisted that he had no intention of doing away with the Law of Moses (Matthew 5:17–18).

- Jesus also showed great reverence for the Temple, referring to it as 'my Father's house' (Luke 2:49) and 'a house of prayer for people of all nations' (Mark 11:17).

- He referred to the offering of sacrifices, implying that his disciples did this (Matthew 5:23).

- He accepted the position and importance of the priests (Mark 1:44).

- He was accustomed to attending the synagogue on the Sabbath (Luke 4:16).

- He celebrated Jewish festivals (Mark 14:12).

Why then should so much tension have arisen between Jesus and the religious leaders? The main reasons were because of the authority which Jesus appeared to claim and because he questioned the oral traditions and laws which had grown up and which were rigidly kept by the Pharisees, in addition to the Law of Moses.

We might wonder why so many conflict stories are included in the Gospels. At the time Mark's Gospel was written, Christians were experiencing serious opposition from Jewish leaders and this would lead them to think about the occasions when Jesus had met with similar opposition. Certain other questions in the early Church, such as Sabbath observance, fasting and whether it was necessary for Gentile Christians to observe Jewish ritual laws, may also have influenced which stories were included in the Gospels.

The early chapters of the Gospels include a number of conflict stories, of which you have already studied the healing of the paralysed man (Topic 12 d) and the call of Levi (Topic 10 b). From Luke's Gospel we have considered the healing of the crippled woman (Topic 13 e) and the man with dropsy (Topic 12 i). In this Topic we shall look at further conflict stories and other accounts of opposition; there will be more on the subject in Topic 21.

'. . . my Father's house'

ACTIVITIES

1 Look up the information about the Pharisees and the scribes in Topic 3. Keep this in mind as you read the accounts in this Topic.

2 Write a paragraph on each of the following questions:

a) What evidence is there in the Gospels that Jesus was a practising Jew?

b) Why do you think Jesus found himself in conflict with the Jewish religious authorities?

3 Begin a list of conflict stories. Include the reference, the title of the story and the cause of conflict. Begin with the accounts you have already studied, as shown below. Complete the list as you continue with the course.

CONFLICT STORIES		
Reference	Title	Cause of conflict
Mark 2: 1-12 or Luke 5:17-26 or Matthew 9:1-8	Paralysed man	Jesus' claim to forgive sins
Mark 2:13-17 or Luke 5: 27-32 or Matthew 9: 9-13	Call of Levi	Mixing with outcasts

To Help You Understand

a) The Question about Fasting

Read Mark 2:18–22, Luke 5:33–9

MARK
LUKE The only requirement in the Law was that Jews should fast on the Day of Atonement:

> *The tenth day of the seventh month is the day when the annual ritual is to be performed to take away the sins of the people. On that day do not eat anything at all; come together for worship, and present a food offering to the Lord.*
>
> Leviticus 23:26–7

In addition to this, the Pharisees encouraged fasting on Mondays and Thursdays. They did not eat between 6 a.m. and 6 p.m., but after that they would take food. Fasting was a sign of repentance; John the Baptist also encouraged his disciples to fast.

Jesus' comment concerning fasting suggests that his presence with his disciples was a time for joy, like a wedding. He had come with good news! The time for fasting would come later. There is a hint of his death in the statement that 'the bridegroom will be taken away from them.'

This teaching was very important for the early Church, when fasting was practised. An early Christian text, the *Didache*, suggested that Christians fasted on Wednesdays and Fridays.

MARK Mark's Gospel adds two short parables. In the days before pre-shrunk materials, all women would understand the folly of patching an old coat with new material. Perhaps the men would appreciate the second illustration more. New, supple animal skins would be used for new, fermenting wine; old, hard skins would crack and burst if fermenting wine was put into them. Jesus' teaching is something new, not an extra to be added to the Jewish faith.

LUKE Luke alters the concluding parables slightly. Perhaps his final comment was to explain why many Jews rejected Jesus.

b) The Question about the Sabbath

Read Mark 2:23–8, Luke 6:1–5

MARK
LUKE Many of the conflicts between Jesus and the religious leaders concerned his actions on the Sabbath. Little detail was given in the scriptures, except that the day was one for rest and worship (Exodus 20:8–11).

> *You have six days in which to do your work, but do not work on the seventh day, not even during ploughing time or harvest.*
>
> Exodus 34:21

There was much discussion at the time of Jesus as to what was meant by 'work'. It was suggested that moving a stool across an earthen floor was work, for this could create a furrow, which was considered to be ploughing! Many scribal rules had been made, and these were put together in the Mishnah, a book of Jewish law, in about AD 200.

> *The rules about the Sabbath are as a mountain hanging by a hair, for scripture is scanty, and the rules many.*
>
> Mishnah, Hagigah 1:8

Plucking the grain was considered as gleaning and rubbing it in the hands as threshing!

In the Mishnah, 39 kinds of work are forbidden on the Sabbath, including reaping and threshing, which the disciples were accused of doing on this occasion. Notice that they were not stealing; gleaning was permitted according to Deuteronomy 23:25.

Today, we might consider working on Sunday to be a petty matter. In Jesus' time, however, Sabbath-breaking was punishable by death. There is an example in the Old Testament of a man being put to death for gathering firewood on the Sabbath.

When answering questions, rabbis often referred to the Old Testament, and here Jesus gave an example from 1 Samuel 21:1–6 in order to show that religious laws could be set aside when people were in need. The bread had been set aside for the use of priests only, but it was given to David and his men who were fleeing from Saul, and were hungry.

As with a number of such incidents, the climax is a saying of Jesus: that the Sabbath is meant for man's good, not as a burden. Some scholars think that the comment which ends the section, about Jesus' authority over the Sabbath, was added by Mark.

LUKE Luke's account is a shortened version of Mark's.

c) The Man with a Paralysed Hand

Read Mark 3:1–6, Luke 6:6–11, Matthew 12:9–14

MARK LUKE MATTHEW This is another example of conflict over Sabbath regulations. Remember that medical aid could be given on this day only if a life was in danger. Jesus was carefully watched to see if he would heal on the Sabbath. Here he did so quite deliberately by calling the man out and suggesting that failure to do good on the Sabbath is the same as doing harm. Jesus hinted that he was more concerned to keep the Law of Moses than the laws of the scribes. Notice that Jesus was both angry and compassionate. The climax of the story is the plan to kill Jesus. So apparently it was against the law to heal on the Sabbath, but within the law to plan a death!

LUKE Luke's version is very similar to Mark's, except that he does not mention Jesus' anger.

MATTHEW Matthew includes the comment that since they would rescue a sheep on the Sabbath, surely the Law would permit aid to be given to a person.

ACTIVITIES

1 If you have started coursework on the authority of Jesus (see Topic 10), include information from this Topic.

2 Add the miracles in this Topic to your list of miracles.

3 Discuss the meaning of this statement: 'The Sabbath was made for the good of man; man was not made for the Sabbath.'

4 Answer the following questions:
   a) When did the Law require Jews to fast?
   b) When did the Pharisees suggest that Jews should fast?
   c) Why did Jesus refer to a wedding in connection with fasting?
   d) What is the main point of the parables of the patch and the wineskin?
   e) Which traditional laws were the disciples breaking in the cornfield?
   f) Why did Jesus refer to David?
   g) What is the meaning of 'the Son of Man is Lord even of the Sabbath'?
   h) What was the difference between the Law of Moses and the laws of the scribes?

5 Discover what you can about the practice of fasting in the Christian Church today.

d) A Crowd by the Lake

Read Mark 3:7–12

MARK In this passage, concerning the crowds who had come from north, south and east, Mark points out Jesus' popularity with the people, in contrast to the attitude of the Pharisees and Herodians (verse 6).

e) Jesus and Beelzebul

Read Mark 3:20–30, Luke 11:14–26

MARK Reference has already been made to
LUKE this passage on p. 90. Jesus was becoming such a controversial figure that apparently his family wished to persuade him to stop his work. In this and the next two passages considerable opposition is shown by Jesus' relatives and those who knew him best.

It seems that Jewish investigators had arrived from Jerusalem. Since they could not deny that Jesus was casting out demons, they claimed that he did so by the power of Satan (Beelzebul was the prince of the demons). Jesus pointed out that Satan would not cast out Satan, as that would be self-destruction, just as a civil war or family strife would destroy the country or family unit.

Another short parable follows in which the suggestion would seem to be that only a power stronger than the Devil himself would be able to overcome him. A warning follows that all sins can be forgiven except the sin against the Holy Spirit. This is probably a reference to the deliberate attitude of calling good evil, or of attributing the work of God to Satan.

LUKE Luke puts this account in the setting of Jesus actually performing miracles. He also includes a question asked by Jesus as to how Jewish exorcists cast out evil spirits. Luke draws the logical conclusion from the Parable of the Strong Man: Jesus drives out demons by the power of God.

A warning is given in Luke 11:24–6 about the danger of spiritual vacuums. When an evil spirit is cast out of a person, something positive must be put in its place.

f) Jesus' Mother and Brothers

Read Mark 3:31–5, Luke 8:19–21, Matthew 12:46–50

MARK Jesus' family seem to have been
LUKE concerned by the conclusion of
MATTHEW some people that he was mad (Mark 3:21). No mention is made of Joseph, so it is thought that he may have died by this time. Jesus shows that within the Christian family there are new ties.

LUKE Luke and Matthew have very
MATTHEW similar accounts to Mark.

Statue, Nazareth.
What do you know about Jesus' family?

g) Jesus Is Rejected at Nazareth

Read Mark 6:1–6, Luke 4:14–30

MARK This is one of the few events of Jesus'
LUKE ministry that is set in Nazareth. The scrolls would be brought from the ark to the bimah, where the reading from the scriptures would take place. Jesus would then sit to teach.

The rejection of Jesus by the synagogue congregation is significant. They saw him as merely the carpenter whose family they knew. Jesus' brothers are named by Mark, and his sisters are mentioned. Look back to p. 52 for comments about this family.

Scrolls being removed from the ark in a modern synagogue

Jesus recognised that it was natural to be rejected by those who knew him best. We are told that he was unable to heal many people because of their lack of faith.

LUKE Luke obviously has more information about this incident. He states that Jesus read from the prophet Isaiah (Isaiah 61:1–2) and then claimed that the prophecy had been fulfilled. Luke includes the proverb 'Doctor, heal yourself', suggesting that Jesus should perform miracles in his home town.

Jesus gave two examples from the Old Testament, first of Elijah helping a Gentile widow and then of Elisha healing a Syrian leper. This incensed the congregation and they dragged him to a nearby hilltop, intending to kill him. However, for whatever reason, Jesus was able to walk away – and, as far as we know, he never returned to Nazareth.

The Mount of the Precipitation, the traditional site of the attempt on Jesus' life.
Why do you think this place was suggested as the site of the incident?

103

ACTIVITIES

1 Discuss Jesus' comment: 'A prophet is respected everywhere except in his own home town and by his relatives and his family.' Why do you think this is so? Does it still apply today?

2 Modern synagogues are still built on the same pattern as those of the time of Jesus. If it is possible, and you have not already done so, visit a synagogue and identify the ark, the scrolls and the bimah. If this is not possible, find illustrations from books on Judaism.

3 Answer the following questions, with reference to Mark 3:31–5, Luke 8:19–21 or Matthew 12:46–50:

a) Why did Jesus' mother and brothers arrive?

b) Name three of Jesus' brothers.

c) Mention two theories about the 'brothers' of Jesus.

d) What new relationships are referred to in this passage?

4 Discuss the theories put forward in this section to account for Jesus' actions in healing and helping people.

h) The Teaching of the Ancestors
Read Mark 7:1–13, Matthew 15:1–9

MARK MATTHEW Here is a good example of the difference between the Law of Moses (the Old Testament Law) and the traditions of the elders. This time the conflict is over keeping the ritual laws, in particular those to do with the ceremonial washing of hands. This had nothing to do with hygiene, but concerns what was considered to be defilement caused by contact with Gentiles or outcasts. Mark explains the details (verses 3 and 4) for the benefit of the Gentiles among his readers. These were laws of the oral tradition, or 'manmade rules' (verse 7). Jesus called the Pharisees and lawyers hypocrites, or play-actors, and quoted from Isaiah 29:13. Their eagerness to keep the details of these manmade rules had taken the place of real faith.

Jesus then gave an example. He quoted the fifth commandment from Exodus 20:12, and the rather extreme punishment for breaking it from Exodus 21:17. Sometimes amounts of money were set aside for God, the practice being called *Corban*, an Aramaic word meaning 'dedicated'. This practice could be used as an excuse for not supporting needy parents. So in order to keep the tradition of *Corban*, people might break the far more important Law of God.

MATTHEW Matthew's account is similar to Mark's except that he leaves out the details about ritual washing.

i) The Things that Make a Person Unclean
Read Mark 7:14–23

MARK By the time Mark's Gospel was written, many Gentiles had become Christians and this passage may have been included to give guidance about eating with Gentiles. The principle stressed here is that nothing from outside can defile a person, but the evil attitudes and thoughts from within are what cause immoral and sinful behaviour.

j) Jesus at the Home of Simon the Pharisee
Read Luke 7:36–50

Oil from the olive was used for dressing hair.

LUKE Again Jesus enjoyed the hospitality of a Pharisee, but Simon did not show Jesus the usual courtesies of offering water to wash his feet, greeting him with a kiss and providing olive oil for his hair. Simon was apparently prepared to consider Jesus as a prophet, at least until Jesus accepted the anointing by the 'sinful woman'.

Some have tried to identify this event with the one recorded in Mark 14:3–9, but there are a number of differences. The woman has also been identified with Mary Magdalene (Luke 8:2), but this is also far from certain.

Jesus told the Parable of the Two Debtors to illustrate that the woman's love sprang from her gratitude that she had been forgiven. Jesus then confirmed that she was forgiven, which gave rise to questions from those present.

ACTIVITIES

1 If you are studying Luke's Gospel, add the above information to any coursework you have started on forgiveness.

2 Add the parables that you have read in this Topic to your list of parables.

3 Answer all sections of this essay:
   a) Name one occasion when Jesus claimed to forgive sins.
   b) Tell the story briefly.
   c) What do you think Christians mean by i) sin and ii) forgiveness?

To Keep You Thinking

1 Christian observance of Sunday
What is the difference between Sabbath observance and Sunday observance? Discuss with as many Christians as possible how they keep Sunday special.

2 Religious traditions
Find out how important traditions are in different Christian Churches.

The Sermon on the Mount

'Jesus saw the crowds and went up a hill, where he sat down. His disciples gathered round him and he began to teach them . . .'

Setting the Scene

When Jesus chose his 12 apostles he 'went up a hill'. Matthew suggests that it was also on a hill that Jesus gave the teaching which we shall consider in this Topic. This may be significant for, as you remember, some scholars consider that Matthew portrays Jesus as a second Moses, and Moses received the Law on Mount Sinai.

Jesus had already started to preach his message of repentance (Matthew 4:17). Those who responded to Jesus in this way found that there was a change in their behaviour, for those who placed themselves under the kingly rule of God were also in a new relationship to other people. The teaching in the Sermon on the Mount concerns these relationships, and is called 'ethical teaching' (teaching about right conduct or behaviour). This is teaching for the disciples, those who were already committed to Jesus. There is no suggestion that it is necessary to keep a lot of rules in order to earn God's approval. Those who are members of the Kingdom will wish to please the King by obeying him.

By the time Matthew's Gospel was written, such a collection of teachings was very necessary to instruct the new believers. However, the Sermon is not a collection of laws, for some of the ideals are of such a high standard that they are almost impossible to keep. The Sermon teaches principles of behaviour which can be applied to any situation, rather than specific rules. T W Manson made an interesting comparison to describe the Sermon on the Mount:

> *. . . a compass rather than an ordnance map; it gives direction rather than directions.*
>
> *From T W Manson*, The Sayings of Jesus

Chapters 5 to 7 cover the first of five blocks of teaching in Matthew's Gospel. It seems that the author gathered the teaching of Jesus together in blocks, so it may be that the teaching in the Sermon was not given all at the same time. There is a similar Sermon in Luke 6:7–49, which is introduced by the words, 'When Jesus had come down from the hill with the apostles, he stood on a level place . . .'. This has therefore

The view from the Mount of the Beatitudes

become known as the Sermon on the Plain to distinguish it from Matthew's account. However, 34 verses from Matthew's account are included by Luke in other places in his Gospel. In the next section of this Topic, To Help You Understand, the references to these passages from Luke are bracketed, so that you can see immediately which sections are *not* part of the Sermon on the Plain.

The Church of the Beatitudes, which is octagonal, each side representing a Beatitude

---

ACTIVITIES

1 Test yourself with the following questions:
   a) Why is Matthew's account called the 'Sermon on the Mount'?
   b) Why is Luke's account called the 'Sermon on the Plain'?
   c) What is significant about the statement that Jesus 'went up a hill'?
   d) What is ethical teaching?
   e) Why is it suggested that the Sermon on the Mount may be a collection of teachings rather than a sermon given at one time?

2 Discuss the meaning of T W Manson's comment about the Sermon on the Mount.

To Help You Understand

a) True Happiness

Read Matthew 5:1–12, Luke 6:17–26

MATTHEW Matthew tells us that Jesus sat
LUKE down and taught his disciples. It was usual in the synagogues for the person reading the scriptures to stand, but then to teach from a sitting position.

The Sermon begins with eight Beatitudes (from a Latin word meaning 'blessing'). Luke includes four of them, which are balanced by four woes, beginning in the *Good News Bible* with the words 'How terrible for you . . .'

In some versions of the Bible, each Beatitude begins with the words 'Blessed are . . .', in others with 'Happy are . . .' This is not intended to convey a bubbling emotion, but rather a deep contentment or permanent spiritual joy. Most of these descriptions of 'happy people' are rather surprising, for they turn upside down our ideas about what brings happiness. Read and think about the following comments on the Beatitudes:

The so-called Beatitudes, which begin the Sermon on the Mount, have been nicknamed the 'Beautiful Attitudes' because they focus far more on character than on behaviour. They are not a list of rules at all, but a set of congratulations from God to those whose standards are high because their attitudes are right.

From D Field, Christianity in the Modern World

In this portrait of the 'happy' man, Jesus is not giving a universal recipe for contentment, but a description of life in the Kingdom of God, the life of a Christian disciple . . . The Beatitudes describe a man who puts God first.

From R T France, The Man they Crucified

We shall now look at each Beatitude in turn in the order given by Matthew:

The Poor in Spirit
Read Matthew 5:3, Luke 6:20

MATTHEW **LUKE** The *Good News Bible* helps us to understand the meaning of this with its translation 'Happy are those who know they are spiritually poor . . .'. Only those who know that they need God are likely to accept his kingly rule. Professor Barclay has suggested the following meaning:

> *Blessed is the man who has realised his own utter helplessness and has put his whole trust in God . . .*
>
> From William Barclay, The Gospel of Matthew

LUKE Luke gives a more down-to-earth statement in 'Happy are you poor . . .' (verse 20), with a corresponding promise, and balances it with a comment about the rich (verse 24).

Pope's Sermon on Mount

from DAVID WILLEY in Rio de Janeiro

ON A STEEP mountainside overlooking the Atlantic Ocean the Pope brought up to date Christ's Sermon on the Mount last week.

The Vicar of Christ walked up a narrow path past the *favelados*, the slum-dwellers of Rio de Janeiro, was showered with yellow and white flower petals, and in a gesture to the poor in all countries of the Third World, gave away the gold ring he had worn every day since one of his predecessors, Paul VI, created him a cardinal.

This spontaneous and unexpected gesture — which surprised even his closest aide — was witnessed by only a handful of the 60 correspondents who had travelled 6,000 miles from Rome with the Pope to report his journey.

The Brazilian Government had actively discouraged journalists from attending this first meeting between the Pope and the urban poor of Brazil. But nothing . . . could disguise the impact of the Pope's attack on world poverty.

The Pope gave his Sermon on the Mount to a tiny congregation of not more than 150 slum-dwellers and their priest. Many of them were in tears as he said: 'The Church wants to be the Church of the Poor.'

Those Who Mourn
Read Matthew 5:4, Luke 6:21

MATTHEW **LUKE** This Beatitude is frequently quoted at funeral services and has comforted many people. Luke refers to those who weep. As well as being appropriate at a time of bereavement, some scholars suggest that this Beatitude could refer to an individual's spiritual grief for his or her own sins and for the sins of others.

The Meek
Read Matthew 5:5

MATTHEW This word is often confused with 'weak', and the modern versions of the Bible more helpfully refer to 'those who are humble'. A promise had been given to the humble in the Psalms:

> *. . . the humble will possess the land and enjoy prosperity and peace.*
>
> Psalm 37:11

The humble people, who realise their need rather than boast about their self-sufficiency, are spiritually strong.

Those who Hunger and Thirst
Read Matthew 5:6, Luke 6:21

MATTHEW **LUKE** Few of us have experienced the intensity of desperate hunger and thirst. Taken at its face value, Luke's statement may seem very uncaring, but Matthew makes it clear that the desperate hunger Jesus refers to concerns being 'righteous' or right with God. Those who are desperate to be right with God will be satisfied.

The Merciful
Read Matthew 5:7

MATTHEW This characteristic is reflected later in the Sermon (Matthew 6:12) and emphasises the importance of compassion and forgiveness towards others if a Christian expects forgiveness from God.

The Pure in Heart

Read Matthew 5:8

MATTHEW Only those who have found God's forgiveness can be described in this way. The promise that they will see God has an echo of a passage in a book from the Apocrypha, which dates from between the Old Testament and the New Testament periods. The author describes the joys of those who have died:

> *... the greatest joy of all will be the confident and exultant assurance which will be theirs, free from all fear and shame, as they press forward to see face to face the One whom they served in their lifetime and from whom they are now to receive their reward in glory.*
>
> *2 Esdras 7:98 (NEB)*

Peacemakers

Read Matthew 5:9

MATTHEW This is speaking not so much of the non-militant, as of those who have found peace with God and seek to pass it on to others and so do all they can to bring reconciliation. The prayer of St Francis of Assisi sums up this characteristic well:

> *Lord, make me an instrument of Thy peace;*
> *Where there is hatred, let me sow love;*
> *Where there is injury, pardon;*
> *Where there is discord, union;*
> *Where there is doubt, faith;*
> *Where there is despair, hope;*
> *Where there is darkness, light;*
> *Where there is sadness, joy.*
>
> *St Francis of Assisi*

The Persecuted

Read Matthew 5:10–12, Luke 6:22–3

MATTHEW At the time Matthew wrote, the
LUKE early Church was suffering much persecution and some Christians were facing death for their faith. A reminder that Jesus had foretold this would therefore be a great encouragement to them. The final Beatitude ends with the same promise as the first '... the Kingdom of heaven belongs to them.'

ACTIVITIES

1 Discuss the meanings of the words 'happiness', 'joy' and 'blessedness'. If necessary, look them up in a dictionary. Which do you think is the most appropriate for the Beatitudes?

2 Carry out a survey on what people consider leads to happiness. Compare the results against the Beatitudes.

3 'The Beatitudes describe a man who puts God first.' Discuss this comment.

4 Write a description of the people Jesus called 'blessed ...' or 'happy ...'.

PERSECUTION OF CHRISTIANS CONTINUES WORLDWIDE

5 Answer the following questions:
   a) Which Beatitude does the above headline echo?
   b) Explain the Beatitude in your own words.
   c) What is a Beatitude?
   d) Why would this Beatitude be important when the Gospels were written?
   e) What kind of persecution do you think Christians suffer today?

b) Salt and Light

Read Matthew 5:13–16 (Luke 11:33, 14:34–5)

MATTHEW
LUKE We are often told that too much salt can injure health; in fact too little can be just as bad. In the book of Ecclesiasticus in the Apocrypha, salt is listed as one of the chief necessities of life. It was used in the ancient world as an antiseptic, as well as to preserve and add flavour to food. Followers of Jesus should have a similar influence in society.

Topic 11 b) dealt with a brief form of the saying about light. Here it is expanded to show the influence that followers of Jesus should have.

'Your light must shine before people.'

c) Teaching about the Law

Read Matthew 5:17–20

MATTHEW Probably writing with Jews in mind, Matthew was eager to point out that Jesus had not come to destroy the Old Testament scriptures. Here he records Jesus' teaching that he had come to 'fulfil' the Law and the Prophets, to give them a deeper meaning or to 'make their teachings come true'. The teaching of the Law on ethical issues was intended to prevent unacceptable behaviour. Jesus emphasised the importance of the motives, attitudes and thoughts which lead to different types of behaviour.

Matthew gives six examples of this, each starting with the words: 'You have heard that people were told in the past . . .', and continuing, 'But now I tell you . . .'. We shall look at each example in turn:

Anger

Read Matthew 5:21–6 (Luke 12:57–9)

MATTHEW
LUKE The disciples are reminded of one of the ten commandments and told that anger and insults are displeasing to God just as murder is. So they are advised to sort out disputes with each other before offering sacrifice to God and before the law catches up with them.

Beliefs about hell will be considered in Topic 18.

ACTIVITIES

1 Look up Psalm 36:9 and John 8:12. Discuss what connection the early Church might make with the saying in the Sermon about light.

2 If you are studying Luke's Gospel, start a list of the sayings from the Sermon on the Mount in Matthew's version which are included in later sections of Luke's Gospel. Copy the following and add to it as you find further examples:

SAYINGS FROM THE SERMON ON THE MOUNT		
Matthew's reference	Subject of saying	Luke's reference
5 : 13	Salt	14 : 34-5
5 : 14-16	Light	11 : 33

Adultery

Read Matthew 5:27–30

MATTHEW Adultery was punishable by death (Deuteronomy 22:22–4). Again, it is the thought which leads to the action that is condemned. The remedy for lust may seem to us to be extreme! It is an example of exaggeration, and humour, often found in Jewish writings. It is not intended to be taken literally, but to show that drastic methods are necessary to bring about self-control and to avoid sinful actions.

The Sermon on the Mount is illustrated in the topiary at Packwood House.
Can you identify the multitude, the disciples, and the evangelists?

Divorce

Read Matthew 5:31–2

MATTHEW The grounds on which divorce could be allowed were a subject of debate in the first century. In this passage the suggestion is made that a divorced wife would be forced to commit adultery as she would need to remarry in order to support herself.

Vows

Read Matthew 5:33–7

MATTHEW This passage is possibly a comment on Leviticus 19:12:

> *Do not make a promise in my name if you do not intend to keep it; that brings disgrace on my name. I am the Lord your God.*
>
> Leviticus 19:12

Jesus suggested that vows should be unnecessary; the word of a disciple should be trustworthy.

Josephus commented that the Essenes avoided making oaths:

> *... whatsoever they say also is firmer than an oath; but swearing is avoided by them, and they esteem it worse than perjury; for they say that he who cannot be believed without [swearing by] God is already condemned.*
>
> *Josephus*, Wars of the Jews 2:8.6

Matthew records that Jesus was 'put on oath' at his trial (Matthew 26:63). Most Christians consider legal oaths are acceptable, although some refuse to make them.

Revenge

Read Matthew 5:38–42, Luke 6:29–30

MATTHEW
LUKE When first given, the laws of Leviticus 24:19–20 and Deuteronomy 19:21 were intended to limit revenge, not to encourage it. By New Testament times, money payments were made as compensation instead of the exact retaliation permitted by the Law. Jesus told his followers not to seek any revenge, even if they were insulted by a backhander on the right cheek, sued for a garment or pressed into service by the Roman occupying forces. A generous attitude would take the sting out of personal injuries.

Love for Enemies

Read Matthew 5:43–8, Luke 6:27–8 and 6:32–6

MATTHEW
LUKE In Leviticus 19:18, Jews were told '... love your neighbour ...', but nowhere in the Old Testament were they

told to hate their enemies. The saying quoted in this passage had probably grown up as an extension of the command of Leviticus 19. One of the Dead Sea scrolls includes the saying '. . . love all the sons of light and hate all the sons of darkness.' Jesus commended 'love' for enemies. It has been suggested that this is an impossibly high standard to set, but the Greek word used in the New Testament for this kind of love is *agape*, which means practical concern, wanting the best for others, rather than an emotional reaction.

LUKE Luke emphasises this positive approach, which is a new aspect in the teaching of Jesus and goes beyond the requirement of the Law.

The final comment is difficult to translate from the Greek, and the word 'perfect' may be misleading. It possibly suggests that Jesus'

disciples should have a perfect love which includes all people and reflects the love of God. Luke's version states, 'Be merciful just as your Father is merciful.'

Church peace call

The deaths of 1,369 civilians, soldiers and Leftist rebels in El Salvador's civil war last year "summons us to keep striving for peace", Archbishop Arturo Rivera Damas said in his New Year homily. About 65,000 lives have been lost since guerrillas began fighting the American-backed regime in 1979.— AP

ACTIVITIES

Note: Activities 1–3 are for those studying Matthew's Gospel.

1 Answer the following questions on Jesus' teaching about the Law:

   a) What sins can lead to murder?

   b) What was the Council (Matthew 5:22)?

   c) Where was the altar (Matthew 5:23)?

   d) What sin can lead to adultery?

   e) Which commandment concerned adultery?

   f) In which book of the Law were instructions given about divorce?

   g) Why should vows be unnecessary?

   h) What was the point of the law 'An eye for an eye . . .'?

   i) Do you think it is possible to '. . . love your enemy . . .'?

   j) What do you think is the meaning of 'You must be perfect . . .'?

2 Answer all sections of this essay:

   a) What, according to Matthew, was Jesus' attitude towards the Law?

   b) Give three examples of Jesus' teaching about the Law.

   c) Do you think this teaching is practicable for Christians today?

3 Make a chart to summarise Jesus' teaching about the Law. Have four columns and fill them in for each of the six examples in this section. Start as follows:

JESUS' TEACHING ABOUT THE LAW			
OT reference	*'You have heard . . .'*	*NT reference*	*'Now I tell you . . .'*
Exodus 20:13	No murder	Matthew 5:21-2	No anger

d) Teaching about Religious Practices

Read Matthew 6:1

MATTHEW In the first part of chapter 6, Matthew includes three examples of Jesus' teaching on religious actions. Again the stress is on motives; religious duties should be performed in private, to please God, and not in public, to gain other people's approval and admiration.

Charity

Read Matthew 6:2–4

MATTHEW Hypocrites are mentioned in each of these examples. Sincerity is vital in the Christian disciple.

Prayer

Read Matthew 6:5–15 (Luke 11:1–4)

MATTHEW As Jews often raised their arms **LUKE** when praying, they could be seen performing this action on street corners and in the Temple. The teaching here is not about meeting for public worship; Jesus told his disciples to carry out their personal devotions in private. Gentiles' prayers were often long, meaningless incantations. Jesus told his followers to avoid such prayers and, like other rabbis of his day, gave them a pattern prayer to follow. The details of the Lord's Prayer will be considered in Topic 19 – look ahead if you need the details now.

Fasting

Read Matthew 6:16–18

MATTHEW The practice of fasting was mentioned in Topic 14 a). Ashes were often put on the head to indicate to everyone that the individual was fasting. A similar practice is carried out today in some Churches on Ash Wednesday, at the start of Lent. Christians were to fast in the same way that they might feast, with joy and not sorrow.

A Derbyshire well-dressing made from flower petals and other natural materials

ACTIVITIES

1 Discuss what you know about current Christian practices of the three types discussed in this section: charity, prayer and fasting. In what ways do you think it is possible for Christians to be hypocrites?

2 Answer the following questions:

a) Explain the significance of any two symbols shown on the illustration of the Derbyshire well-dressing on p. 113 which are referred to in the Sermon on the Mount.

b) Describe any other two symbols which remind you of teaching in the Gospels.

c) What did Jesus say about prayer in the Sermon?

d) What was Jesus' teaching in the Sermon on other religious practices?

e) How do you think Christians can put this teaching into practice today?

e) Teaching about Priorities

The Sermon on the Mount does not arrange itself neatly into sections from this point, but there is a common theme about the need for Christian disciples to give priority in life to God. In a number of passages a contrast is drawn between differing approaches to life.

Riches in Heaven

Read Matthew 6:19–21 (Luke 12:33–4)

MATTHEW LUKE A contrast is drawn between a life based on possessions and one where spiritual concerns take priority. Luke, with his stress on providing for the needy, suggests that Christians should sell their possessions in order to give the money to the poor.

The words from Matthew are sometimes read in churches during a communion service, when an offering is made for the poor.

The Light of the Body

Read Matthew 6:22–3 (Luke 11:34–6)

MATTHEW This is a warning to Jesus' followers that they should allow the light of God to shine into every part of their lives.

God and Possessions

Read Matthew 6:24–34 (Luke 16:13 and 12:22–31)

MATTHEW LUKE The Christian disciple is faced with a choice between serving God and serving money (the word 'mammon' given in some versions of the Bible could also mean property). Warnings are given about the futility of worry. There are examples from the natural world: birds are provided for and flowers bloom beautifully, if briefly. (Grass was often cut and dried to provide fuel for ovens.)

Anemones, possibly the wild flowers referred to in the Sermon on the Mount

Judging Others

Read Matthew 7:1–6, Luke 6:37–42

MATTHEW
LUKE This is a warning about undue criticism of others and the hypocrisy of seeing others' faults but not one's own. Jesus illustrated this in a humorous way with flying sawdust in a carpenter's workshop.

LUKE Luke emphasises that a Christian should treat others as he would wish God to treat him. He goes on to suggest that a teacher needs to understand clearly before passing on his teaching.

Ask, Seek, Knock

Read Matthew 7:7–12, Luke 6:31
(Luke 11:9–13)

MATTHEW
LUKE This passage is another encouragement to prayer. The beginning could be misunderstood to lead to the idea that prayer could be used for selfish ends. As a father gives only what is good to his son, so God gives only what is good to his children. Luke suggests that what God wants to give is the Holy Spirit.

The last verse has become known as the Golden Rule. Jesus suggested that this sums up the ethical teaching of the Law and the Prophets. Other religions have a similar rule; for instance, centuries before Jesus, Confucius wrote:

> *What you do not like when done to yourself, do not do to others.*

An ancient story tells of how a Gentile asked the Rabbi Hillel to teach him the Jewish Law while he stood on one foot. Hillel replied, 'Whatever is hateful to you, do not do to your fellow-man.'

Rabbi Hillel and the Gentile.
What question did the Gentile ask?

Jesus gave a new emphasis to the teaching by turning these negative sayings into a positive command: 'Do for others what you want them to do for you.'

ACTIVITIES

1 Discuss what is meant by '. . . riches in heaven' (Matthew 6:20, Luke 12:33).

2 Make a list of the things about which the disciples were told not to worry.

3 Make a list of the examples of hypocrisy about which warnings were given to the disciples.

4 Discuss the Golden Rule. How do you think this should affect the life of a committed Christian today?

5 Answer the following questions, with reference to Matthew 6:24 or Luke 16:13:
  a) What is the context of this saying in the Gospel you are studying?
  b) Give two other words which could be used instead of 'money'.
  c) Give three examples from the Sermon of how a disciple should give priority to God.
  d) Suggest some ways in which a person today may be a slave to material things.

f) Warnings

The Sermon ends with a number of warnings to the people listening. It may be that this teaching was meant for the crowds as well as the disciples.

The Narrow Gate

Read Matthew 7:13–14 (Luke 13:22–30)

MATTHEW A choice between life and death
LUKE is presented in a number of passages in the Old Testament and the Apocrypha:

> *I am now giving you the choice between life and death, between God's blessing and God's curse, and I call heaven and earth to witness the choice you make. Choose life.*
>
> Deuteronomy 30:19
>
> *Listen! I, the Lord, am giving you a choice between the way that leads to life and the way that leads to death.*
>
> Jeremiah 21:8
>
> *He has set before you fire and water; reach out and take which you choose; before man lie life and death, and whichever he prefers is his.*
>
> Ecclesiasticus 15:16–17 (NEB)

The choice in this part of the Sermon is between the easy way leading to hell (see Topic 18) and the narrow way which is hard to find and follow but which leads to life.

A Tree and its Fruit

Read Matthew 7:15–20, Luke 6:43–5

MATTHEW Disciples are here warned to
LUKE beware of false prophets who may easily deceive them. They have to decide how genuine they are by the lives they lead.

I Never Knew You

Read Matthew 7:21–3 (Luke 13:25–7)

MATTHEW This passage concerns a day of
LUKE judgement and suggests that only those obedient to God will enter the Kingdom of heaven (notice the future emphasis here). Those rejected are the 'wicked', who have not done the will of God.

The Two House Builders

Read Matthew 7:24–9, Luke 6:46–9

MATTHEW The conclusion to the Sermon
LUKE suggests that obedience to the teaching of Jesus is crucial. A good foundation was essential for a building, then as now. The Sermon suggests that the only firm foundation for a life is the teaching of Jesus. This was, and is, a startling claim to make, and the final comment about the amazed reaction of the crowd to the authority of Jesus is therefore appropriate.

A modern house in Bethany built on rock

ACTIVITIES

1 It has been suggested that the ethical teaching of Jesus can be summarised under two headings:
   - Attitudes and behaviour of which he approved
   - Attitudes and behaviour which he 'hated'

   Try to summarise the teaching in the Sermon in two columns under these headings.

2 If you are studying Matthew's Gospel, be sure to fill in your sheets headed 'Jewish Emphasis' and 'Teaching'.

3 Discuss whether you think the Sermon on the Mount/Plain is teaching for committed Christians only, or for society in general.

4 If you are studying Luke's Gospel, check that you have completed the list of passages which appear outside the Sermon on the Plain (Activity 2 on p. 110). What does the list show about the way Matthew and Luke used their sources of information?

5 Make a chart of the attitudes and choices illustrated in these four 'warning' accounts. Start it in this way:

WARNINGS	
Reference	Attitudes and choices
Matthew 7:13-14 or Luke 13:24	The narrow gate — life. The wide gate — hell.

To Keep You Thinking

Ethical issues
Make a list of the ethical, or moral, issues in the Sermon and discuss their relevance to Christians today.

Who is Jesus?

'Who do you say I am?'

Setting the Scene

Sooner or later in life we all have to face important issues and make decisions or reach conclusions. The early chapters of the Gospels picture the disciples making important decisions about following Jesus. Later on they find themselves faced with further questions about who Jesus is. Having heard his teaching, watched him in his daily life and experienced his power, they can only ask each other, 'Who is this man?' (Mark 4:41).

The disciples were not alone in their questionings. Wherever Jesus went, people were amazed by him. We have already noticed questions asked about him (e.g. Mark 6:3) and conclusions reached by crowds and religious leaders alike (e.g. Mark 3:21–2).

In this Topic we shall consider questions asked and conclusions reached about Jesus. 'Peter's Declaration about Jesus' has been called the watershed of the Gospels, for what precedes it is rather different from what follows it.

After the Declaration or Confession of Peter, conclusions reached by the disciples are examined, explained and illustrated in the remainder of the Gospels. If you are studying Mark, you have reached almost precisely the halfway point, which is certainly a turning point in the Gospel. Up to here it has been concerned largely with the teaching of parables for the crowds and accounts of conflicts and miracles. After Peter's declaration there is mainly teaching for the disciples and an account of the last week of Jesus' life, when much teaching was also given, but very few miracles are included.

A watershed – from a ridge, rivers flow in opposite directions.
What is the watershed of the Gospels?

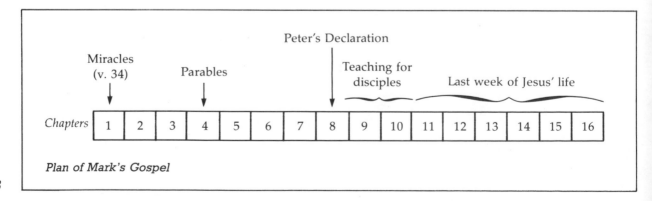

Plan of Mark's Gospel

ACTIVITIES

1 If you are studying Mark's Gospel, copy the diagram on p. 118 and add to it the number of miracles recorded in each chapter. Notice also where the main blocks of teaching are. This will help you to revise the first half of the Gospel.

   If you are studying Luke or Matthew, construct a similar diagram and add the appropriate details.

2 Revise the section 'The Expected Messiah' in Topic 4. Check that your lists of information on the titles used of Jesus are up to date. Add information from this Topic as you find it.

3 Make a list of the opinions expressed in the passages you have studied so far under the heading 'Who is Jesus?'.

To Help You Understand

a) The Messengers from John the Baptist

Read Luke 7:18–35, Matthew 11:2–6

LUKE MATTHEW This account has already been referred to on p. 80. Earlier, in Luke 3:18–20, the information is given that John the Baptist had been imprisoned by Herod Antipas. Josephus tells us that John was imprisoned in the fortress at Machaerus, to the east of the Dead Sea, which had been rebuilt in the time of Herod the Great. Apparently John's disciples were still free to visit him and they acted as messengers to express John's doubts to Jesus about his Messiahship. The reply is that they should tell John of the evidence they have seen in the miracles they have witnessed.

Luke 4:18–19 records that in the synagogue at Nazareth Jesus referred to Isaiah 61:1. Here there is a combination of that passage with Isaiah 35:5–6. It is interesting that, unlike the occasion in Nazareth, no reference is made here to the end of Isaiah 61:1, where there is a promise of freedom for those in prison. Jesus could hold out no such hope for John.

After the messengers had left, Jesus commented about John. He was not a weak man, like the reeds swaying in the wind; neither was he a richly dressed courtier. He was the prophet who prepared the way for the Messiah and, as such, the greatest man who had lived up to that point. However, the humblest Christian believer would have greater privileges than John, for he would see the fulfilment of the coming of the Christ.

Some Jews rejected both John, who lived a life of self-denial, and 'the Son of Man', who feasted and mixed with all groups in society. Jesus likened them to children who cannot agree about their games – whether they want to play at weddings or funerals!

MATTHEW Matthew's account is a briefer version of Luke's.

ACTIVITIES

1 Discuss John the Baptist's doubts about Jesus. How would you account for them?

2 Discuss the meaning of 'God's wisdom, however, is shown to be true by all who accept it.'

Reeds swaying in the wind

SECTION F: REACTIONS TO THE GOOD NEWS

b) Herod's Confusion

Read Mark 6:14–29, Luke 9:7–9

MARK **LUKE** Jesus had sent out his 12 disciples on a mission in Galilee and Herod Antipas had therefore heard about Jesus. Some people were saying that John the Baptist had come back to life – and Herod, too, believed this when he heard what was happening.

Mark then records the details of the death of John. He had been imprisoned because of criticism of Antipas for marrying his brother's wife, a forbidden relationship according to Leviticus 18:16. (Look back at the chart on p. 10, 'Sons of Herod the Great', for details of the family concerned.) Herodias gained her opportunity for revenge on John when her daughter, whom Josephus names as Salome, was made a generous offer by Antipas.

Josephus suggests that Herod Antipas had a political motive for killing John:

> *Now some of the Jews thought that the destruction of Herod's army came from God, and that very justly, as a punishment of what he did against John, that was called the Baptist; for Herod slew him who was a good man . . . Herod, who feared that the great influence John had over the people might put it into his power and inclination to raise a rebellion, (for they seemed ready to do anything he should advise) thought it best by putting him to death, to prevent any mischief he might cause. . . . Accordingly, he was sent a prisoner, out of Herod's suspicious temper, to Macherus, the castle . . . and was there put to death.*
>
> *Josephus*, Antiquities of the Jews 18:5.2

Herod's former father-in-law, Aretas, an Arabian king, had defeated Herod in battle after he divorced his first wife, Aretas' daughter. It was this defeat which some saw as a punishment on Herod for his actions against John.

LUKE Luke's account is briefer than Mark's. The fact of John's imprisonment and the reason for it have already been stated in Luke 3:18–20.

ACTIVITIES

Antipas makes rash offer of half kingdom: Salome asks for Baptist's head

JOHN BEHEADED AT PALACE PARTY

By Jashub ben Aram

JOHN the Baptist is dead. He was beheaded by order of Herod Antipas at the climax of an all-night party given at the castle of Machaerus to honour the 30th anniversary of the Tetrarch's accession.

1 Imagine you are a journalist writing the above front-page article. Complete it!

2 Discuss why you think Herod was confused.

3 Add opinions expressed in this section to your list headed 'Who is Jesus?'.

c) Peter's Declaration about Jesus

Read Mark 8:27–30, Luke 9:18–21, Matthew 16:13–20

MARK **LUKE** **MATTHEW** Mark locates this event 25 miles (40 km) north of the Sea of Galilee, near Caesarea Philippi, the capital of Herod Philip's territory (see the map on p. 86). Near the main source of the River Jordan was a settlement formerly known as Paneas in honour of the god Pan. It was rebuilt and renamed by Philip in honour of both Augustus Caesar and Herod Philip.

> *Philip . . . built the city Caesarea, at the fountains of Jordan, and in the region of Paneas.*
>
> *Josephus*, Wars of the Jews 2:9.1

Near Caesarea Philippi

It was here that Jesus faced his disciples with two critical questions. They were in a unique position to answer the first – 'Who do people say I am?' – since it is very likely that they would mingle with the crowds and hear comments as Jesus was teaching and healing. The replies given were:

- **John the Baptist** We noticed the reasons for this in the previous section.

- **Elijah** We have discovered that the Jews were waiting for Elijah to return as the forerunner of the Messiah (Malachi 4:5).

- **Jeremiah** Matthew adds this name to the list. Some scholars see similarities between the Old Testament prophet Jeremiah's suffering and rejection and that of Jesus, which may be the connection.

- **One of the prophets** Many people saw Jesus as another of the ancient prophets.

Then came the question to which the earlier part of the Gospels has been leading: 'Who do you say I am?' Peter, as the spokesman, gave the answer, 'You are the Messiah [or Christ].' This is the first use of the term by Mark since his introduction in Mark 1:1, and is a momentous confession on the part of the disciples.

LUKE Luke's is a shortened version of Mark's account.

MATTHEW Matthew adds to 'the Messiah' 'the Son of the living God', and goes on to give the commendation made to Peter. This includes two difficult verses (18 and 19) which are interpreted differently by different Churches. We have, incidentally, the first reference in the Gospels to the Church in verse 18 (the only other is in Matthew 18:17). Perhaps it is not surprising that Matthew should be the writer who includes this term, since he seems to have been very interested in Church organisation.

There is a pun on the name Peter (Greek *Petros*) and the rock foundation (Greek *petra*). The Roman Catholic Church therefore believes that the Church was founded on Peter, who became the first Bishop of Rome. Most Protestant Churches believe that 'this rock foundation' is referring to Peter's confession of faith, that the Church is built on Jesus the Messiah, the Son of the living God. There is a statement in verse 19 concerning the keys of the Kingdom of heaven, which have become the symbol of Peter.

The symbol of St Peter. Find out why this symbol is used.

However, the consequence of having such 'keys', both prohibiting and permitting (which may mean having authority to practise Church discipline or to proclaim guilt or innocence), is said in Matthew 18:18 to apply to all the apostles.

All three Gospels end with the statement that the disciples were not to tell anyone of their new knowledge of Jesus – another example of the Messianic secret. This again may be due to a misunderstanding of Jesus' Messianic role.

Since the time of the Gospels, people have been seeking the answer to the same question, 'Who is Jesus?', and have reached vastly different conclusions. Here is a very small selection of the opinions that have been expressed. The first four were written by children in a junior school:

Jesus is the man who as got holes in his hands. He was pinned on a cross.

Anthony, aged 7½

Jesus is a man who is a Lord.

Kalvinder, aged 7½

I think Jesus is a magic man and he can do enithing.

Daniel, aged 8½

I think Jesus is God's Son. He is a loverly person like his farther.

Louise, aged 8½

He's a man – he's just a man
He's not a king – he's just the same
As anyone I know.

Mary's song from the soundtrack of Jesus Christ Superstar

Jesus Christ was more than a man.

Napoleon

The greatest man who ever lived.

I respect Jesus' teaching but can't believe that he was the Son of God.

A man who was merely a man and said the sort of things Jesus said would not be a great moral teacher. . . . Either this man was, and is, the Son of God: or else a madman or something worse.

From C S Lewis, Mere Christianity

ACTIVITIES

1 Answer the following questions, referring to the passage you have just studied:
   a) How did Caesarea Philippi get its name?
   b) What was the first question Jesus asked his disciples?
   c) What replies did they give?
   d) What was the second question Jesus asked his disciples?
   e) Who answered it?
   f) What was the reply?
   g) What do you think was the reason for the prohibition that followed?

2 Discuss the very varied opinions about who Jesus is.

3 Carry out a survey on what people think about Jesus. This could be a class project. Make sure to include people of all ages and of differing beliefs. Present the results in an interesting manner.

4 Write a paragraph about your own answer to the question, 'Who is Jesus?'. If you are not sure what you think, explain why.

d) Jesus Speaks about His Suffering and Death

Read Mark 8:31 – 9:1, Luke 9:22–7, Matthew 16:21–8

MARK **LUKE** **MATTHEW** The disciples had expressed their belief that Jesus was the Messiah, and here we are given Jesus' teaching about what his Messiahship will involve. Jesus uses the term 'Son of Man' rather than Messiah, and identifies himself with the suffering servant of Isaiah (see p. 24). This gave a completely new meaning to contemporary ideas about the Messiah. Peter rebuked Jesus for suggesting that he would suffer and die, and in this Jesus saw a temptation. Peter, in turn, was given a strong reprimand, and the suggestion was made that he was seeing things from the wrong point of view.

*Crucifixion was common in first-century Palestine.
Find out which people could not be crucified.*

Crucifixion was a fairly common sight during the Roman occupation of Palestine. It was used particularly for those who revolted against Roman rule. We are told of the actions of a particular Roman commander after one such revolt:

> *Varus sent a part of his army into the country . . . those that appeared to be the least concerned in these tumults he put into custody but such as were the most guilty he crucified; these were in number about two thousand.*
>
> *Josephus*, Wars of the Jews 2:5.2

The cross-beam of a cross was often carried to a crucifixion. Jesus spoke of his followers needing to carry the cross, either physically or metaphorically, as Luke suggests. This is the first hint that Jesus' death might be by crucifixion. Messiahship will involve suffering and death, and those who follow must be prepared to do so literally.

Some consider that the last verse of this passage refers to the Transfiguration, the Resurrection or Pentecost, or the fact that the early Christians expected the Second Coming to take place in their own lifetime.

ACTIVITY

Begin a chart of the predictions made by Jesus about his suffering and death. First use the above passage from Mark, Luke or Matthew. Note the reference and then make a brief note of each point of the prediction. Do the same for later passages.

ACTIVITIES

1 Discuss the meaning of:

   a) *'Whoever wants to save his own life will lose it; but whoever loses his life for my sake will save it.'*

   b) *'Does a person gain anything if he wins the whole world but loses his life?'*

2 One of the suggested readings at a confirmation service in the Church of England is Matthew 16:24–7. Write a paragraph to show how this is relevant.

e) The Transfiguration

Read Mark 9:2–13, Luke 9:28–36, Matthew 17:1–13

MARK
LUKE
MATTHEW   About a week later, Jesus and three of his disciples had another mountain-top experience. Tradition suggests that this event took place on Mount Tabor in Galilee, but that is very unlikely since archaeologists have found evidence of a settlement on the flat-topped mountain in the first century. Mount Hermon is a more likely setting, a much higher, former volcanic mountain 14 miles (22 km) north of Caesarea Philippi.

Mount Hermon – a possible site of the Transfiguration   123

We do not know exactly what happened on the snow-capped summit, but a vivid experience, perhaps a vision, confirmed the faith that Peter had so recently expressed. Jesus was transfigured – his appearance changed – and Elijah and Moses appeared. Both of these men had had similar dramatic experiences on mountains. After he had received the ten commandments, we are told:

> *Moses went up Mount Sinai, and a cloud covered it. The dazzling light of the Lord's presence came down on the mountain.*
>
> *Exodus 24:15–16*

After a dramatic demonstration of the power of his God on Mount Carmel, Elijah, a prophet of the eighth century BC, fled to Mount Sinai, where he also experienced the presence of God (I Kings 19:8–12).

Elijah on Mount Carmel – the ceiling of a side chapel in the Church of the Transfiguration on Mount Tabor. See Topic 4 for the corresponding illustration of Moses.

124

The Samaritans believed that Moses would return, and the Jews were expecting Elijah to herald the coming of the Messiah. Moses represents the Law, Elijah the Prophets.

It has been suggested that the Transfiguration may have taken place near the time of the Feast of Tabernacles, for Peter, not knowing what to say, suggested putting up three shelters such as might be built at that time of year. A cloud then appeared (remember the Baptism?). This is linked with the *shekinah*, the glory of God, as referred to in Exodus 24:15–16 (quoted above) and in a large number of other passages in the Old Testament. The voice from the cloud confirms that Jesus is the Son of God, and encourages the disciples to listen to him, rather than to Moses and Elijah.

An encouragement to secrecy follows, on this occasion with a time limit. A discussion took place about Elijah being the Messianic fore-runner. Jesus assured them that Elijah had come already. (Notice another association of the term 'Son of Man' with suffering.)

LUKE Luke tells us that Moses and Elijah talked with Jesus about his death in Jerusalem.

MATTHEW Matthew adds the note that the disciples realised that Jesus was in fact referring to John the Baptist when he spoke of Elijah's coming.

The following extract from the preface to the Mass for the second Sunday of Lent is used in the Roman Catholic Church:

> *Father, all-powerful and ever-living God,*
> *we do well always and everywhere to*
>   *give you thanks*
> *through Jesus Christ our Lord.*
> *On your holy mountain he revealed*
>   *himself in glory*
> *in the presence of his disciples.*
> *He had already prepared them for his*
>   *approaching death.*
> *He wanted to teach them through the*
>   *Law and the Prophets*
> *that the promised Christ had first to suffer*
> *and so come to the glory of his resurrection.*

ACTIVITIES

1 Answer the following questions, with reference to Mark 9:7-9, Luke 9:34-6 or Matthew 17:5-8:

   a) Which three disciples accompanied Jesus on this occasion?

   b) On which earlier occasion had there been a voice from a cloud?

   c) What would be the significance of the cloud for the disciples?

   d) Who had been talking with Jesus?

   e) Why are the words 'listen to him' important?

   f) Why do you think the disciples were to keep this experience a secret for some time?

2 Discuss the ways in which you think this experience might confirm the declaration of faith made earlier by the disciples.

3 Check on which earlier occasion the three disciples mentioned here were singled out to be with Jesus.

The Titles of Jesus

We have found a number of answers to the question 'Who is Jesus?' in this Topic. In addition, many hints are given in the titles used of Jesus in other parts of the Gospels as well as in these passages. This subject was introduced in Topic 4 (see p. 24).

One title which is often used is 'Son of Man'. This title was used by the prophet Ezekiel of himself and indicated that he was an ordinary human being. (In the *Good News Bible* the title used is 'mortal man'.) The title is also used in Daniel 7:13, where it indicates a figure with divine authority, some think the Messiah. 'Son of Man' is used widely in the Synoptic Gospels, always by Jesus and in three different ways:

• when speaking of his ministry on earth, often in terms of his authority, for example Mark 2:10 and 2:28,

• when speaking of his suffering and death, for example Mark 8:31, 9:9 and 9:12,

• when speaking of his future glory and return to the world, for example Mark 8:38.

Jesus' use of this term could merely indicate that he was a human being, but his reply to the High Priest in Mark 14:62 would suggest that it is to be seen as a Messianic title.

Christ before Caiaphas, *van Honthorst. What question did the High Priest ask Jesus?*

ACTIVITIES

1 Check that your lists concerning the titles of Jesus (see Topic 4) are up to date by adding vital information from this Topic.

2 Refer to the list of references to the title 'Son of Man' that you have already made. Add a key to indicate whether the reference is to the authority of Jesus (A), his suffering (S) or his future glory (G).

3 Discuss what you think is the meaning of the concept of the Son of Man in the Gospels.

4 Make a list of other titles that could be added to the following ones: The Messiah, Son of God, Son of Man.

5 Answer all sections of this essay:

   a) Give four titles used of Jesus in the Gospel you are studying.

   b) Explain the meaning of any two of the titles.

   c) How and why do you think these titles came to be used by the early Church?

To Keep You Thinking

Who is Jesus?
Discuss views held by people today about who Jesus is.

Discipleship

TOPIC 17

'Whoever does not carry his own cross and come after me cannot be my disciple.'

Setting the Scene

In Topic 10 you studied the call of the disciples, when they first 'left everything and followed Jesus'. After Peter's declaration at Caesarea Philippi and Jesus' transfiguration, much more narrative is included in the Gospels concerning commitment to discipleship. In this Topic we shall consider some of the accounts of the work given to the disciples, and the demands made on those who wished to become followers of Jesus.

To Help You Understand

a) Jesus Sends out the Twelve Disciples

Read Mark 6:7–13, Luke 9:1–6, Matthew 10:5–15

MARK
LUKE
MATTHEW

This account, recorded in all three Synoptic Gospels, concerns a mission of the 12

disciples which took place in Galilee, before the time of Peter's confession.

In the days before newspapers, radio and other means of mass communications, one of the few ways of letting people know what was happening was by word of mouth. Although crowds of people flocked to hear Jesus' message, his impact was limited by the number of places he could visit. So the disciples were sent out in pairs to help spread the Good News of repentance, as preached by Jesus, to exorcise evil spirits and to heal.

Instructions were given for the journey. The disciples had to travel light, with no extra baggage, and rely on the hospitality of those to whom they were to take the message. Apparently, the Essenes travelled in a similar style, relying on help from other Essenes:

. . . they carry nothing with them when they travel into remote parts. . . .
Accordingly there is, in every city where they live, one appointed particularly to take care of strangers, and provide garments and other necessities for them.

Josephus, Wars of the Jews 2:8.4

People in that part of the world were, and are, exceptionally hospitable, so what we might consider to be sponging on others was quite acceptable and, in fact, tested the faith of the disciples in God's ability to provide for them (Matthew 6:31–2).

It was a practice of Jews to shake the dust from their feet when leaving a Gentile area. To carry out such a symbolic action against Jews was intended to help them realise the seriousness of rejecting Jesus' messengers.

MATTHEW Matthew suggests that at this point in Jesus' ministry the message was to be taken only to Jews. Look up Matthew 28:19 and notice that a different instruction is given there.

Matthew's account is more detailed than those of Mark and Luke. This is possibly in order to give the early Church guidance about hospitality to travelling preachers. *Shalom* (peace) is a Jewish greeting and the apostles have to carry this peace with them (see Matthew 5:9). The horrific events which overtook Sodom and Gomorrah, recorded in Genesis 19:23–8, are used to illustrate the seriousness of rejecting the message.

According to several biographers of St Francis of Assisi, it was the reading of this passage from Matthew's Gospel in 1209, when Francis was 27 years old, that convinced him that he must become a wandering preacher like the apostles.

ACTIVITIES

1 Discuss the connection between St Francis, the mission of the 12 and the Beatitudes.

2 Answer the following questions, with reference to the passage you have read:

a) In which area did this mission take place?

b) What message did the disciples take?

c) What did the disciples have to do to help those to whom they went?

d) What other instructions were they given?

e) Why do you think they were given these instructions?

f) What do you think was the point of shaking the dust from their feet?

3 If you are studying Matthew's Gospel, be sure to add information from this passage to your list about Matthew's Jewish emphasis. Check that you have included information from the Sermon on the Mount.

Ploughing a straight furrow (see Luke 9:62)

b) The Would-be Followers of Jesus

Read Luke 9:57–62

LUKE The remaining accounts in this Topic are in the setting of Jesus' final journey to Jerusalem before his death. In this passage we are given three examples of would-be followers:

- The first showed great commitment, but Jesus encouraged him to count the cost; he would be homeless if he followed Jesus.

- The second was invited to follow Jesus, but it seems likely that he wanted to wait until his father had died. He would have been busy with funeral arrangements if his father had already died, since burials normally took place within 24 hours. Jesus realised that if the man delayed, it could be too late. 'Let the dead . . .' was probably a proverb. The emphasis is that discipleship should have priority over even the closest family ties.

- The third is a volunteer who made what seems to be a reasonable request to say good-bye to his family. A similar request was granted when Elijah called Elisha to be a prophet (1 Kings 19:19–20). Perhaps Jesus suspected that the man might be dissuaded by his family, and warns him that, like a ploughman, if he looks back he will not reach his goal successfully. (Look back at the photograph on p. 128).

c) Jesus Sends Out the Seventy-two

Read Luke 10:1–24

LUKE Some scholars think there are so many similarities between this and the mission of the 12 that they must be two accounts of the same event. However, there are a number of differences. The mission of the 12 may symbolise the mission to the 12 tribes of Israel, and that of the 72 the mission to the Gentile world.

The 72 were sent ahead of Jesus, possibly into Judaea, to prepare for his arrival amongst hostile people (wolves). There is a sense of urgency; they were not to stop to exchange lengthy greetings on the way. Comments are inserted about Chorazin, Bethsaida and Capernaum, whose people have had every opportunity for repentance but have failed to respond (see p. 84).

The 72 returned, full of their success. Jesus commented on his authority over powers of evil and told his disciples to rejoice that their names are written in heaven. This would have meant a great deal to the disciples, with their knowledge of the Old Testament:

The Lord answered, 'It is those who have sinned against me whose names I will remove from my book.'

Exodus 32:33

At that time the great angel Michael will appear . . . When that time comes all the people of your nation whose names are written in God's book will be saved.

Daniel 12:1

Jesus rejoiced and thanked God that his comparatively uneducated followers had understood the significance of his coming, and he reminded them of their privileges.

ACTIVITIES

1 If you are studying Luke's Gospel, make two parallel lists to show the similarities and differences between the instructions to the 12 and to the 72 when sent out on their mission.

2 Include information from this Topic on your list headed 'Discipleship'. Begin some coursework on discipleship. Use the material you have already collected, as well as material in this Topic and the next. Think of and discuss interesting ways to present the information.

3 Discuss the demands and warnings made by Jesus in Luke 9:57–62.

d) Jesus Visits Martha and Mary

Read Luke 10:38–42

LUKE The fourth Gospel tells us that Mary and Martha lived in Bethany (John 11:1). Martha was very concerned that Mary had left her to do all the work for the visitors. When Jesus suggested that only one thing was needed, it may be a reference to one dish: perhaps Martha's preparations were too elaborate. He commends Mary for her desire to listen to him.

e) The Cost of Being a Disciple

Read Luke 14:25–33

LUKE It is made quite clear in this passage that total commitment was essential for the disciple of Jesus. Notice that the teaching was given to the crowd. Again, the priority of love for Jesus over human relationships is stressed.

Two parables are given to illustrate that it is important to 'count the cost' before embarking on Christian discipleship. The first concerns the building of a tower, something outside the experience of most of us today, but in those days it was a common practice to construct a watchtower in a corner of a vineyard.

The second parable concerns a king going to war. He will not go into battle unless he has enough forces to face the enemy.

So Jesus encouraged people to consider very carefully before becoming disciples. There was no room for hangers-on; a willingness to make great sacrifices was essential.

Perhaps the Christian Church today does not expect the same standard of commitment from

A vineyard watchtower

its members. One Christian denomination has an annual Covenant service (a renewal of promises made to God), and a prayer, which is the climax of the service, includes these words:

> *I am no longer my own, but yours.*
> *Put me to what you will, rank me with*
>   *whom you will;*
> *put me to doing, put me to suffering;*
> *let me be employed for you or laid aside*
>   *for you, exalted for you or brought*
>   *low for you;*
> *let me be full, let me be empty;*
> *let me have all things, let me have*
>   *nothing;*
> *I freely and whole heartedly yield all*
>   *things to your pleasure and disposal.*
>
> From the Methodist Service Book

ACTIVITIES

1 Discuss '. . . none of you can be my disciple unless he gives up everything he has.' What do you think this implies? What is the connection with the prayer quoted above?

2 Answer the following questions, with reference to Luke 14:25–7:

 a) Where was Jesus going to at this time?

 b) On which previous occasion did Jesus state that a disciple must 'carry his own cross'?

 c) Which two parables are included to illustrate the cost of discipleship?

 d) Do you think it is possible for a Christian today to follow the teaching of verse 26?

3 Interview any willing, committed Christians about what they understand by Christian discipleship.

f) The Rich Man

Read Mark 10:17–31, Luke 18:18–30

MARK This is an illustration of what is stated
LUKE in the passage you have just studied.
Luke adds the detail that this man was a Jewish
leader, perhaps a member of a local council, or
even of the Sanhedrin. The details recorded by
Mark are vivid: the man 'ran up', 'knelt before
him', Jesus 'looked straight at him with love',
and we are told of the man that 'gloom spread
over his face'. This might suggest that this is an
account given to the author by an eye-witness.

The man wanted to know how he could gain
eternal life. The answer makes it clear that
eternal life is received by those who put God
first in their lives.

Jesus' first question to the man, 'Why do you
call me good?', is probably intended to make the
man think about Jesus' relationship to God,
rather than a denial that Jesus is good. The
group of commandments referred to by Jesus
concern duty towards others, and the man was
probably sincere in saying that he had obeyed
them from childhood. Jesus saw that it was his
money that was keeping him from God and
suggested a remedy.

Jesus' comment that it would be difficult for
rich people to enter the Kingdom of God would
amaze and shock those who heard it, for it was
generally believed by Jews that wealth was a
sign of God's favour. Jesus completely reversed
that idea by suggesting that money can become
a god itself (see also Luke 16:13). There is a

Jewish saying about an elephant going through the eye of a needle. The camel was the largest animal in Palestine, so this exaggeration would have been meaningful. There is a theory that 'the eye of a needle' was a name given to a small wicket gate set into one of the main gates of Jerusalem. A traveller arriving after dark would have to unload his camel before he could get it through. This vividly illustrates the point Jesus was making, although we cannot be certain of its validity.

What did Jesus say in his teaching about a camel?

Jesus went on to suggest that salvation is a gift of God; no person can attain it for themselves. Peter was tempted to boast about the sacrifices made by the disciples. He was assured that many blessings would come their way – but that suffering would come as well. A final warning is given against pride.

Notice that the man asks about eternal life (Mark 10:17, Luke 18:18), Jesus speaks of entering the Kingdom of God (Mark 10:23, Luke 18:24) and the disciples ask who can be saved (verse 26). Think about the connection between these three terms.

A modern collect (prayer) says:

> *Lord, save us from the sorrow of keeping our possessions and losing You; keep before us a vision of Your love, the love which makes all things possible, even our free response to Your death on the Cross. Amen.*
>
> 'Collect for fourth Sunday after Trinity' in Susan Williams, Lord of our world

Jericho, the city of palm trees

g) Jesus and Zacchaeus

Read Luke 19:1–10

LUKE This event happened as Jesus was passing through Jericho, one of the oldest cities on earth, an oasis called 'the city of palm trees'.

> *Jericho, where the palm tree grows, and that balsam which is an ointment of all the most precious . . .*
>
> *Josephus*, Antiquities of the Jews *14:4.1*

Look up the section on tax collectors in Topic 2. There is considerable humour in the situation of this short man climbing a sycomore fig tree to see Jesus and being spotted by him. The reaction from the crowd is the same as on the occasion when Jesus visited Levi's home.

Zacchaeus shows his willingness to change direction by giving away half his belongings. He takes seriously a comment recorded in the scriptures concerning someone who had cheated another of his property:

> *For having done such a cruel thing, he must pay back four times as much as he took.*
>
> *2 Samuel 12:6*

Zacchaeus' attitude contrasts with that of the rich man who was unwilling to give anything away. Jesus said that Zacchaeus had found salvation.

ACTIVITIES

1 Look up the ten commandments (Exodus 20:1–17). Discuss which of these commandments the rich man had broken.

2 Write definitions of eternal life, the Kingdom of God, salvation. Write a paragraph to explain the connection between them.

3 Answer the following questions, with reference to Mark 10:23–7 or Luke 18:24–7:

a) What led to Jesus giving this teaching?

b) Why were the disciples shocked?

c) What is the point of the illustration about the camel?

d) How did Jesus answer the question, 'Who, then, can be saved?'?

e) Do you think it is difficult for a person to be a Christian today?

To Keep You Thinking

Wealth

Discuss whether you think Jesus' teaching about wealth is relevant in today's society.

Teaching about Discipleship

'. . . he was teaching his disciples.'

Setting the Scene

Life is sometimes pictured as a journey, and in many religions pilgrimage (making a journey for a religious purpose) is very important. Many Christians would see a visit to the Holy Land, for instance, as a pilgrimage, whilst Muslims try to go on a pilgrimage to Mecca at least once in a lifetime.

After the visit to the area around Caesarea Philippi, Jesus and his disciples travelled through Galilee and then made their way south, towards Jerusalem, although the route followed is not easy to ascertain. There is a growing feeling in the accounts that this journey is of great significance.

Throughout the journey, it is suggested that Jesus is teaching his disciples to prepare them for the future. In Mark's Gospel, the end of Mark 9 and most of Mark 10 concerns such teaching; whilst Luke devotes nine chapters to this period, including many parables peculiar to Luke which will be studied later. Matthew has three chapters on this journey.

Modern pilgrims in Jerusalem.
Why is Jerusalem a place of pilgrimage today?

ACTIVITIES

1 As you read the passages in this Topic, make a list of the references to the journey made by Jesus and his disciples. Note what is said on each occasion when the journey is mentioned.

2 Look back at the diagram you made of the various chapters of the Gospel you are studying (see p. 119). Indicate on it which chapters concern the teaching given to the disciples on their journey to Jerusalem.

To Help You Understand

a) Jesus Speaks Again about His Death

Read Mark 9:30–2, Luke 9:43–5

MARK Jesus' first specific prediction about
LUKE his death was studied in Topic 16 d). On that occasion, and again in this passage, the disciples did not understand the teaching. A new idea is introduced here – that Jesus will be handed over to those who would put him to death. This may be a reference to the actions of Judas Iscariot. Notice the use of the term 'Son of Man'.

LUKE Luke includes no actual reference to death or resurrection in his account.

ACTIVITIES

1 Add this information to your list of predictions of Jesus' suffering and death, begun in Topic 16.

2 Add information to your list of the uses of the term 'Son of Man', begun in Topic 4.

b) Who Is the Greatest?

Read Mark 9:33–7, Luke 9:46–8

MARK You will remember that some of the
LUKE disciples lived in Capernaum, and it may be that this teaching was given in Peter's home, possibly with one of his children playing an important part. Status was as important in society then as it is now, and this had been the cause of an argument between the disciples. Jesus suggested that greatness can be measured by service offered to others, including children.

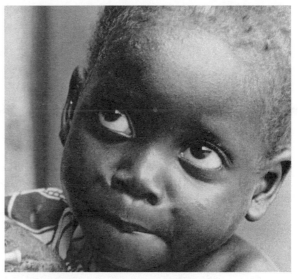

'He took a child . . .'

c) Whoever Is Not Against Us Is For Us

Read Mark 9:38–41, Luke 9:49–56

MARK This passage shows the intolerant
LUKE attitude shown by the disciples towards an exorcist who was not one of the 12. Jesus taught against such intolerance with the often-quoted sentence: 'For whoever is not against us is for us.'

LUKE Luke illustrates the attitude of revenge shown by James and John. A direct journey from Galilee to Jerusalem, via Samaria, would have taken some three days and it was often difficult to find hospitality in Samaria. James and John, living up to their nickname (see Topic 10) and possibly thinking of an event recorded in 2 Kings 1:9–16, wanted the Samaritans punished. They were rebuked for their attitude.

135

A large millstone

ACTIVITIES

1 Discuss the attitudes illustrated in the previous two accounts. Do you find anything surprising in Jesus' teaching?

2 If you are studying Luke's Gospel, add information to your list of references to Gentiles in the Gospel.

d) Temptations to Sin

Read Mark 9:42–50, Luke 17:1–4

MARK This is a warning about destroying **LUKE** the faith either of children or of young believers. The seriousness of this is emphasised by the reference to the 'large millstone', one which could be turned only by an animal. At this point Mark uses the same type of exaggeration as is found in Matthew's Sermon on the Mount (e.g. Matthew 5:29–30).

It is important at this stage to consider teaching given about 'hell'. The Greek word used here is *Gehenna*, meaning 'the valley of the sons of Hinnom'. In this valley in the seventh century BC, the kings Ahaz and Manasseh had encouraged the offering of human sacrifice. When the young king, Josiah, came to the throne, he determined to stop this practice, and desecrated the valley so that no worship of any kind would be conducted there:

The Valley of Hinnom today. Why do you think buildings were not erected here until the twentieth century?

> *King Josiah also desecrated Topheth, the pagan place of worship in the Valley of Hinnom, so that no one could sacrifice his son or daughter as a burnt offering to the god Molech.*
>
> 2 Kings 23:10

The valley, which was to the south-west of Jerusalem (see the plan on p. 166), later became the local rubbish tip, with continuous fires and creepy-crawlies! So it became a very vivid illustration for the worst possible existence that could be imagined.

This teaching is followed by three sayings about salt. Look up the comments made about salt on p. 110.

LUKE Luke omits the comments about hell but includes teaching about forgiveness for those who repent.

e) Jesus Speaks a Third Time about His Death
Read Mark 10:32–4, Luke 18:31–4

MARK **LUKE** There is a stress here on the foreboding of the disciples and the fear of the people who followed, possibly fellow-pilgrims going up to Jerusalem. There are more predictions about Jesus' suffering.

LUKE Luke stresses the failure of the disciples to understand this teaching.

f) The Request of James and John
Read Mark 10:35–45, Matthew 20:20–8

MARK **MATTHEW** As the second prediction about Jesus' death is followed by an argument about rank and status (see sections a) and b) in this Topic), so the third prediction is followed by a similar discussion about position, after a question asked by James and John.

The two were rebuked for their failure to understand the implications of what they asked. To drink a cup of suffering implied sharing in a bitter experience. We know from Acts 12:2 that James was put to death for his faith.

The other disciples were understandably angry with James and John. Jesus stressed his teaching about humility and service.

Dr Vincent Taylor suggested that the last verse of this passage is one of the most important sayings of the Gospels. A ransom was the price paid for the redemption and release of a slave. The language used is similar to that used of the suffering servant in Isaiah:

> *But because of our sins he was wounded, beaten because of the evil we did.*
> *We are healed by the punishment he suffered, made whole by the blows he received.*
>
> Isaiah 53:5

MATTHEW Matthew follows Mark's version closely, except that the request about position is made by the mother of James and John.

ACTIVITIES

1 Discuss Mark 10:45 or Matthew 20:28. Why do you think it has been suggested that this is one of the most important sayings in the Gospels?

2 Add more information to your chart about the predictions of Jesus' suffering and death.

3 Answer the following questions, with reference to Mark 9:47–8:
   a) What Greek word is used for 'hell' in this passage?
   b) Explain the origin and meaning of the word.
   c) Why are worms and fire mentioned?
   d) What do you understand to be the Christian belief about hell?

137

g) True Happiness

Read Luke 11:27-8

LUKE In these verses, a woman showed a very human reaction in pronouncing a blessing on Jesus' mother. The comment of Jesus implies that those who obeyed the word of God would be equally blessed.

h) The Demand for a Miracle

Read Luke 11:29-32

LUKE Two examples from the Old Testament are given here. The first is of Jonah who eventually went to preach to the Assyrians in Nineveh:

> *The people of Nineveh believed God's message. So they decided that everyone should fast, and all the people, from the greatest to the least, put on sackcloth to show that they had repented.*
>
> *Jonah 3:5*

Jesus claimed to be greater than Jonah, and contrasted the attitudes of the people of his day with the repentance of the Ninevites.

The story of the Queen of Sheba's visit to King Solomon is recorded in 1 Kings 10:1-10. Like the Ninevites, the Queen of Sheba was a Gentile, and was commended for her desire to hear the teaching of Solomon.

i) Jesus Accuses the Pharisees and the Teachers of the Law

Read Luke 11:37-54

LUKE This passage comes before a warning against hypocrisy which appears in Luke 12. We have already noticed a criticism made of Jesus' disciples for failing to practise Jewish ritual washings (see Topic 14). The Pharisees were criticised for:

- being concerned more with outward appearances than with inner purity,

- carefully tithing (a tithe = $\frac{1}{10}$) all produce, even herbs, but neglecting justice and love for God – this may be a reference to Micah 6:8,

- desiring prestige and respect but having a corrupting effect on other people.

There are other criticisms made of the teachers of the Law. One concerns the building of fine tombs for prophets who were murdered by previous generations of Jews. Since the teachers of the Law still persecute prophets, they are seen as guilty of the murders.

A first-century tomb, traditionally that of Zechariah, in the Kidron Valley, outside Jerusalem. This gives us an idea of the monuments erected at that time.

The murders of Abel and Zechariah are the first and last murders recorded in the Jewish scriptures.

j) A Warning against Hypocrisy

Read Luke 12:1-3, Matthew 10:26-7

LUKE
MATTHEW The previous passage leads up to this warning. Hypocrisy has always been a particular danger for believers of any faith.

'. . . not one sparrow is forgotten by God'

ACTIVITIES

1 Look up the following Old Testament references:

a) Jonah 3:1–5   b) 1 Kings 10:1–10

c) Micah 6:8   d) Genesis 4:8

e) 2 Chronicles 24:20–2

List the references and make a comment beside each as to how the passage is used in Luke's Gospel.

2 Make lists of the criticisms made against a) the Pharisees and b) the teachers of the Law in Luke 11:37–54. Explain each criticism briefly.

3 Discuss the danger of hypocrisy for people with a religious faith.

l) Confessing and Rejecting Christ

Read Luke 12:8–12, Matthew 10:32–3

LUKE MATTHEW Christian followers were told of the need to acknowledge their faith publicly and were warned of the consequences of not doing so. Luke adds the saying about the sin against the Holy Spirit, included earlier in Mark (see Topic 14 e). There follows teaching about persecution. The disciples are warned that they may be brought to trial for their faith, but they are encouraged not to be afraid.

k) Whom to Fear

Read Luke 12:4–7, Matthew 10:28–31

LUKE MATTHEW Jesus' followers were told not to fear those who might persecute them, but rather to respect the authority of God.

Sparrows and other small birds were sold very cheaply for food, yet all were known to God. His concern for the individual was stressed, so there was no need for fear.

m) Jesus the Cause of Division

Read Luke 12:49–53, Matthew 10:34–6

LUKE MATTHEW You will remember that fire is used in the Gospels as a symbol of judgement. The 'baptism' which Jesus said was to come is probably a reference to his suffering. Although Jesus came to bring peace (see Luke 2:14), not all would accept this peace, and the consequence would therefore be division, often within families.

ACTIVITIES

1 If you are studying Luke's Gospel, look up Luke 2:14 and 12:51. Discuss the following questions:

a) In what sense did Jesus bring 'peace on earth'?

b) In what sense did Jesus bring division?

2 If you are studying Luke's Gospel, add information from these passages to your list headed 'The Holy Spirit'.

3 Answer the following questions, with reference to Luke 12:4–7 or Matthew 10:28–31:

a) What should the disciples not fear?

b) What Greek word is used for 'hell'?

c) What is considered here to be worse than death?

d) What point does the reference to sparrows illustrate?

e) What do you think is the difference between fear of God and fear of other people?

n) Understanding the Time

Read Luke 12:54–6

Rain clouds. In a dry country, these are seen as a blessing, not a disaster.

LUKE Clouds from the Mediterranean to the west, bring rain. A sirocco wind from the desert brings scorching heat. There was fairly accurate weather-forecasting, even in the first century, but people failed to recognise the signs of the Messiah's coming.

o) Turn from Your Sins or Die

Read Luke 13:1–5

LUKE It was a common belief that suffering was the result of an individual's sin. The book of Job in the Old Testament discusses the problem of suffering. Eliphaz 'comforts' Job with these words:

> *Think back now. Name a single case where a righteous man met with disaster.*
>
> *Job 4:7*
>
> *It is not because you fear God that he reprimands you and brings you to trial.*
> *No, it's because you have sinned so much; it's because of all the evil you do.*
>
> *Job 22:4–5*

Jesus' comments on two incidents which are otherwise unknown are included in this passage in Luke. Given Jewish beliefs, it would follow that the victims deserved the disasters which overtook them. Jesus denied this and used the incidents to encourage all to repent.

An incident similar to the first one mentioned in the passage is recorded by Josephus. This happened some time later in the Temple in Jerusalem:

> *... he [a certain John] had such engines as threw darts and javelins and stones ... these darts that were thrown by the engines came with that force ... insomuch that many persons who came thither with great zeal from the ends of the earth, to offer sacrifices at this celebrated place ... fell down before their own sacrifices themselves and sprinkled that altar ... with their own blood.*
>
> *Josephus*, Wars of the Jews 5:1.3

The tower of Siloam was probably part of an aqueduct constructed by Pilate, using Temple funds:

> *After this he [Pilate] raised another disturbance by expending that sacred treasure which is called Corban upon aqueducts, whereby he brought water from the distance of four hundred furlongs ...*
>
> *Josephus*, Wars of the Jews 2:9.4

p) Faith

Read Luke 17:5–6

LUKE This brief saying suggests that quantity is not a significant measure of faith; it is the quality of faith that matters.

An aqueduct of the time of Jesus. This one was built by Herod the Great to bring a water supply to Caesarea.

ACTIVITIES

1 Discuss the popular belief about suffering at the time of Jesus.

2 Write a definition of faith. Which of the following definitions corresponds most nearly to your own?

'To have faith is to be sure of the things we hope for, to be certain of the things we cannot see.'

Hebrews 11:1

'Faith is believing a promise.'

'Faith is belief in God.'

'Faith is trust in and commitment to God's love.'

'Christian faith is to accept what God has revealed of himself in Jesus.'

'Faith is trust in Jesus.'

To Keep You Thinking

1 **The problem of suffering**
Discuss what the following suggest about the problem of suffering:

a) Jesus' comments about his own death,

b) Jesus' comments about the Galileans killed by Pilate.

2 **Pilgrimage**
In what ways could discipleship be considered a pilgrimage?

Teaching about Prayer, the Family and the Future

'Lord, teach us . . .'

Setting the Scene

This Topic brings together Jesus' teaching on prayer, the family and the future. Most of this teaching is given in the context of the journey to Jerusalem, and for the benefit of the disciples.

As has been discovered, the new faith brought by Jesus concerned God's kingly rule over the individual. To the offer of forgiveness, both John the Baptist and Jesus suggested that the individual should respond with repentance. So there is a relationship between the individual and the Lord. This relationship is to be continued through prayer.

142   *'They were continuing towards Jerusalem'*

A new relationship between a person and God also results in new relationships with other people, and there is teaching for Jesus' followers about family relationships.

Important teaching about the future was given at this point and during the last week of Jesus' ministry.

To Help You Understand

a) Jesus' Teaching on Prayer
Read Luke 11:1–13, Matthew 6:5–15 and 7:7–11

LUKE MATTHEW We have already considered briefly the teaching on prayer given in the Sermon on the Mount. Look back at Topic 15 d), **Prayer,** and e), **Ask, seek, knock,** and revise these sections thoroughly.

It is necessary at this point to consider the details of what has become known as the Lord's Prayer. It was a common practice for rabbis to teach their disciples a prayer for their personal use. Luke suggests that the disciples, seeing Jesus at prayer, asked him to teach them to pray. Since Luke and Matthew both have a version of the prayer, it probably comes from their common source. However, the fact that there are differences in the two versions would suggest that the prayer was not used in the early Church in quite the same repetitive way that it is used in the Church today.

Luke's version is the shorter of the two. The prayer may be divided into two sections. The

A community prayer

first consists of adoration and begins with the word 'Father', suggesting that the relationship in prayer should be as natural as with a father. To the Jews a name signified the whole character of a person, so the prayer is that God may be honoured and worshipped, and that his rule may be accepted.

The second section concerns requests, supplications or intercessions. These are in the plural, for example, 'Give us . . .', which suggests this is meant to be a community prayer.

First there is a prayer for basic physical needs, then for spiritual needs. This prayer for forgiveness will involve confession of sins. Notice the statement that Christians forgive others. Forgiveness from God cannot be expected if it is withheld from other people. There is a final request that there should not be 'hard testing' – possibly a reference to persecution.

LUKE Luke follows the Lord's Prayer with the Parable of the Friend at Midnight (verses 5–8), which illustrates persistence in prayer.

MATTHEW Matthew's version of the Lord's Prayer is the most commonly used. It is preceded by a comment that prayer should not consist of 'meaningless words', and the prayer is given as a pattern to follow. It has a number of additions to the version given by Luke:

- To the words 'Our Father' is added 'in heaven'.

- Verse 10 is extended to include a prayer that God's will may be done.

- The prayer ends with a request for protection from the Evil One.

Some manuscripts add a further section to verse 13, which is often used in Christian worship: '. . . for yours is the kingdom and the power and the glory forever. Amen.' This may well reflect the doxology (offering of praise to God) from an Old Testament prayer of King David:

> *You are great and powerful, glorious, splendid and majestic. Everything in heaven and earth are yours, and you are king, supreme ruler over all. . . . Now, our God, we give you thanks, and we praise your glorious name.*
>
> *1 Chronicles 29:11, 13*

143

ACTIVITIES

1 If you are studying Luke's Gospel, add this information to your list headed 'Joy, Praise, Prayer and Worship'.

2 The version of the Lord's Prayer which you have read may be different from the one you may have learnt in childhood. Collect together as many versions of the Lord's Prayer as you can find in different versions of the Bible, or as modern versions set to music. Discuss the differences.

3 Some biblical scholars from time to time query the origin of sayings which have been attributed to Jesus down the ages. The following brief report illustrates this continuing process. Read it carefully and discuss it, bearing in mind that not all biblical scholars would agree with the conclusions:

> A group of 25 American scholars, meeting recently in Atlanta, questioned how much of the Lord's Prayer can be traced back to Jesus. A paper presented by a Jesuit priest suggested that some of the prayer may have been composed by the early Christians, rather than by Jesus himself, including the phrases 'thy Kingdom come, thy will be done' and 'deliver us from evil'.

Discuss which version of the Lord's Prayer this group of scholars would consider to be closest to the original.

4 Think of the Lord's Prayer as a pattern on which Christians might base their prayers:
   a) List the different types of prayer included in the Lord's Prayer.
   b) Write a modern prayer which a Christian might use, based on the pattern of the Lord's Prayer.

b) The Parable of the Widow and the Judge

Read Luke 18:1–8

LUKE There are two more parables peculiar to Luke on the subject of prayer. The judge referred to in the first of these parables is probably an example of one appointed by Herod or by the Roman authorities. Such judges were well-known for their corrupt practices, unlike the town elders who judged most cases and who were very fair. The cause of the widow's trouble is not given. The judge eventually helped her merely to get rid of her! Notice that God's willingness to answer prayer is emphasised. He is contrasted with the judge, not likened to him.

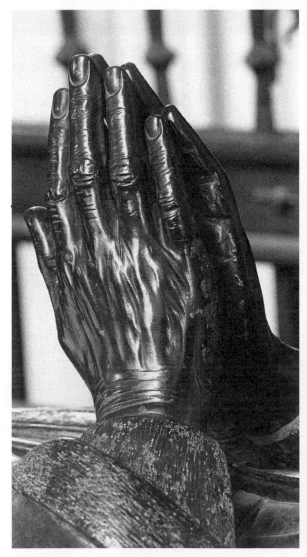

Praying Hands of Lady Margaret Beaufort from a tomb in Westminster Abbey.

c) The Parable of the Pharisee and the Tax Collector

Read Luke 18:9–14

LUKE Here, in the second of these two parables, we have a further example of Luke's interest in outcasts. (Remind yourself of the two other passages about tax collectors that you have read in Luke's Gospel.) People would gather in the Temple courtyards at the special hours of prayer: 9 a.m., noon and 3 p.m. This story illustrates two attitudes to prayer. An early seventeenth-century verse was written about this parable:

> Two Went Up Into The Temple To Pray
>
> *Two went to pray? O rather say,*
> *One went to brag, th'other to pray.*
> *One stands up close, and treads on high,*
> *Where th'other dares not send his eye.*
> *One nearer to God's altar trod,*
> *The other to the altar's God.*
>
> *Richard Crashaw (1613–49)*

ACTIVITIES

1 Add information from this Topic to your list of parables and to your list headed 'All sections of society'.

2 Answer all sections of this essay:
   a) Name two parables about persistence in prayer and narrate one of them briefly.
   b) What attitudes are illustrated in the Parable of the Pharisee and the Tax Collector?
   c) Suggest a definition of prayer.
   d) Why do you think Christians are encouraged to pray?

3 Attempt some coursework on Jesus' teaching about and practice of prayer.

Include what you have discovered in this Topic and in Topic 15. First decide on an interesting way of presenting your material and then carefully list what you will include under headings, before writing up your work.

4 Head a sheet of paper 'The Prayers of Jesus'. Look up each of the following references and list the occasions when we are told that Jesus prayed:

Luke 6:12–13;
Mark 1:35, 6:41 and 8:6;
Luke 10:21–2 and 11:1;
Mark 14:35–6 or Luke 22:42;
Mark 15:34;
Luke 23:34, 23:46 and 24:30.

Start in this way:

THE PRAYERS OF JESUS		
Reference	*Details*	*Occasion*
Luke 6: 12-13	A night of prayer	Before choosing the 12

d) Jesus Teaches about Divorce

Read Mark 10:1–12, Luke 16:18

MARK We now turn to two passages which **LUKE** concern family relationships. We have already discovered that there was a debate going on at the time of Jesus about the grounds for divorce. Look back to Topic 15 c), **Adultery** and **Divorce,** if necessary. You will be aware that divorce is a subject about which much discussion still takes place today.

Lawyers back 'divorces on demand' plan

By Terence Shaw
Legal Correspondent

LAW COMMISSION proposals for changes in the law allowing divorce on demand a set period of time after starting proceedings, would be "widely acceptable" to the public and lawyers, a conference of family law solicitors was told at the weekend.

Professor Brenda Hoggett, the Law Commissioner with responsibility for family law, said that responses to the Law Commission's proposals last May on reform of the grounds for divorce had indicated widespread support for a solution of divorce as a "process over time".

'Make divorce harder' plea

By Our Home Affairs Correspondent

DIVORCE should be made harder, not easier, in order to restore the stability of marriage and arrest moral decay, says a report today by the Social Affairs Unit, a Right-wing think tank which tries to influence Tory thinking.

Special family magistrates' courts should look at the conduct of people seeking divorce and assign blame in an inquisitorial fashion, it says.

Assigning blame to the party is necessary for morality and for a fair distribution of property, writes Mr George Brown, a barrister and author of the report.

The ground for divorce in the county court should be a finding before the magistrates followed by an interval for reconciliation.

> *So God created human beings . . . He created them male and female.*
>
> *Genesis 1:27*
>
> *That is why a man leaves his father and mother and is united with his wife, and they become one.*
>
> *Genesis 2:24*

The question asked by the Pharisees may have been designed to trap Jesus into making a comment against the Law, or to bring him into conflict with Herod, who had married a divorced woman. In his reply, Jesus referred to two passages from Genesis:

The suggestion would seem to be that, although divorce was allowed at the time of Moses, this was not God's original intention. Jesus suggested to his disciples that remarriage was the same as adultery. This appears in both Mark's Gospel and Luke's Gospel.

ACTIVITIES

1 Discuss the two newspaper extracts. What is your opinion about the following?

   a) divorce on demand,

   b) making divorce more difficult.

2 Try to find a copy of a church marriage service (a prayer book or service book will normally include one). List all the references to the passage in Mark that are included in the service.

3 Add this to your list of conflict stories.

4 Discuss any differences between this teaching of Jesus and the current practice concerning the marriage of divorcees.

e) Jesus Blesses Little Children

Read Mark 10:13-16, Luke 18:15-17

MARK **LUKE** It is significant that Mark inserts this account immediately after Jesus' teaching about divorce. Already, in Mark 9, there have been two occasions when Jesus made comments about children (look them up if you have forgotten the details). Such a concern for the young is not often found in ancient writings.

When this event happened, the disciples apparently wished to protect Jesus from being bothered by children. However, a rebuke followed, with the comment that it is necessary to receive the Kingdom of God like a child. Children show great trust in adults, and receive gifts without question.

Children in Israel

ACTIVITIES

1 This passage is read in some churches at the baptism of an infant, in others at the funeral of a child. Discuss the appropriateness of the passage to each of these two occasions.

2 Answer the following questions, with reference to Mark 10:13-16 or Luke 18:15-17:

   a) Mention two previous occasions when Jesus referred in his teaching to children.

   b) On which occasions might this passage be read in a church service?

   c) What does this passage show about Jesus' attitude towards children?

   d) What do you think is the meaning of '. . . whoever does not receive the Kingdom of God like a child will never enter it'?

3 Discuss what you consider to be the Christian attitude towards children.

4 Find out all you can about any one Christian children's charity.

f) The Coming of the Kingdom

Read Luke 17:20-37

LUKE We have discovered that, in the teaching of Jesus, the Kingdom of God is shown as both a present reality and as something to be set up in the future. This passage suggests both aspects.

In reply to a question from the Pharisees, Jesus suggested that the Kingdom was present 'within you', which may mean that it is the rule of God accepted by the individual, or that it is inside, among, or within the grasp of the believers.

Jesus then taught the disciples about the day of the Son of Man, or a future revelation of the Kingdom. This probably refers to the *Parousia*, or Second Coming of Jesus (see Topic 11 l). Before the coming, which will be a revelation to all, yet unexpected, Jesus must suffer and be rejected. Two examples are given from the Old Testament which illustrate the unexpectedness of judgement. The *Parousia* will bring judgement and division when it comes. The passage ends with a proverb. As vultures gather around a corpse, so the *Parousia* will occur when conditions are right.

147

g) Predictions Concerning the Future

Read Mark 13:1–37, Matthew 10:16–25

MARK   Mark sets this teaching during
MATTHEW   the last week of Jesus' ministry.
When the disciples comment about the magnificence of the Temple, Jesus predicts that it will be destroyed. After further questions, he teaches four of his disciples from a point on the Mount of Olives, overlooking the Temple area.

The type of teaching in these passages and in parts of Luke 17 is sometimes called 'eschatological teaching' (teaching about the last things); another term often used is 'apocalyptic' (revelation of the future). Mark 13 is sometimes known as the 'Little Apocalypse', as compared with the 'Great Apocalypse', which is a name sometimes given to the book of Revelation.

It has been suggested that various sayings have been combined in this chapter, as the subject moves from the destruction of the Temple to the *Parousia*. The return of Jesus is the subject of verses 5–13 and various warnings are given about conditions which would precede the *Parousia*.

The passage in Matthew 10 is parallel to that of Mark 13:9–13.

Mark 13:14–33 moves on to the destruction of Jerusalem. This begins with a warning about 'The Awful Horror' or the 'abomination of desolation' being set up. This may be a reference to verses in Daniel and 1 Maccabees:

> *The Awful Horror will be placed on the highest point of the Temple and will remain there until the one who put it there meets the end which God has prepared for him.*
>
> *Daniel 9:27*
>
> *On the fifteenth day of the month Kislev in the year 145 [167 BC] 'the abomination of desolation' was set up on the altar.*
>
> *1 Maccabees 1:54 (NEB)*

The book of Maccabees refers to a statue set up in the Temple by Antiochus Epiphanes. However, in Mark 13:14, the warning is about a besieging Roman army (see the parallel passage in Luke 21:20). The Roman standards which would be carried by the Roman army besieging Jerusalem in AD 70 may have reminded the Christians of the day of this teaching. They took the warning and fled to the mountains of Pella and so escaped the destruction. Josephus gives a vivid description of the siege and destruction of Jerusalem in his *Wars of the Jews*.

In 1970 a dwelling was excavated in Jerusalem which had been destroyed by fire. It has become known as the Burnt House. Among the burnt debris were cooking pots, and coins which dated from AD 67, 68 and 69. Archaelogists

'The Son of Man will appear, coming in the clouds with great power and glory.'

consider that this was part of the Roman destruction of AD 70.

The tragedy of the period, especially for pregnant and nursing mothers, is commented on. Christians were to pray that the events would not happen during the winter rains. There is a further warning that false Messiahs will appear at that time. The theme of the *Parousia* is returned to in verses 24–7, and more preceding events are listed.

The Parable of the Fig Tree is included in verses 28–31. Some see here a reference to the destruction of Jerusalem, as many people who heard Jesus were still alive when it occurred.

The conclusion of the chapter is a warning to be watchful, for no one knows when the master will return. The Parable of the Doorkeeper is included here.

Burnt House debris

ACTIVITIES

1 Make a list of events and conditions which will precede the *Parousia*, using Mark 13:5–13 and 24–7.

2 Answer the following questions:

   a) What Greek word describes the Second Coming of Jesus?

   b) What word is used to describe teaching about the end of the world?

   c) What word is used to describe teaching which reveals the future?

   d) Which four disciples heard the teaching described as the 'Little Apocalypse'?

   e) Name two occasions when clouds are mentioned in the Gospels.

   f) What is meant by 'The Awful Horror'?

   g) What did Christians in Judaea do in AD 70?

   h) Which parable in this section is about watchfulness?

   i) Which parable in this section is about interpreting the signs of the times?

3 Add information from this section to your lists of parables, references to the Kingdom of God, and predictions of Jesus' suffering and death.

To Keep You Thinking

1 Prayer

Try to find out when Christians might pray and what different types of prayer they may use.

2 Marriage

Find out what vows couples make when they are married in church. How do the vows reflect the teaching of Jesus?

3 Children

Share your views about the abuse of children in our society and how Christians can help to overcome such abuse.

Parables from Luke

'Jesus told them this parable . . .'

Setting the Scene

T he 'Journey to Jerusalem' section of Luke's Gospel includes many parables. We looked at the ones to do with prayer in Topic 19; we shall consider the remainder in this Topic.

Most of these parables are found only in Luke's Gospel, and so are from Luke's special source. A few have parallels in Matthew's Gospel, and so may be Q material. It is probable that Jesus told the same parable on several occasions, varying the details. The Parable of the Great Feast (Luke 14:15–24) has many similarities to the Parable of the Wedding Feast (Matthew 22:1–14), and the Parable of the Gold Coins (Luke 19:11–27) has many parallels with the Parable of the Three Servants (Matthew 25:14–30).

To Help You Understand

a) The Parable of the Good Samaritan

Read Luke 10:25–37

LUKE   This is perhaps the best-known parable in the Gospels and its details are so vivid that it is easy to fall into the trap of thinking of it as an actual event, rather than a story told by Jesus. The story has very much affected our thinking, and we make frequent references to the 'Good Samaritan'.

Youths turned out to be Good Samaritans for veteran, 74

By Paul Stokes

AN OLD soldier found kindness and generosity of spirit in the last people he expected as he footslogged eight miles home after missing his last bus.

Mr Willie Willmott, 74, a veteran of the Burma campaign in the 1939–45 War, thought his number was up when he was confronted by a dozen youths.

He feared he was about to be mugged, but the youngsters saw the Burma Star emblem he was wearing and then clubbed together to raise £5 to pay for a taxi to take him home.

Mr Willmott, of Ashley Road, Ilfracombe, North Devon, had been left stranded after an evening out with comrades at the Royal British Legion club at Wrafton, near Barnstaple.

"I saw these youths skylarking," said the former sergeant in the Royal West African Force. "I was a bit worried. Luckily, instead of mugging me, they helped me out.

"I could not believe a thing like that could happen in the world today."

Samaritan clergyman attacked

By Paul Stokes

A CLERGYMAN was beaten up because he stopped to tend an injured schoolgirl who had fallen from her bicycle.

The Rev David Butcher, 42, was set upon by two men when their car was delayed by his at the scene of the accident on the outskirts of Gloucester. One of them drew a knife.

He was hit in the face, knocked to the ground and kicked.

'Samaritan' drivers may escape bans

Police drop fine for motorway Samaritan

An inn, known as the Inn of the Good Samaritan, has stood on this spot for centuries.

The parable is introduced with a question about receiving eternal life. The scriptures referred to are those of the Shema (see Topic 3). The teacher of the Law, wishing to justify his original question, went on to ask, 'Who is my neighbour?' The parable is an answer to that question. Most Jews of the period would have defined a neighbour as a fellow-Israelite. A very different idea is given in the parable.

The story is set on the 15-mile (24 km) stretch of road descending 3600 feet (1080 m) between Jerusalem and Jericho, which passes through the desert of Judaea (see the map on p. 2). This was the scene of frequent muggings, and a lone traveller was easy prey for groups of robbers. The priest and Levite were probably afraid of contamination, which would explain their attitude:

> **Whoever touches a corpse is ritually unclean for seven days.**
>
> *Numbers 19:11*

To be ritually clean was more important to them than making sure that the traveller was dead. It was the despised Samaritan, who the listeners would probably have expected to be the villain of the story, who took pity on the injured man. Using olive oil and alcohol, he dressed the man's wounds (we notice Luke's medical interest here) and took him to an inn.

This story has some similarities to an account in the Old Testament and Jesus may have had this in mind. Some prisoners were being returned from Israel to Judah, and we are told:

> **They gave them clothes and sandals to wear, gave them enough to eat and drink and put olive oil on their wounds. Those who were too weak to walk were put on donkeys and all the prisoners were taken back to Judaean territory at Jericho, the city of palm trees.**
>
> *2 Chronicles 28:15*

Jesus concludes the parable with a question. Which of the three passers-by acted as a neighbour? It is interesting that the teacher of the Law did not name the Samaritan, but rather referred to 'the one who was kind to him'.

151

ACTIVITIES

1 Write a modern version of the Parable of the Good Samaritan.

2 Try to find examples from newspapers and magazines of people who have acted as Good Samaritans.

3 Answer all sections of this essay:

a) Describe briefly one occasion when Jesus befriended a Samaritan.

b) Explain the meaning of a parable that Jesus told about a Samaritan.

c) Explain why you think Luke puts so much emphasis on Jesus' concern for Samaritans and Gentiles.

d) What do you think Christians can learn today from what Luke records of Jesus' teaching about Samaritans?

4 Discover what you can about the work of the Samaritans. Write a paragraph about the significance of the name of the organisation.

Stressful farmers told to seek help from Samaritans

By Colin Wright

THE NATIONAL Farmers' Union, alarmed at the rising number of suicides among farmers unable to deal with pressures brought on by declining incomes, falling land prices and growing liabilities, is urging its members to contact the Samaritans rather than attempt to cope alone with stress.

b) The Parable of the Rich Fool

Read Luke 12:13–21

LUKE This parable was told in response to a request. Rabbis sometimes settled disputes, but Jesus refused to be drawn into this quarrel about property, instead giving a warning about greed. The rich man pictured in the parable is completely self-centred (count the number of times he uses the words 'I' and 'my'!).

ACTIVITIES

1 Discuss why this is usually known as the Parable of the Rich Fool.

2 Make a note of any TV commercials that you see in a set period of time. Compare them against the saying of Jesus, 'A person's true life is not made up of the things he owns.'

3 Discuss what is meant by a) a materialistic society and b) the consumer society. What do you think should be a Christian's attitude towards possessions?

4 Answer the following questions, with reference to Luke 12:16–21:

a) Why did Jesus tell this parable?

b) What word is used to describe a person who is concerned mainly about possessions?

c) What would happen 'this very night'?

d) What do you think was wrong with this man's attitude?

e) What do you think it means to be 'rich in God's sight'?

c) Watchful Servants

Read Luke 12:35–40

LUKE This parable concerns a master returning from a wedding feast. Jews often thought of the time of the coming of the Messiah as a feast or banquet. The servants should be watchful and ready for the master's return, no matter how delayed it may be.

The passage ends with another short parable (verse 39) sometimes called the Parable of the Thief in the Night. Again it illustrates readiness. The return of the Son of Man (the *Parousia*) will be at an unexpected time and disciples must be ready.

d) The Faithful or the Unfaithful Servant

Read Luke 12:41–8

LUKE This follows on from the previous parable and is given in response to a question from Peter. Again there is a prediction about a delay in the master's return. There are serious warnings given to those who abuse their position by ill-treating others. The final two verses suggest that privilege brings responsibility.

ACTIVITIES

1 Revise the parables that you have read so far in the course. Check that your list is up to date. As you revise them, make a note of those that were told in answer to a question. Note the question and explain briefly how the parable answers it.

2 'Privilege brings responsibility.' Discuss this in relation to these parables and to life today.

---

e) The Parable of the Unfruitful Fig Tree

Read Luke 13:6–9

LUKE Just as we may have all kinds of plants growing in a garden, a vineyard would often have fruit trees other than vines. A fig tree takes

An unfruitful fig tree

about three years to mature, so at that age it should be producing fruit. The gardener pleaded that it should be given one further chance to fruit.

Both vines and fig trees were used in the Old Testament as symbols of Israel. This parable therefore suggests that either Israel as a whole or individuals should repent whilst the opportunity exists. Notice that this parable follows a section about repentance and judgement.

f) The Parable of the Great Feast

Read Luke 14:7–24

LUKE This parable is given the setting of a Pharisee's home where Jesus was a guest (see verses 1–6). It is preceded by comments about humility – not seeking the seats nearest to the host at a wedding feast (verses 7–11). There is also advice about offering hospitality to those who are unable to repay you (verses 12–14).

The Messianic banquet is referred to in verse 15. The parable which follows is sometimes called the Parable of the Great Supper. It was a

'... *invite the poor*'

mark of courtesy to send a servant to summon the guests when a feast was ready. In the situation of the parable, three excuses were given, concerning business, possessions and relationships. Because the original guests had refused the invitation, it was extended to those mentioned earlier, in verse 13, perhaps representing outcasts, and then to any who would accept the invitation, perhaps this time representing the Gentiles.

ACTIVITIES

1 Remembering that a parable teaches one main point, discuss which of the following you consider to be the main point of the parable of the Great Feast:

- The invitation to enter the Kingdom

- Not everyone will enter the Kingdom of God

- The extension of the invitation to outcasts and Gentiles

- The Gentile mission of the Church

- Excuses that were made for not entering the Kingdom

2 Answer the following questions, with reference to Luke 14:12–14:

a) Where was Jesus when he made these comments?

b) Which miracle had he already performed?

c) What teaching had he given about humility?

d) Summarise, briefly, the teaching of the parable which follows this passage.

e) What is meant by the 'Messianic banquet'?

f) What do you think is suggested in this passage about who would be invited to the Messianic banquet?

g) The Lost Sheep

Read Luke 15:1–7

LUKE In Luke 15 there are three parables about the lost. It is suggested by Luke that comments from the Pharisees and lawyers concerning Jesus' friendship with outcasts led to this teaching. The search for a lost sheep would be familiar to all who heard this parable, as would the idea of God searching for his scattered people:

> *I, the Sovereign Lord, tell you that I myself will look for my sheep and take care of them in the same way as a shepherd takes care of his sheep that were scattered and are brought together again.*
>
> *Ezekiel 34:11*

The emphasis of the parable is on God's concern for the straying sinner and the joy over the one who repents.

h) The Lost Coin

Read Luke 15:8–10

LUKE This parable, with a very similar meaning to the Parable of the Lost Sheep, would be particularly meaningful to women. The silver coin was probably from a woman's head-dress, presented to her upon her marriage. The loss of the coin would therefore be similar to the loss of a wedding ring. The emphasis here is on the initiative God takes to find the sinner.

i) The Lost Son

Read Luke 15:11–32

LUKE The Parable of the Lost Son, or the

Runaway returns

A TEARFUL mother spoke of her relief today after her daughter returned home after eight days on the run.

Prodigal Son, has been called the greatest short story ever written. The family tragedy of a young person leaving home and getting into difficulties was as common in the first century as it is today.

The following is an extract from a Roman papyrus of AD 100:

> *Antonius Longus to Nilous, his mother, greeting. Continually I pray for your health. I had no hope that you would come up to town. On this account I did not enter the city either. I was ashamed to come for I am going about in rags. I beseech you, mother, forgive me. I know what I have brought upon myself. I have been punished, in any case. I know I have sinned. . . .*

The elder son in this story would inherit two thirds of his father's property and the younger son one third. After he left home, the young man wasted his money (prodigal means wasteful) and needed to work for a Gentile. He did a job which would have been considered unclean for a Jew, for pigs were forbidden animals.

Rembrandt's Prodigal Son. What aspects of the story do you think the artist emphasises?

In contrast to the sheep and the coin, the young man in this story was lost through his own deliberate action. He was able to be found when he came to his senses, repented and decided to return home with a confession. The welcome, however, was not dependent on the confession, and the young man was accepted back as a son and given a welcoming feast, as well as a ring which was a sign of authority.

The elder brother plays an important part in this story, for he resented the welcome given to his brother, whom he called 'this son of yours'. It has been suggested that the elder brother represents Israel, or the Pharisees, or the Jewish religious leaders.

Remember that a parable was intended to teach one main point. Work out what you think is the main point of this parable.

ACTIVITIES

1 This parable has been given various titles: the Prodigal Son, the Lost Son, the Loving Father, the Elder Brother. Make notes under each of the four titles to show how appropriate they are.

2 Discuss a modern, parallel situation to that of the Parable of the Lost Son. Act or mime it. Perhaps you could present it in an assembly?

3 Answer the following questions:

a) Narrate, briefly, the parable which is illustrated in the photograph of the well-dressing.

b) Name two other parables of the lost.

c) For whose benefit were the three parables taught?

d) It has been suggested that the most effective way of emphasising a point is to say it in three different ways. What point do you think is being emphasised in these three parables?

e) What do you consider to be the significant differences between the three parables?

j) The Shrewd Manager

Read Luke 16:1–17

LUKE The Parable of the Shrewd Manager, sometimes called the Parable of the Unjust Steward, has been described as the most difficult parable in the Gospels. It was taught for the benefit of the disciples. The steward, or manager of an estate, was faced with losing his job, so he used his common sense to get back some of his master's property. At the same time he made 'friends' (those who were let off their debts lightly) who would later be in his debt. His master praised him for his resourcefulness.

The difficulty comes in working out the point of the parable, which would seem to be in verses 8–12. Notice that the disciples are not told to be like the shrewd manager, but to be resourceful, to use wealth to 'make friends' (verse 9). The Greek could mean 'make friends for yourselves *apart* from worldly wealth' rather than '*with* worldly wealth'. The disciples are also told to be faithful in handling money and to serve God rather than money.

Verses 14–17 include comments about self-justification and the relationship of the Good News to the Law of Moses.

ACTIVITIES

1 Discuss which of the following statements you consider to be an appropriate comment on this parable:
   - Follow the example of the Shrewd Manager.
   - You cannot serve God and money.
   - Faithfulness in this life is a good preparation for the next.
   - Christians should use their common sense.
   - Buy friends for yourself.
   - Be resourceful.

2 Make a list of things which you think people value most. Compare your list with others'. Then discuss the saying that '. . . the things that are considered of great value by man are worth nothing in God's sight.'

---

k) The Rich Man and Lazarus

Read Luke 16:19–31

LUKE This parable is sometimes given the title 'Dives and Lazarus', *dives* being a Latin word meaning 'wealthy'. Some think the narrative had its origins as a folk story and that Jesus used it to show that doing nothing for those in need is as sinful as ill-treating them. Another interpretation of the parable is that it is an attack on the Jewish leaders because of their attitude to outcasts.

A contrast is drawn between Lazarus, sitting with Abraham at the feast in heaven, and the rich man in *Hades* (a Greek word meaning 'the place of the departed', not the same as the word for hell, which is *Gehenna*). The separation of the two is stressed. The suggestion in verses 30 and 31 concerning someone rising from death hints at the rejection of Jesus even after his resurrection.

A beggar. What other teaching did Jesus give about such people?

157

l) A Servant's Duty

Read Luke 17:7-10

LUKE Sometimes called the Parable of the Unprofitable Servant, this short account suggests that a slave gets no respite from his work, nor thanks for completing it. The follower of Jesus should not hope for reward nor expect to gain merit for his service to God.

m) The Parable of the Gold Coins

Read Luke 19:11-27

LUKE This parable is sometimes called the Parable of the Pounds and is a variation on the Parable of the Talents or Three Servants in Matthew 25:14–30. It may well be based on an actual historical event. After the death of Herod the Great, one of his sons, Archelaus, travelled to Rome in order to be confirmed as king. Josephus tells us that a Jewish deputation also went to Rome to oppose Archelaus' claim, since he was unpopular.

Luke suggests that the reason this parable was told was because Jesus was about to reach Jerusalem and people were expecting that he would set up the Kingdom of God. We therefore have another example of a parable concerning a master going away, this time to receive a kingdom, and returning. In this story, each servant was given the same amount of money and told to trade with it.

The teaching at the end of the account is very similar to that in Matthew 25:26–30. There is, in Luke 19:27, the additional comment concerning the fate of the enemies of the King.

ACTIVITIES

1 Make sure that all of these parables are added to your list of parables.

2 Answer the following questions:

a) Name two parables which include reference to a feast.

b) Name two parables which are about the *Parousia*.

c) Name two parables which refer to rejoicing over the sinner who repents.

d) Name two parables which concern money.

e) What question does the Parable of the Good Samaritan answer?

f) What is the main point of the Parable of the Thief in the Night?

g) Which parable suggests that privilege brings responsibility?

h) Which parable concerns the invitation to enter the Kingdom of God?

i) Why was the rich man (Dives) criticised?

j) What happened to the third servant in the Parable of the Gold Coins?

To Keep You Thinking

1 God's forgiveness

The Parable of the Lost Son suggests the possibility of forgiveness for those who repent. Look in any prayer books you may have and find examples of prayers asking for forgiveness.

2 Stewardship

In the twentieth century the Church rediscovered the importance of stewardship. Try to find out what is meant by a 'stewardship campaign'.

In Jerusalem

TOPIC 21

'. . . it is not right for a prophet to be killed anywhere except in Jerusalem.'

Setting the Scene

The tension which has been noticed in the last few Topics reaches a climax in this section of the Gospels. We have considered a number of chapters, particularly from Luke's Gospel, which include teaching given on the journey to Jerusalem and predictions of trouble when Jesus arrived there. Now the destination is reached and the drama builds up.

After the time of Jesus' visit to Jerusalem at the age of 12, the Synoptic Gospels do not record any further visits until this point in the ministry of Jesus. The fourth Gospel, however, suggests that Jesus frequently visited Jerusalem, especially at festival time. It is very probable that this was so, and hints of such visits are given in the Synoptic Gospels.

Mark's Gospel suggests a timetable of one week for the events in Jerusalem leading up to the death and resurrection of Jesus. Some scholars suggest that the events covered several months. Approximately one third of Mark's Gospel is taken up with this Passion narrative, as it is sometimes called ('passion' in this context means suffering), and only a slightly smaller proportion of Luke and Matthew. Look back at the diagram on p. 26.

This Topic begins with comments made by Jesus about Jerusalem, set by Luke at the beginning of the journey to Jerusalem. The entry into the city and the events of the early part of the week are included, building up to various controversies with the Jewish leaders.

Jerusalem – the narrow streets would be very crowded at Passover time.

ACTIVITIES

1 Whichever Gospel you are studying, look quickly through Mark 11:1 – 16:8. List the days of the week into which the events are slotted, and the events which occurred on each day.

2 Discuss why such a large proportion of the Gospels is taken up with the Passion narratives.

159

To Help You Understand

a) Jesus' Love for Jerusalem

Read Luke 13:31–5

LUKE Jesus was warned by some friendly Pharisees that Herod wanted to kill him. This event may have happened in Perea, which was part of the territory of Herod Antipas. Jesus showed little respect for Herod, referring to him as a fox. This term was used of a sly, devious or destructive person. The phrase 'on the third day' was often used to mean 'in a short time'. Jesus had to complete his work before moving on to Jerusalem, where he would be killed. In his lament over Jerusalem there is a suggestion that Jesus had often tried to give his message to the people of that city, but had been rejected.

'How many times have I wanted to put my arms round all your people, just as a hen gathers her chicks under her wings, but you would not let me.' What does this suggest about Jesus' visits to Jerusalem?

A prediction follows that the Temple will be abandoned and that the next time Jesus is seen in Jerusalem will be when he is greeted with words from Psalm 118, which were used as a blessing on pilgrims visiting Jerusalem for the festivals:

> *May God bless the one who comes in the name of the Lord! From the Temple of the Lord we bless you.*
>
> *Psalm 118:26*

This quotation of the psalm by Jesus is usually taken as referring to the Entry into Jerusalem, but since the parallel passage in Matthew's Gospel is set during the last week in Jerusalem, after the Entry, some scholars believe that it is a reference to the *Parousia*, which will occur after the destruction of the Temple.

b) The Triumphant Entry into Jerusalem

Read Mark 11:1–11, Luke 19:28–40, Matthew 21:1–11

MARK
LUKE
MATTHEW From the instructions given to the disciples, it is obvious that Jesus had deliberately planned this procession, perhaps as the first public proclamation of his Messiahship. A king, going into battle, would ride a horse, but the normal form of everyday transport was and is a donkey.

In entering Jerusalem in this way, Jesus was fulfilling two prophecies:

> *I will send my messenger to prepare the way for me. Then the Lord you are looking for will suddenly come to his Temple. The messenger you long to see will come and proclaim my covenant.*
>
> *Malachi 3:1*
>
> *Rejoice, rejoice, people of Zion! Shout for joy, you people of Jerusalem! Look, your King is coming to you! He comes triumphant and victorious, but humble and riding on a donkey – on a colt, the foal of a donkey.*
>
> *Zechariah 9:9*

There would have been many pilgrims travelling to Jerusalem at this time and they spread cloaks on the road, as was customary to greet a king:

> ... *Jehu's fellow-officers spread their cloaks at the top of the steps for Jehu to stand on, blew trumpets, and shouted 'Jehu is king!'*
>
> 2 Kings 9:13

Approaching Jerusalem from the east, pilgrims would have passed through Jericho, the city of palm trees, and possibly used palm-fronds as fans on the 15-mile (24-km) journey through the desert of Judaea to Jerusalem. The crowd appears to have recognised that this was an important event. The cry 'Praise God' is the Hebrew *'Hosanna'* which means 'Save now!' Perhaps the crowd hoped that Jesus would take action against the Romans. Certainly Jesus' peaceful visit to the Temple and his return to Bethany, where his friends Mary, Martha and Lazarus lived and where he appears to have spent each night, was an anti-climax after the earlier events.

Christians celebrate the events of the day that Jesus entered Jerusalem as 'Palm Sunday'.

LUKE Luke's account is very similar to that of Mark, except that he adds an echo of the song of the angels (Luke 2:14) to the shouts of praise. He also adds that Pharisees asked Jesus to silence the disciples.

MATTHEW Two animals are mentioned by Matthew, who also includes the quotation from Zechariah 9:9, and a reference to Jesus as 'David's Son'.

ACTIVITIES

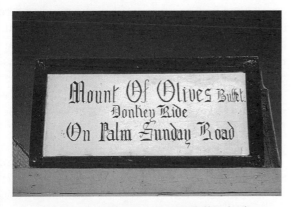

An example of modern commercialisation!

1 Answer the following questions:

a) Where did Jesus ride from on Palm Sunday?

b) What was Jesus' destination on Palm Sunday?

c) What evidence is there that Jesus deliberately organised the triumphant entry?

d) Describe briefly the reactions of the disciples and the crowd to the events of Palm Sunday.

e) Why do you think the crowd behaved in this way?

f) What do you think was the significance of the triumphant entry?

2 Add information from Luke 13:31–5 to your list of predictions of the suffering and death of Jesus, started in Topic 16.

3 Discuss what reasons Jesus had for making the comments about Herod recorded in Luke 13:31–5.

View from inside the Church of Dominus Flavit, 'The Lord wept'. Why is this an appropriate location for the church?

c) Jesus Weeps over Jerusalem

Read Luke 19:41–4

LUKE This passage appears only in Luke's Gospel. Jesus weeps, not for himself, but because of the coming suffering of Jerusalem.

Josephus gives a long description of the destruction of Jerusalem in AD 70, including details of the wall built around Jerusalem which effectively blockaded it and caused many people to die of starvation before the final destruction and burning of the city. The details given by Luke correspond so well with Josephus' account that it seems evident that Luke wrote after the events of AD 70.

d) Jesus Goes to the Temple

Read Mark 11:12–25, Luke 19:45–8, Matthew 21:12–17

MARK LUKE MATTHEW Mark suggests that these events occurred on the day after Palm Sunday, although Luke and Matthew give no details of time.

The incident recorded in Mark 11:15–19 would have taken place in the Court of Gentiles in the Temple (see the diagram on pp.14 and 15). Merchants had set up a market for the sale of sacrificial animals to pilgrims who had travelled too far to bring their own animals. It is likely that high prices were charged. There were also money changers who provided specially minted coins for the Temple treasury, so that coins bearing the image of Caesar need not be used. The Temple authorities received rents from this activity. The reason why Jesus removed these traders was that the Court of Gentiles was the only place where Gentiles were allowed to worship in the Temple, and the merchants' activities made prayer impossible. Jesus was angry that the Temple should be misused in this way.

There is an interesting passage at the end of the prophecy of Zechariah which looks forward to a future deliverance of Jerusalem and suggests:

> *When that time comes, there will no longer be any merchant in the Temple of the Lord Almighty.*
>
> *Zechariah 14:21*

Understandably, this action of Jesus provoked a reaction from the Temple authorities, who now sought a way to kill him.

LUKE Luke's account is briefer than that of Mark.

MATTHEW Matthew adds that Jesus healed in the Temple and that the authorities were angry that children were still shouting his praises there.

MARK Mark also records that, on the way to Jerusalem, Jesus cursed a fig tree that had no fruit. The following day (verses 20–5) the tree had died. This is a difficult story, which should perhaps be seen as Jesus acting out a parable rather than as a miracle. As we saw in the Parable of the Unfruitful Fig Tree, in Topic 20 e), a fig tree often typifies Israel. The uselessness of this unfruitful fig tree may be a warning of the failure of Israel and its consequences. Jesus used the incident to teach lessons about faith, prayer and forgiveness.

ACTIVITIES

1 Look up the Old Testament quotations in the passage you are studying, either by means of footnotes in your Bible or by using a concordance.

2 Discuss why Jesus wept over Jerusalem.

3 Study carefully the photograph of a well-dressing (below) and answer the following questions:

a) What event is depicted?

b) When did this event happen?

c) Where did the event take place?

d) Why were traders involved?

e) Why do you think Jesus took such extreme action?

f) What were the consequences of this event?

4 Study the border of the illustration carefully and discuss the symbolism which is used.

A Derbyshire well-dressing

e) The Question about Jesus' Authority

Read Mark 11:27–33, Luke 20:1–8, Matthew 21:23–7

MARK
LUKE
MATTHEW Mark suggests that a planned attempt was made on the following day to trap Jesus into incriminating himself. Various groups of people asked a series of questions which were probably prearranged. The setting was probably the Court of Gentiles and the first question was asked by a deputation from the Sanhedrin. Jesus was asked who gave him the right, presumably to drive out the traders from the Temple. This was a difficult question for Jesus. If he claimed that it was his own idea or that of another person, he could be charged with sacrilege; if he claimed that God had given him the right to do it, he could be charged with blasphemy. The pattern of question and answer which follows was a typical form of discussion used by Jewish rabbis.

Jesus' question concerned John the Baptist's right to baptise. Their refusal to answer this, suggesting that they did not accept that John was sent by God, implied that they would not accept that Jesus was sent by God either.

f) The Parable of the Tenants in the Vineyard

Read Mark 12:1–12, Luke 20:9–18, Matthew 21:33–46

MARK
LUKE
MATTHEW This is the final parable we shall study; it is sometimes known as the Parable of the Wicked Husbandmen. It was an indirect answer to the question put by the chief priests, the teachers of the Law and the elders. The parable is based on Isaiah's Song of the Vineyard (Isaiah 5:1–7), which all Jews would know well and where the vineyard represents Israel. In the setting of the last week of Jesus' life, the meaning is obvious and a warning to the Jewish authorities is implied. The quotation concerning the stone rejected by the builders is from Psalm 118:22–3, a psalm already referred to in this Topic.

LUKE Luke adds a comment concerning the effect of the 'stone' of the prophecy, which includes ideas from the Old Testament.

MATTHEW Matthew adds the comment that the Kingdom of God will be taken from those who were originally offered it, and given to others.

ACTIVITIES

1 Add this to your list of conflict stories begun in Topic 14. Add other appropriate accounts from this Topic as you study them.

2 Design a chart headed THE QUESTIONS OF 'HOLY WEEK' to illustrate the four questions studied in this Topic. Use the following headings:

- Question
- Asked by
- Why difficult to answer
- Reply given

Fill in the information as you read each of the questions. Start now with the question about authority.

A model of the Temple showing part of the portico where Jesus may have taught

ACTIVITIES

1 Read the Song of the Vineyard, Isaiah 5:1–7. Notice the similarities to the Parable of the Tenants in the Vineyard.

2 Discuss the meaning of the Parable of the Tenants in the Vineyard. Do you think this is a parable or an allegory?

3 Add information from this parable to your list of parables and to your list of predictions of Jesus' suffering and death.

A denarius. It has been suggested that strict Jews should not have had such a coin in the Temple. Why not?

g) The Question about Paying Taxes

Read Mark 12:13–17, Luke 20:19–26, Matthew 22:15–22

MARK LUKE MATTHEW The next question was asked by a group of Pharisees and Herodians, an alliance which had earlier wanted to kill Jesus (see Mark 3:6). Luke and Matthew suggest that a trap was deliberately set. The group began with flattery and then asked whether the Law allowed payment of taxes to the Roman emperor. This was very much a political question, for some 20 years earlier, Judas the Galilean had started the Zealot movement with a refusal to pay taxes to the Romans. Look back at the quotation from Josephus' *Wars of the Jews* on p. 11.

If Jesus suggested that taxes should not be paid, he would be allying himself with the Zealots, and be in trouble with the Romans. If, on the other hand, he accepted the payment of taxes, he could have been seen as a collaborator, which would have made him very unpopular with the Jews. In his reply, Jesus asked his questioners to produce a silver denarius (the daily wage for a worker), which had the Emperor's head on it. Jesus then suggested that taxes should be paid where they were due (the Romans had brought many benefits to the Jews), but that the Jews' main duty was to worship God.

h) The Question about Rising from Death

Read Mark 12:18–27, Luke 20:27–40,

MARK LUKE MATTHEW A group of Sadducees approached Jesus next. They had particular beliefs, especially concerning life after death, as we saw in Topic 3. They asked a question about the levirate law (*levir* = brother-in-law) which provided for a childless widow to be married to or supported by her brother-in-law (Deuteronomy 25:5–6). It was again a trick question, encouraging Jesus to speak against the Law of Moses. The rather absurd situation of a woman marrying each of seven brothers in turn was suggested. Despite the fact that the Sadducees did not believe in life after death, they asked whose wife the woman would be at the resurrection. Jesus' reply was a rebuke for implying that the future life is a continuation of the present physical life. Notice that Jesus did not say that the dead would become angels, but that they would be 'like the angels'.

Then Jesus argued that there is an existence beyond death. He referred to Exodus 3:6, where Moses was addressed by God centuries after the deaths of Abraham, Isaac and Jacob. The words used were: 'I am the God of Abraham . . .', not 'I was the God of Abraham . . .', demonstrating that Abraham and his descendants lived on in the presence of God.

165

ACTIVITIES

1 Discuss why these two questions were difficult for Jesus to answer.

2 Add the information from the two questions to your chart.

3 Answer the following questions, referring to Mark 12:18–27, Luke 20:27–40 or Matthew 22:23–33:

a) What name is given to the law concerning the marriage of a widow to her brother-in-law?

b) How was this question intended to trap Jesus?

c) Why was the question hypocritical?

d) What teaching did Jesus give in his reply concerning life after death?

4 'Pay the Emperor what belongs to the Emperor.' Discuss the implications of this teaching for Christians today.

5 Refer to the locations suggested on the plan (below) to trace the events of the last week of Jesus' ministry.

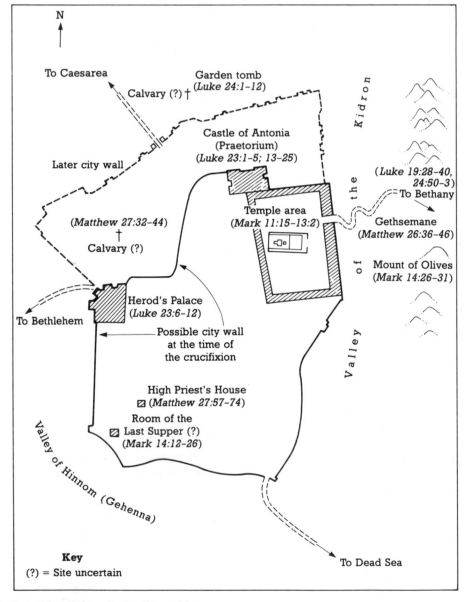

Annotated plan of Jerusalem in the time of Jesus

i) The Great Commandment

Read Mark 12:28–34

MARK This was probably a genuine question concerning the ritual and moral commandments – which were the most important? Jesus replied in the words of the Shema (see p. 13). There are many similarities here to the question asked before Jesus taught the Parable of the Good Samaritan. The teacher of the Law agreed that love for God and one's neighbour is more important than keeping the ritual law (for example, offering sacrifices). Jesus commended the man for his reply.

j) The Question about the Messiah

Read Mark 12:35–7, Luke 20:41–4

MARK This time the question is asked by
LUKE Jesus, and on the surface it seems that he is denying that he is descended from David. He was possibly trying to encourage people to think about the Messiah. Will he be merely another king of the family of David, or will he be greater than David? Psalm 110:1 is quoted, where the suggestion is that David called the Messiah 'my Lord', thus making David less important than the Messiah.

k) Jesus Warns against the Teachers of the Law

Read Mark 12:38–40, Luke 20:45–7

MARK Here the scribes or teachers of the
LUKE Law are criticised for three things:

- believing themselves to be superior to others,
- oppressing those who need their help,
- their hypocrisy.

l) The Widow's Offering

Read Mark 12:41–4, Luke 21:1–4

MARK The reference to a widow in the
LUKE previous account is a link with this incident. Look up the diagram of the Temple on pp. 14 and 15 and find the Temple treasury. Jesus used the incident to teach his disciples that the amount of money given is less important than the sacrifice involved.

ACTIVITIES

1 Discuss how the widow's offering was 'more . . . than all the others'.

2 With reference to Mark 12:38–40 or Luke 20:45–7, list the criticisms made of the teachers of the Law under the headings given in k) above.

To Keep You Thinking

1 **The celebration of Palm Sunday**
   Palm Sunday is celebrated by Christians as the beginning of Holy Week. Make a diary of how Christians might commemorate the various days of Holy Week.

2 **Belief in life after death**
   Hints are given in this Topic and elsewhere in the Gospels of Jesus' teaching about life after death. Discuss the concept.

Preparations

'The time was near for the Festival of Unleavened Bread. . .'

Setting the Scene

There is much similarity between the Synoptic Gospels in the Passion narrative. Some scholars think that this part of Mark's Gospel was the first part to be written down, since the events recorded in this section are so important for Christian beliefs. Look back at the list of points you made concerning the *Kerygma* (p. 22) and notice how many of them concern information in this final section of the Gospels.

Mark tells us that the events we are about to consider took place 'two days before the Festival of Passover and Unleavened Bread', Matthew says something similar and Luke tells us that the Festival of Unleavened Bread was near. Originally the two festivals mentioned were separate, but it seems that the beginning of the week-long Festival of Unleavened Bread had become combined with the Passover celebrations.

Writing of an event before the time of Jesus' ministry, Josephus said:

> *. . . this happened at the time when the feast of unleavened bread was celebrated, which we call the Passover.*
>
> *Josephus*, Antiquities of the Jews 14:2.1

To Help You Understand

a) The Plot against Jesus
Read Mark 14:1–2, Luke 22:1–2, Matthew 26:1–5

MARK LUKE MATTHEW The questions which were considered in Topic 21 had failed to trap Jesus into incriminating himself. The authorities decided that they must arrest Jesus secretly and put him to death either before or after the feast.

MATTHEW Matthew often uses a formula similar to that in verse 1, 'When Jesus had finished teaching all these things', to indicate the end of one section and the beginning of another. Jesus then predicts the crucifixion.

Bethany, showing old and new-style housing. Which friends of Jesus lived in Bethany?

b) Jesus Is Anointed at Bethany
Read Mark 14:3–9, Matthew 26:6–13

MARK MATTHEW By Mark's reckoning, these events took place on the Wednesday of Holy Week, when Jesus remained in Bethany. The account is set in the home of Simon, who was perhaps a leprosy sufferer once cured by Jesus.

The woman who anointed Jesus is not named in the Synoptic Gospels, but a Mary is mentioned in the fourth Gospel. Tradition suggests that this was either Mary Magdalene or Mary who lived at Bethany. The perfume was probably of a kind used to anoint the dead and may have been provided ready for the woman's own burial. It was very expensive, worth the equivalent of a year's wages (the silver coin would be the denarius). This was a tremendous sacrifice, as it takes a long time to save a year's wages! If you remember the meaning of the word 'Messiah' or 'Christ' you will realise the significance of the woman's action.

An alabaster jar from Egypt.
For what purpose would it have been used?

Matthew suggests that the disciples grumbled about the waste of money, whilst the fourth Gospel suggests that Judas objected. Jesus commended the woman, seeing in her action a preparation for his death. By the time the story was written down by Mark it had probably been repeated many times, which adds weight to the comment made in verse 9.

LUKE Luke does not include this account, but has an earlier, similar story (Luke 7:36–50).

c) Judas Agrees to Betray Jesus

Read Mark 14:10–11, Luke 22:3–6, Matthew 26:14–16

MARK
LUKE
MATTHEW It is difficult to know why Judas decided to betray Jesus. He may have been disappointed that Jesus had not taken action against the Romans after entering Jerusalem on Palm Sunday, it may have been greed, or perhaps he hoped to force Jesus into taking some action by bringing events to a climax.

No account is given of the discussion with the authorities, but it seems that Judas was prepared to give information about where and when Jesus could be arrested quietly. He may also have reported Jesus' acceptance of Peter's suggestion that he was the Messiah, for a question was asked about this at the subsequent trial. It seems probable that the authorities decided to take action immediately, before the feast, when the opportunity was there.

LUKE Luke suggests that Judas' action was due to the power of Satan.

MATTHEW Matthew gives the detail of the 30 silver coins, which was the amount a slave was worth:

> *If the bull kills a male or female slave, its owner shall pay the owner of the slave thirty pieces of silver.*
>
> Exodus 21:32

ACTIVITIES

1 Discuss why the authorities wished to kill Jesus.

2 Answer the following questions, with reference to Mark 14:3–9 or Matthew 26:6–13:

a) Where did this event take place?

b) What can be assumed about the host on this occasion?

c) Why was the woman criticised?

d) How did Jesus interpret the woman's action?

e) What is suggested in this passage about attitudes to the poor?

3 If possible, find a copy of the song 'Said Judas to Mary . . .' You may find this in a modern hymn book. Think about the meaning and relevance of the words.

4 List as many possible reasons as you can think of as to why Judas betrayed Jesus.

d) Jesus Eats the Passover Meal with His Disciples

Read Mark 14:12–21, Luke 22:7–13, Matthew 26:17–25

MARK
LUKE
MATTHEW
In comparing the Synoptic Gospels with the fourth Gospel, there is uncertainty as to when this meal took place. However, Mark suggests that it was a Passover meal. The Passover meal was a time to celebrate with family and friends, so the disciples asked where they would celebrate it.

Again, Jesus had made prior arrangements. Luke identifies Peter and John as the two disciples who were sent to follow a man carrying a water-pot (men would normally carry water in a leather bottle) to discover the venue for the meal. It has been suggested that the house used was that of Mary, the mother of John Mark (the probable author of Mark's Gospel), where Christians often gathered (Acts 12:12).

When the meal began in the upper room, Jesus warned that one of the 12 would betray him. There is a comment about Jesus' death which shows that, although he must die, the traitor is still responsible for his actions.

MATTHEW Matthew makes no mention of the man with the jar of water, but does emphasise Judas' reaction to Jesus' comments about the traitor.

> *. . . the Lord Jesus, on the night he was betrayed, took a piece of bread, gave thanks to God, broke it, and said, 'This is my body which is for you. Do this in memory of me.' In the same way, after supper he took the cup and said, 'This cup is God's new covenant, sealed with my blood. Whenever you drink it, do so in memory of me.' This means that every time you eat this bread and drink from this cup you proclaim the Lord's death until he comes.*
>
> *1 Corinthians 11:23-6*

Jews have specific blessings for bread and wine and these would have been used by Jesus. The emphasis on the bread as the body of Jesus and the wine as his blood stresses that the death of Jesus would be a sacrifice. In the Old Testament, blood was seen as sealing the covenant (agreement) made between God and his people at Mount Sinai:

> *This is the blood that seals the covenant which the Lord made with you when he gave all these commands.*
>
> *Exodus 24:8*

e) The Lord's Supper

Read Mark 14:22–6, Luke 22:14–23, Matthew 26:26–30

MARK
LUKE
MATTHEW
These are some of the most important passages in the Gospels for Christians today. The service of Holy Communion (also known as the Eucharist, Mass, Lord's Supper or Breaking of Bread) is based on these verses. You will remember the significance of the idea of the Messianic banquet. This is not the earliest written account of the Lord's Supper (or the Last Supper). An account of it was included by Paul in his letter to the Corinthians, some 15 years before Mark's Gospel was written:

Christians receiving communion. Why are bread and wine used?

Later, the prophet Jeremiah saw that a new covenant was necessary since God's people had broken his commands:

> *The time is coming when I will make a new covenant . . . I will put my law within them and write it on their hearts. I will be their God and they will be my people . . . I will forgive their sins and I will no longer remember their wrongs.*
>
> *Jeremiah 31:31, 33, 34*

So Jesus' disciples would interpret these words of Jesus as referring to the promised new covenant.

LUKE Luke refers first to one of the four cups of wine which would be used at a Passover celebration, before following Mark's account. Then there follows a warning about the betrayer.

MATTHEW Matthew adds that Jesus' blood would be poured out for many 'for the forgiveness of sins'.

The hymn which followed the supper would be part of the Hallel, Psalms 114–18, which was traditionally sung at Passover.

An area of recent excavations in Jerusalem. In 1988, archaeologists discovered the remains of a gate dating from before the time of Jesus. This is thought to be the Gennath or Garden Gate mentioned by Josephus in a description of Jerusalem. It may have been used by Jesus and his disciples on their way to the Garden of Gethsemane, after the Last Supper.

ACTIVITIES

1 Discuss why there was so much secrecy about the location for the Passover meal.

2 If you have a copy of either *The Gospels: A GCSE Activities Pack* or *Judaism: A GCSE Activities Pack* (both by Eileen Bromley, published by Stanley Thornes & Hulton), use the resource sheet 'A Simplified Form of Seder' to experience a Passover celebration.

3 Look carefully at the illustration of a well-dressing on p. 172, and answer the following questions:

   a) At the Last Supper, what did Jesus refer to as i) 'my body' and ii) 'my blood'?

   b) Why do you think the title 'Communion' is used?

   c) How does the illustration emphasise the ideas of i) suffering and ii) sacrifice?

   d) Why do you think the account in the Gospels is so important for Christians today?

4 Look up the Hallel, and discuss how this was particularly appropriate for the Passover celebrations.

5 Discuss the meaning of 'This is my blood which is poured out for many, my blood which seals God's covenant.'

A well-dressing at Wirksworth, Derbyshire.

The Chapel of Christ the Servant, Coventry Cathedral.
In what ways was Jesus a servant?

172

f) The Argument about Greatness

Read Luke 22:24–30

LUKE A rebuke was necessary even at this late date after an argument about status. The disciples of Jesus should not be power-seekers, but servants, following the example of their master. However, their loyalty would result in participation in the joys and responsibilities of the Kingdom.

g) Jesus Predicts Peter's Denial

Read Mark 14:27–31, Luke 22:31–4,
Matthew 26:31–5

MARK   Another warning is given here –
LUKE   that the disciples would desert
MATTHEW Jesus. However, there is also a hint of the Resurrection. After Peter's strong complaint, he is told that he will three times deny knowing Jesus.

MATTHEW Matthew follows Mark's account closely.

LUKE Luke's version is rather different from Mark's, suggesting there will be Christian work for Peter to do in the future, even after his failure.

h) Purse, Bag and Sword

Read Luke 22:35–8

LUKE Jesus reminded his disciples of the occasion when they were sent out on a mission. He obviously did not intend his disciples to arm themselves literally in order to defend him (see verses 50 and 51). Perhaps he was warning them to be prepared for trouble, which they misunderstood, as verse 38 suggests.

The quotation from Isaiah 53:12 identifies Jesus with the Suffering Servant (see Topic 4).

ACTIVITIES

1 Find the origin of the quotation in Mark 14:27 or Matthew 26:31 and then look it up.

2 If you are studying Luke's Gospel, look back at and revise the two occasions when the disciples were sent out on a mission (Topic 17).

3 Discuss in what sense the passages you have studied in this Topic are preparations.

4 Answer the following questions, briefly:

a) Where was Jesus anointed?

b) What could have been sold for a year's wages?

c) Which two festivals were celebrated at this time?

d) How did Jesus' disciples find the location for the Last Supper?

e) Where was the room which was to be used?

f) What warning was given at the Last Supper?

g) What was the significance of the bread?

h) What was the significance of the wine?

i) What is a covenant?

j) What hymn would be sung after the supper?

To Keep You Thinking

1 **Christian observance of Maundy Thursday**
Try to find out the meaning of 'Maundy' and how the day is commemorated.

2 **The celebration of Holy Communion**
Find out how the different Churches carry out the command of Jesus: 'Do this in memory of me' (Luke 22:19).

3 **Archaeology and the Gospels**
The Gospels are such ancient documents that it is easy to overlook the fact that new discoveries are still being made today in connection with them. Archaeology is just one area of research. We have referred already to the Kinneret boat (Topic 10), the Burnt House (Topic 19) and the Last Supper Gate. In 1991 there was a report from the Israeli Department of Antiquities of a burial cave having been found near Jerusalem. It contains a number of inscriptions of the name Caiaphas, the High Priest who is referred to in the next Topic. This may well be the Caiaphas family tomb which has now been excavated. Discuss the significance of these archaeological discoveries.

Arrest and Trials

'In accordance with his own plan, God had already decided that Jesus would be handed over to you.'

Setting the Scene

As we have seen, according to the Gospels, Jesus predicted on many occasions that he would be put to death. When the time came for his arrest, he took no action to escape his captors. At his trials he made little attempt to defend himself. The question arises, why should Jesus have taken this attitude towards his own death? Hints are given in the Gospels; look out for them as you study this Topic and the next one.

To Help You Understand

a) Jesus Prays in Gethsemane

Read Mark 14:32–42, Luke 22:39–46, Matthew 26:36–46

MARK
LUKE
MATTHEW The name Gethsemane means 'olive press', and the setting for this event was in all probability an olive grove which has been identified with an area on the lower slopes of the Mount of Olives (see photograph).

Other occasions have been noted when Peter, James and John were alone with Jesus. Notice that Jesus commented to them about the sorrow in his heart, not about fear. Jesus' prayer is very important. He addressed God as *'Abba'*, the familiar form of Father. His request to avoid the cup of suffering (see p. 137) could refer to both the physical and the spiritual suffering that he is about to endure, and emphasises Jesus' humanity. Notice that this request is followed by a willingness to do what God wants. The disciples, who by this time must have been exhausted, had fallen asleep. Notice that Peter is singled out for criticism by Mark.

On previous occasions, Jesus commented

that his hour had not yet come. Notice that this is the point at which he states: 'The hour has come!'

MATTHEW Matthew's version is similar to Mark's.

LUKE Luke's version is shorter than Mark's. He adds a comment about an angel (remember the interest shown in angels in the early chapters of his Gospel). Note that verses 43 and 44 may not have been part of the original Gospel.

Gethsemane today. In what ways might the area have been different in the first century?

b) The Arrest of Jesus

Read Mark 14:43–52, Luke 22:47–53, Matthew 26:47–56

MARK
LUKE
MATTHEW From Gethsemane it would be possible to see an approaching crowd coming from the city. A kiss was the usual greeting, especially of a disciple for his rabbi. The fourth Gospel tells us that Peter struck the High Priest's slave, Malchus. The young man mentioned here has been identified by some as John Mark. If the Last Supper were held in his mother Mary's home, Mark may well have followed Jesus and the disciples to Gethsemane.

LUKE Luke adds the interesting details that it was officers of the Temple guard who arrested Jesus, that the slave's right ear was healed by Jesus (remember Luke's interest in healing), and Jesus' comment that the authorities would only act under the cover of darkness.

MATTHEW Matthew emphasises the fulfilment of prophecy in the events that occurred, and adds the comment about armies of angels.

ACTIVITIES

1. Follow the events as recorded in the Gospel you are studying on the plan on p. 188.

2. Discuss the significance of:
   a) *'Not what I want but what you want.'*
   b) *'The hour has come!'*

3. Discuss why you think Mark singles out Peter for rebuke (Mark 14:37). Why do you think the writers of the other two Synoptic Gospels make no mention of Peter in this connection?

4. Answer the following questions:
   a) Describe briefly the event commemorated in the chapel pictured below.
   b) Who does the figure represent?
   c) What is the importance of the chalice?
   d) What is the significance of the metal work in the foreground?
   e) What do you think Christians can learn about prayer from the event illustrated here?

5. Make a chart to compare the events in Gethsemane with those on the Mount of the Transfiguration (Mark 9:2–13, Luke 9:28–36 or Matthew 17:1–13).

6. To help revise your work, make lists of:
   a) occasions when Jesus was tempted,
   b) occasions when Peter, James and John were alone with Jesus.

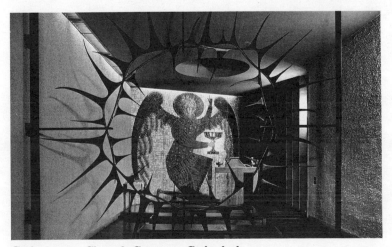

Gethsemane Chapel, Coventry Cathedral

c) Jesus before the Council

Read Mark 14:53–64, Luke 22:66–71, Matthew 26:57–66

MARK
LUKE
MATTHEW In the 1930s, excavations were being carried out for the building of a new church in Jerusalem, when some remains of an extensive building were found. It has been suggested that this was the house of the High Priest. Various levels have been excavated, including underground dungeons, and a flight of steps dating from the first century was unearthed nearby.

The event recorded by Mark may have been a full trial by the Sanhedrin or a preliminary examination. There were many illegalities in this trial. Although Jesus had been arrested, there was no evidence to convict him of an offence.

> *One witness is not enough to convict a man of a crime; at least two witnesses are necessary to prove that a man is guilty.*
>
> Deuteronomy 19:15

Jesus' silence would be another reminder to the readers of the Gospel of the Suffering Servant of Isaiah:

> *Like a lamb about to be slaughtered, like a sheep about to be sheared, he never said a word.*
>
> Isaiah 53:7

Eventually, the High Priest asked a leading question, 'Are you the Messiah, the Son of the Blessed God?' Jesus' reply used words from Daniel 7:13, implying that when he had used the term 'Son of Man' he had meant that he was the Messiah. This understandably infuriated the High Priest and the Council, as they would consider this to be blasphemy.

LUKE Luke suggests that this trial took place in the morning.

MATTHEW Matthew suggests that the Council encouraged false evidence to be presented, and that the High Priest put Jesus on oath before asking him the question about Messiahship.

Steps leading to the probable site of the High Priest's house, near the church of St Peter in Gallicantu ('at the cock-crow'). Why do you think the church was given this name?

d) Jesus Is Mocked and Beaten

*Read Mark 14:65, Luke 22:63–5,
Matthew 26:67–8*

MARK   The early Christians would see
LUKE   further significance in pro-
MATTHEW   phecies from the Servant Songs:

> *I bared my back to those who beat me.*
> *I did not stop them when they insulted
>   me,*
> *when they pulled out the hairs of my
>   beard*
> *and spat in my face.*
>
>   *Isaiah 50:6*

ACTIVITIES

1 Revise your list of references to the
Son of Man and the information on the
subject in Topic 4. Make use of the
index if necessary. Then write the
following essay:

   a) Why do you think Jesus used the
term 'Son of Man' of himself?

   b) Explain the three contexts in which
the term 'Son of Man' is used in
the Gospels.

   c) What do you think Jesus meant by
his reply to the High Priest at his
trial?

2 Look up John 2:19. Discuss the
connection between this verse and
Jesus' trial.

3 As you read the accounts of the trials
of Jesus, make a list of the charges
brought against him, at which trial and
by whom. Assess the fairness of the
charges and write a paragraph about
each. What do you think would happen
if such a series of 'trials' took place
today?

e) Peter Denies Jesus

*Read Mark 14:66–72, Luke 22:54–62,
Matthew 26:69–75*

MARK   Peter can be admired for follow-
LUKE   ing Jesus to the High Priest's
MATTHEW   house, and for remaining even
after three accusations that he was associated
with Jesus. It seems that he was recognised as a
disciple – his Galilean accent probably gave him
away. Even today, weather-cocks are often
placed on church steeples, as a reminder of the
need for loyalty. When Peter remembered
Jesus' warning about the denials, he was
overcome with remorse.

*What is the significance of this weather-vane on a
church steeple?*

ACTIVITIES

1 Discuss Peter's denial. Try to account
for his behaviour on this occasion.

2 Answer the following questions, with
reference to Mark 14:66–72, Luke
22:54–62 or Matthew 26:69–75:

   a) What was the name of the High
Priest?

   b) Where did this event take place?

   c) How was Peter recognised?

   d) Why do you think Peter denied
knowing Jesus?

   e) What was the reason for Peter's
remorse?

f) Jesus Is Brought before Pilate

Read Mark 15:1–5, Luke 23:1–5,
Matthew 27:1–14

MARK Pilate was the Roman governor
LUKE or procurator of Judaea. He had
MATTHEW been tactless and brutal in
dealing with the Jews. Josephus reports an
earlier occasion:

Now Pilate, who was sent as procurator
into Judaea by Tiberius, sent by night
those images of Caesar that are called
ensigns into Jerusalem.

Josephus, Wars of the Jews 2:9.2

Jesus was taken to Pilate's residence, probably
in the Castle of Antonia, by about 6 a.m. It is
probable that permission had to be obtained
from the Roman governor before a person could
be put to death. A charge of blasphemy would
mean nothing to a Roman, so the charge was
apparently changed from a religious to a
political one. Jesus was accused of treason by
reference to a Messianic title, King of the Jews.
Again Jesus avoided giving a direct answer to
his questioner.

LUKE Luke notes a number of charges made
before Pilate, and that Jesus was declared
innocent.

MATTHEW Matthew inserts an account of
the suicide of Judas before Pilate's questioning
of Jesus.

g) Jesus Is Sent to Herod

Read Luke 23:6–12

LUKE Only Luke records this account. Look
back at p. 160 to remind yourself of Herod
Antipas' attitude towards Jesus. Jesus refused
to answer any of Herod's questions, and so he
was treated with contempt.

h) Jesus Is Sentenced to Death

Read Mark 15:6–20, Luke 23:13–25,
Matthew 27:15–31

MARK Apparently Pilate was in the
LUKE habit of releasing a prisoner at
MATTHEW Passover time and it was
probably for this reason that a crowd had
gathered. We are told that Barabbas was a rebel
and a murderer. Yet he was the one who was
granted his freedom, after the chief priests had
brought pressure to bear on the crowd. Pilate,
weakly listening to the crowd, handed over for
crucifixion, after having him whipped or
scourged, the man he had already proclaimed to
be not guilty.

Every ten years, a Passion Play is performed in Oberammergau in Bavaria. What is happening in this scene?

The soldiers, who would probably be from various Roman provinces outside Palestine, dressed Jesus in royal purple (or perhaps a soldier's scarlet cloak would fit Matthew's suggestion) and crowned him with thorns, rather than a laurel wreath, before mocking him as a King.

LUKE Luke emphasises that Jesus was innocent and that Pilate wished to release him.

MATTHEW Matthew tells us that Barabbas was also called Jesus! He also includes details of Pilate's wife's dream, and that Pilate washed his hands to indicate that he was not responsible for Jesus' death.

ACTIVITIES

1 Answer the following questions, briefly:

   a) What is the meaning of the name 'Gethsemane'?

   b) Which disciples were selected to pray with Jesus in Gethsemane?

   c) What did Jesus pray in Gethsemane?

   d) Who kissed Jesus and why?

   e) Suggest a possible identity of the naked young man.

   f) Who followed Jesus to the High Priest's house?

   g) Name two charges brought against Jesus at his trial.

   h) What direct question was asked by the High Priest at the trial?

   i) On what charge did the Sanhedrin find Jesus guilty?

   j) What charge was made against Jesus before Pilate?

   k) Why was Barabbas in prison?

   l) Name two ways in which the soldiers mocked Jesus.

2 Discuss why Jesus refused to defend himself at his trials.

3 Write paragraphs to explain the part played in the trials of Jesus by a) Caiaphas, b) Pilate and c) Herod (if you are studying Luke's Gospel).

Who Is Responsible for the Death of Jesus?

At the time the Gospels were written, there was considerable misunderstanding of Christian beliefs by the Romans. One of the aims of Luke's Gospel in particular seems to have been to show the Romans that Christianity was not against their laws. There is therefore an emphasis on Jewish responsibility for the death of Jesus, although it was obviously Pilate's judgement that led directly to Jesus' crucifixion.

Over the centuries, some Christians have blamed the Jews for the death of Jesus, and horrifying persecution (anti-Semitism) has taken place. The Second Vatican Council of the Roman Catholic Church made this statement:

Even though the Jewish authorities and those who followed their lead pressed for the death of Christ (John 19:6), neither all Jews indiscriminately at that time, nor Jews today, can be charged with the crimes committed during his passion.

Declaration on the Relation of the Church to Non-Christian religions, para 4

A more recent statement was made by the Archbishop of Canterbury and the head of the Roman Catholic Church in Britain at a joint meeting with the Chief Rabbi and other Jews. They expressed the sorrow of Christians over the persecution of Jews through the centuries, and especially the failure of the Churches to protest against anti-Semitism and the Holocaust.

A group of 13–16-year-olds were asked to list who they thought was responsible for the death of Jesus. These are their suggestions:

- Judas
- Caiaphas
- Herod
- The crowd
- Pilate
- The disciples
- The Jewish priests
- God
- Jesus
- Everyone

179

ACTIVITIES

1 Discuss the suggestions given on p. 179. Reach your own conclusions – who do you think was responsible for the death of Jesus?

2 Discuss the statements made by Churches concerning the persecution of Jews. What is meant by a) anti-Semitism and b) the Holocaust?

To Keep You Thinking

The problem of suffering

Discuss the relevance of Jesus' prayer in the Garden of Gethsemane to the problem of suffering.

Crucifixion

'. . . Christ died for our sins, as written in the Scriptures; . . . he was buried.'

Setting the Scene

In the passage from which the above quotation is taken, written a considerable time before the Gospels, Paul was listing for the Corinthians the main points of the Good News which had been passed on to him.

As we saw at the beginning of this book, there is evidence not only from Christians but also from Roman and Jewish sources that Jesus was put to death by crucifixion. Crucifixion was a method of execution used by the Romans, who had taken it over from the Phoenicians. It was a particularly cruel death, as victims often stayed alive for 36 hours or more before dying of exhaustion or suffocation. There is some discussion about the form of the cross, but a first-century skeleton of a crucified man suggests that nails were placed through the wrists and heels. No Roman citizen could be crucified; this horrific practice was used only for slaves and subject peoples. Jews, basing their ideas on a passage from the Old Testament, believed that anyone crucified was cursed of God:

> **And if a man has committed a crime punishable by death and he is put to death and you hang him on a tree, his body shall not remain all night upon the tree, but you shall bury him the same day, for a hanged man is accursed by God . . .**
>
> *Deuteronomy 21:22–3 (RSV)*

ACTIVITIES

1 Look back at Topic 4. Which Roman and Jewish writers refer to Jesus' death?

2 List as many examples as you can find of crosses in your community. If possible, sketch them and then find out about the different types. As a group, make a collage to display the information you have discovered.

A modern sculpture in the Roman Catholic cathedral in Middlesbrough shows the possible position in which victims were crucified.

To Help You Understand

a) Jesus Is Crucified

Read Mark 15:21–32, Luke 23:26–43,
Matthew 27:32–44

MARK **LUKE** **MATTHEW** There was a Jewish community in the North African town of Cyrene in what is today called Libya. Simon may have been a pilgrim on his way to Jerusalem. Mark gives the information that Simon had two sons, Alexander and Rufus, who may have been known to the Church in Rome (see Romans 16:13). It seems that the cross-beam of the cross would be carried by the victim to his crucifixion. Simon was forced to carry this for Jesus, possibly because Jesus was exhausted after the scourging (or whipping).

Golgotha, or *Calvaria* in Latin, may have been given this name meaning 'the place of the skull' because of the purpose to which the site was put or because of the shape of a rock formation.

This is one of two sites suggested as possibilities for the place of crucifixion. Why do you think this was identified as a possible site?

Jesus refused the mixture of wine and myrrh which was intended to deaden the pain. The soldiers on crucifixion duty had the right to the victim's clothing, and in this the early Christians saw a fulfilment of a verse from Psalm 22:

> *They gamble for my clothes*
> *and divide them among themselves.*
>
> *Psalm 22:18*

It may well be that someone carried a notice before the condemned person on the journey to the cross to explain the crime. This would then be nailed on the cross. Jesus' notice read 'The King of the Jews' or 'Jesus of Nazareth, the King of the Jews' (John 19:19). The initial letters from the Latin words *Iesus Nazarenus Rex Iudaeorum* have become an important Christian symbol:

JESUS OF NAZARETH,
THE KING OF THE JEWS

Look out for examples of this symbol.

Two bandits, possibly Zealots, were crucified with Jesus. Crowds would gather to watch the entertainment provided by a crucifixion and it was customary to hurl insults at those on the cross. The insults against Jesus reflected the accusations against him, reminding the early Christians once more of Psalm 22. There was a further temptation, this time for Jesus to save himself.

MATTHEW Matthew's account is very similar to Mark's.

LUKE Luke seems to have had additional information to that used by Mark. He records that women wept, but that Jesus, in a prophecy concerning the destruction of Jerusalem, said that they would have cause to weep for themselves and for their children. It would have been better not to have had children than to see them suffering so badly. Things would be so bad that people would wish themselves dead (Hosea 10:8). If suffering such as this could happen to a person who was innocent of any crime, what might happen in a time of revolution (verse 31)?

Luke also tells us of Jesus' first saying from the cross. As he was being crucified, he said: 'Forgive them, Father! They don't know what they are doing.' Luke gives further details of the insults of one of the criminals crucified with Jesus and of his assurance to the other. Paradise was a Persian word meaning a garden, and it came to signify a place of bliss.

ACTIVITIES

1 If possible, visit a place where the stations of the cross can be seen. This is most likely to be in a Roman Catholic church. Make a note of those stations which reflect the accounts you have read in the Gospels.

2 Look at the photograph below and answer the following questions:

a) What is a Passion Play?

b) At what time was Jesus crucified?

c) Which people were crucified with Jesus and what do you know of them?

d) What temptation did Jesus face on the cross?

e) *'He saved others, but he cannot save himself.'*

  i) Give examples of people saved by Jesus in various ways, as recorded in the Gospels.

  ii) What is your opinion of the second part of the above quotation?

3 Design a banner or a poster to represent any aspect of the Gospels that has made a particular impact on you.

A banner created for the Methodist Church, Sherborne, by Margaret Bacon. In what ways does this banner reflect the events of the crucifixion?

Crucifixion scene from the Oberammergau Passion Play

b) The Death of Jesus

*Read Mark 15:33–41, Luke 23:44–9,
Matthew 27:45–56*

**MARK
LUKE
MATTHEW** We are told of an unnatural eclipse of the sun which lasted for three hours. Mark records another cry of Jesus from the cross, which is a quotation from Psalm 22:1. This gives a glimpse into the spiritual suffering of Jesus on the cross; this is the only time he felt himself separated from God. The bystanders misunderstood this cry, thinking he was calling for Elijah. There was an idea that Elijah would protect the righteous in time of trouble.

Mark records that, at the time of Jesus' death, the veil of the Temple was torn in two. This curtain separated the Holy Place from the Holy of Holies (see the plan on pp. 14 and 15), which represented the presence of God. Only the High Priest ever entered the Holy of Holies, and so there was much significance in being able to see into it. Jesus' death had made a way into the presence of God – an idea emphasised by a later New Testament writer:

> *We have then, my brothers, complete freedom to go into the Most Holy Place by means of the death of Jesus. He opened for us a new way, a living way, through the curtain – that is, through his own body.*
>
> *Hebrews 10:19–20*

Christ of St John of the Cross, *Salvador Dali.
Discuss the symbolism of this painting.*

The impression made on the centurion is emphasised. He saw Jesus as 'the Son of God', 'a son of God', or 'a good man' as some manuscripts suggest. We are told of some women who remained faithful to Jesus.

LUKE Luke tells us of Jesus' cry from the cross as he died.

MATTHEW Matthew adds details of an earthquake at the time of the death of Jesus, and of a resurrection, symbolising that death was now conquered.

184

ACTIVITIES

1 Look up Psalm 22. Make a note of all the verses paralleled in the accounts of the crucifixion.

2 List the words Jesus spoke from the cross, as suggested in the Gospel you are studying. Write a paragraph about each to show its significance.

ACTIVITY

Answer the following questions, with reference to Mark 15:33–9, Luke 23:44–7 or Matthew 27:45–54:

a) What unusual event happened between noon and 3 p.m.?

b) What is the significance of the cry of Jesus beginning, 'Eloi, Eloi . . .'?

c) What interpretation did the Christian Church put on the tearing of the veil of the Temple?

d) What was the reaction of the army officer?

e) What other reactions to Jesus are suggested in the passages you have read in this Topic?

c) The Burial of Jesus

Read Mark 15:42–7, Luke 23:50–6, Matthew 27:57–66

MARK LUKE MATTHEW Joseph of Arimathea appears to have been a member of the Sanhedrin and was a secret disciple of Jesus. It was necessary to bury the body before the Sabbath began at 6 p.m., so Joseph showed considerable courage in requesting permission and placing the body in a rock tomb, protected by a large stone. The fact that the women saw where the body was placed is stressed, in preparation for the events of Easter Sunday.

LUKE Luke emphasises that the women prepared the necessary spices for the anointing, and then rested on the Sabbath.

MATTHEW Matthew says that the new tomb used for the burial of Jesus had been prepared by Joseph for his own use. Matthew also includes details of the guarding of the tomb, possibly because at the time his Gospel was written the common theory was that the disciples had stolen the body of Jesus (see Matthew 28:11–15).

ACTIVITIES

1 A recent newspaper article reported that scholars have now fixed the date of the crucifixion to either 7 April AD 30 or 3 April AD 33, both Fridays. These are the only possible dates which fit the biblical evidence. Look back at the chart you made in Topic 7, p. 44, and discuss the implications of this new evidence.

2

Out of Reach

Reaching – I can't reach far enough.
So someone stretched out a hand.
And someone put a nail in it!

John Dutton

Discuss the meaning of this very short poem.

3 It has been suggested that Jesus did not die when he was crucified and that he later revived in the cool tomb. Look through the passages you have read in this Topic and then write a paragraph on what you think of this suggestion.

4 Find as many Christian hymns as you can about the death of Jesus. 'There is a green hill far away' and 'When I survey the wondrous cross' are two examples. For each hymn, list:

a) information included from the Gospels;

b) the Christian interpretation given to the stories;

c) encouragements given to Christian response and commitment.

ACTIVITIES

Coventry Cathedral – charred cross.

1 Discuss why the cross has become the symbol of Christianity.

2 Answer the following questions, briefly:

a) Who carried Jesus' cross?

b) What is the meaning of the name 'Golgotha'?

c) Who had Jesus' clothing?

d) What was written on the notice on the cross?

e) At what time did Jesus die?

f) What happened in the Temple at the time of Jesus' death?

g) Who witnessed both the crucifixion and the burial?

h) What do you know about Joseph of Arimathea?

i) Why was Pilate surprised that Jesus was dead?

j) Where was the body of Jesus buried?

To Keep You Thinking

1 **Christian observance of Good Friday**
Consider why the name 'Good Friday' was given to the day of the crucifixion and how Christians commemorate it today.

2 **The Christian doctrine of the atonement**
Christians believe that Jesus, through his death, brought about a reconciliation between people and God. Find some Christian hymns that suggest this doctrine.

The End and the Beginning

'Christ . . . was buried and . . . was raised to life three days later, as written in the Scriptures . . .'

Setting the Scene

The writers of the Gospels agree that the end of their accounts is the beginning of another story. Luke continues the story in a second volume, the Acts of the Apostles. For Jesus, death was not the end, for he was raised from the dead and gave his followers instructions to spread the Good News throughout the world. Paul, writing to the Christians in Corinth some 20 years after the death of Jesus, said, 'Christ . . . was raised to life three days later . . .'. More recently, the comment has been made that the Gospels end not with a funeral but with a festival.

Many theories have been suggested as to what happened on the Sunday after the crucifixion of Jesus, some of which we shall consider briefly in this Topic. The evidence of the Gospels is that, when the first disciples visited the tomb, they found it empty, and that Jesus appeared alive to many of his followers. Paul, writing before the Gospels were written, suggests that over 500 people saw him on one occasion (1 Corinthians 15:6).

There are a number of differences between the accounts in the Synoptic Gospels. This does not necessarily mean that there are contradictions. It may indicate that we have independent reports of what happened, and the differences between them are similar to the differences between various modern newspaper reports of the same event.

To Help You Understand

a) The Resurrection

Read Mark 16:1–8, Luke 24:1–12, Matthew 28:1–15

MARK
LUKE
MATTHEW It is significant that the first visitors to the tomb were women. It has been suggested that the early Christians were so convinced of the continuing presence of Jesus with them after his death that they invented the Resurrection accounts to explain their experience. If this had been the case, it is unlikely that women would have been given the privilege of being first at the tomb and of seeing the risen Jesus, for women were considered to be unreliable witnesses.

After 6 p.m. on the Saturday it would have been possible for the women to buy the necessary spices. At first light they took them to the tomb. On the way they realised that they would be unable to move the vast stone which sealed the entrance. To their amazement, however, they found that the stone had already been removed, and when they entered the tomb they were further alarmed by the presence of a young man. He announced that Jesus had been raised: the climax of the Gospel. A message was to be given to the disciples that Jesus would meet them in Galilee (look back at Mark 14:28). Peter is singled out to be given this news. The story ends on a strange note in Mark's Gospel, for the women leave the tomb, absolutely terrified.

A first-century tomb.
Why would it have been so difficult for women to move such a stone?

LUKE Luke records that there were two men in the tomb who reminded the women of Jesus' predictions about his suffering and resurrection. The women reported to the disciples what had happened, but the reaction of the disciples was that their story was nonsense. However, Luke records that Peter then visited the tomb – a story that is given in more detail in the fourth Gospel (John 20:1–10).

MATTHEW Matthew includes a comment about an earthquake (see also Matthew 27:51). The young man is said to be an angel (do you remember what the word 'angel' means?). Matthew also includes an account of an appearance of Jesus to the women and of their joyous worship.

Matthew also gives details of the soldiers guarding the tomb: that they fainted with fear at the appearance of the angel and that they were later bribed by the chief priests to say that the disciples had stolen the body while they slept! Matthew includes these comments as apparently this was the official explanation being given at the time he wrote his Gospel.

The Garden tomb, at a site to the north of Jerusalem, gives a good impression of a first-century tomb.
Why do you think some Christians prefer to remember the Resurrection in this setting rather than within the Church of the Holy Sepulchre?

In 1878 a Greek inscription was discovered in Nazareth which probably dates from the reign of the Emperor Claudius (AD 41–54). The following are extracts from the decree, which is now in the Louvre in Paris:

> *Ordinance of Caesar. It is my pleasure that graves and tombs remain undisturbed in perpetuity . . . If any man lay information that another has either demolished them, or has in any other way extracted the buried, or has maliciously transferred them, or has displaced the sealing or other stones, against such a one I order that a trial be instituted . . . Let it be absolutely forbidden for anyone to disturb them. In the case of contravention I desire that the offender be sentenced to capital punishment on charge of violation of sepulture [tomb].*

It may be of great significance that this decree was found near Nazareth, the home town of Jesus, whose disciples had apparently been accused of grave-robbing!

The Nazareth decree.

ACTIVITIES

1 Answer the following questions, briefly:

   a) Name two women who visited the tomb early on the Sunday morning.

   b) Why had there been a delay between Jesus' burial and this visit?

   c) Why did the women visit the tomb?

   d) Why were they concerned as they arrived?

   e) What puzzled them at the tomb?

   f) What frightened them at the tomb?

   g) What message was given to them?

   h) Who did they have to pass the message on to?

   i) Why were they unlikely to be believed?

   j) What official story accounted for the disappearance of the body?

2 Imagine that you are a detective hired by the authorities in Jerusalem to investigate what has happened to the body of Jesus. As you study the accounts in this Topic, imagine that you are able to interview the key witnesses. Write a report on the case.

b) The Ending of Mark's Gospel
Read Mark 16:9–20

MARK These verses do not appear in many old manuscripts of Mark's Gospel. Mary Magdalene is reintroduced in verse 9, having already appeared in verse 1. The style of these verses, in the form of a list of appearances, is very different from the rest of the Gospel. In fact, as we shall see, the list is compiled from the other Gospels and the Acts of the Apostles. For these reasons, many scholars believe that these last 12 verses of the Gospel were added by a later writer.

If verse 8 was the original end of the Gospel, it would seem very unsatisfactory – the women leaving the tomb and saying nothing to anyone because of their fear. For this reason it has been suggested that perhaps the original ending was lost, or that Mark was unable to complete the Gospel, so it was completed by a later writer who summarised the other accounts which were in existence at that time:

- **Jesus Appears to Mary Magdalene** (see John 20:11–18),

- **Jesus Appears to Two Disciples** (see Luke 24:13–35),

- **Jesus Appears to the Eleven** (see Luke 24:36–49, Matthew 28:16–20, John 20:19–23 and Acts 1:6–8),

- **Jesus Is Taken up to Heaven** (see Luke 24:50–3 and Acts 1:9–11).

A Celtic cross. What do you think this empty cross with a circle symbolises?

c) The Walk to Emmaus
Read Luke 24:13–35 (Mark 16:12–13)

LUKE Emmaus was about seven miles **MARK** (11 km) from Jerusalem, according to Luke, but the site cannot be identified with any certainty. Only one of the disciples, Cleopas, is named. It may well be that the other was his wife (look up John 19:25 to find out a possible name). They would not have expected to be joined by Jesus so, preoccupied with their conversation, they did not recognise him as he joined them. In explaining recent events to Jesus, Cleopas referred to him as a prophet and the one who was going to set Israel free. They were reminded of the teaching of the scriptures that the Messiah must suffer before entering his glory.

It was the saying of the blessing and the breaking of the bread that helped them to recognise Jesus. This is an interesting reminder of the Last Supper and of the teaching about the Messianic banquet.

Jesus then disappeared, and Cleopas and his companion returned to Jerusalem to be told that the Lord was alive and had appeared to Simon Peter.

ACTIVITIES

1 Look up the references given above and notice how the compiler of the list used the material available to him.

2 Discuss the reasons why Mark 16:9–20 was probably not part of the original Gospel.

3 Read again Mark 16:14–18. Make a list of the consequences that would follow the preaching of the good news.

ACTIVITIES

1 Answer the following questions:

a) Name two of the people shown in this well-dressing.

b) Where were they travelling to?

c) Where had they come from?

d) What conversation were they having?

e) Why did they not recognise the mysterious stranger?

f) Explain the significance of what happened later in their home.

2 Discuss the importance of the three titles used of Jesus in the passage you have just read.

The Church Missionary Society headquarters in London. When you have studied section d) on p. 192, discuss the appropriateness of this inscription.

The Triangular Lodge, Rushton. The builder of this unusual lodge wished to express his belief in the doctrine of the Trinity, so everything is in threes. What is the doctrine of the Trinity?

d) Jesus Appears to His Disciples

Read Luke 24:36–49, Matthew 28:16–20 (Mark 16:14–18)

LUKE When Jesus appeared to his **MATTHEW** disciples he used the familiar **MARK** greeting 'Shalom . . .'. They were invited to touch him and he ate, so providing convincing evidence that he was not a ghost. Again there is teaching from the scriptures to help them to see that suffering and resurrection were in the plan of God. They were then given instructions for the future. They are witnesses of the risen Lord and must take the message about repentance and forgiveness of sins to all nations, after the promised Holy Spirit has come to them.

MATTHEW Matthew's account is set in Galilee. It is interesting that some followers still doubted at this point. As well as preaching, the disciples were told here to baptise in the name of the Father, the Son and the Holy Spirit. Some scholars believe that this was a later addition to the Gospel, as it states a belief in the Trinity.

Matthew ends his Gospel with the assurance that the presence of Jesus will remain with his followers to the end of the age, a reminder of the phrase from the first chapter of the Gospel, 'God is with us' (Matthew 1:23).

ACTIVITIES

1 Discuss the following quotation from Tertullian, who lived in the second century AD:

> *The Son of God was crucified. I am not ashamed, because it is shameful. The Son of God died. It is credible because it is absurd. He was buried and rose again. It is certain because it is impossible.*
>
> *Tertullian*, The Flesh of Christ, 5

2 Answer the following questions, with reference to Mark 16:14–18, Luke 24:36–49 or Matthew 28:16–20:

   a) Where is this account set?

   b) How did Jesus try to convince his followers that he was alive?

   c) What commission was given to the disciples?

   d) What response was expected from those who heard their message?

   e) What do you think actually convinced the disciples that Jesus was alive?

Belief in the Resurrection

We discussed, opposite, a comment by an early Christian, Tertullian, that it is impossible that Jesus could rise again. Many people today might well agree with his comment, but not necessarily with the conclusion which he draws from it!

Many theories have been put forward to explain the accounts we have studied. The following are just a few of them:

- Jesus did not actually die, but revived in the cool tomb and got out of it, perhaps with help from the disciples.

- The disciples stole the body and then invented the stories to convince people that Jesus was alive.

- The women did not find the body of Jesus because they went to the wrong tomb.

- The followers of Jesus experienced a series of hallucinations or visions because they expected Jesus to rise from the dead.

- The stories are not to be understood literally but simply indicate that the spiritual Jesus lives on.

Some of the ideas put forward by Christians who believe that Jesus actually rose from the dead are:

- The differences between the Gospels suggest that the disciples did not produce an 'agreed version' of the stories or invent them but that they are reliable accounts.

- The empty tomb, together with the accounts of the appearances, are convincing evidence.

- The disciples were soon preaching that Jesus was alive, and the authorities were unable to produce the dead body of Jesus to prove them wrong.

- The disciples were soon fearlessly risking death for their beliefs. This is difficult to explain if Christianity is based on a fraud.

- *It is certain because it is impossible.*

  Tertullian

  God raised him from death

  Acts 3:15

I know that.....
My Redeemer Liveth

What Christian beliefs and symbolism are illustrated on this card?

ACTIVITIES

1 Discuss the above theories.

2 Answer all sections of this essay:

   a) Which people saw the empty tomb?

   b) Describe two appearances of the risen Jesus.

   c) Discuss two of the theories put forward to explain the Resurrection stories.

   d) What arguments are put forward to show that it is unlikely that the disciples invented the Resurrection accounts?

e) Jesus Is Taken up to Heaven

Read Luke 24:50–3 (Mark 16:19–20)

LUKE These two brief passages end the
MARK Gospels of Luke and Mark. The
Ascension has been described as a necessary
conclusion to the story of Jesus. After the
Resurrection it was important that the disciples
should understand that the physical presence of
Jesus would not remain with them for long. So
at Bethany, on the Mount of Olives, they were
convinced that he had returned to the presence
of the Father. Luke continues this account at the
beginning of Acts where he says, '. . . a cloud hid
him from their sight.' He emphasises the
worship and joy of the disciples and ends his
account where he began in chapter 1: with a
scene of worship in the Temple.

ACTIVITIES

1 It has been suggested that rather than
   the 'Ascension of Jesus' this event
   should be referred to as the 'Exultation
   of Jesus'. Discuss the difference
   between the two terms.

2 Find a hymn about the Ascension.
   Discuss what it suggests about the
   significance of this event.

3 Obtain a copy of either the Apostles'
   Creed or the Nicene Creed (you will
   find both in a prayer or service book).
   List the points of the creed which
   seem to be based on events recorded
   in the Gospels.

What do clouds symbolise in the Gospels? Look back to pp. 124–5.

To Keep You Thinking

1 **Celebration of Easter**
   Discuss with Christians how they celebrate this festival.

2 **Celebration of the Ascension**
   Discuss what you think this festival means to Christians.

ACTIVITIES

1 Check that you have completed all the lists of information from the Gospels, and revise them!

2 Look back at the introduction to the Gospel you are studying. Check that you understand how the writer develops his theme throughout the Gospel.

3 Write a paragraph to answer the following question on the Gospel you are studying:

MARK How successful do you consider the author of Mark's Gospel to have been in outlining 'the Good News about Jesus Christ, the Son of God' (Mark 1:1)?

LUKE What do you consider to be Luke's particular contribution in writing his 'orderly account' (Luke 1:3)?

MATTHEW How does the author of Matthew's Gospel present 'Jesus Christ, a descendant of David, who was a descendant of Abraham' (Matthew 1:1)?

4 Ask any Christians you know when, where and why they might read or listen to readings from the Gospels.

5 The Resurrection and Ascension began a new chapter in the lives of the followers of Jesus, who were to be his witnesses. Study carefully the outline of their preaching (below) as recorded in the Acts of the Apostles. Use it to revise the text you have studied, making notes of passages in the Gospel which give details of the points made in the *Kerygma*.

Christ in Glory, *Llandaff Cathedral, by Epstein. How successful do you consider the artist to have been in presenting his subject?*

An Outline Of The Kerygma (The Preaching Of The Early Christians):

The prophecies are fulfilled, and the New Age has begun.
The Messiah, born of David's line, has appeared.
He is Jesus of Nazareth, God's Servant, who
Went about doing good and healing by God's power,
Was crucified according to God's purpose,
Was raised from the dead on the third day,
Is now exalted to God's right hand,
And will come in glory for judgment.
Therefore let all repent, believe and be baptised for
the forgiveness of sins and the gift of the Holy Spirit.

Appendix

Source Details of Extracts Quoted in the Text

Quotations from Josephus are from either *Antiquities of the Jews* or *Wars of the Jews*, translated by William Whiston and published in *The Works of Flavius Josephus* by Fleming H Revell Company, New York, in the nineteenth century. Josephus wrote towards the end of the first century AD and gives us a unique insight into Jewish life in that period.

Topic 2
The extract from an article by Tom Fleming about Jerusalem, 'City where the past is always present', was written for the Easter edition of the *Radio Times*, 14 April 1984.

Topic 4
The extract from an Arabic passage from Josephus' *Antiquities of the Jews* was translated by Professor Shlomo Pines and published in the *Journal of the Israeli Academy of Science and Humanities*, 1973.
The letter from Ignatius, Bishop of Antioch, to the church at Tralles was written as Ignatius was being taken to his martyrdom in Rome. The *Letter of Ignatius to Tralles*, the *Epistles of Pliny*, the *Annals of Tacitus* and Suetonius' *Life of Claudius* and *Life of Nero* are all quoted in *Documents of the Christian Church* edited by Henry Bettenson and published by Oxford University Press.

Topic 5
Also quoted in *Documents of the Christian Church* (see above) are Eusebius, *Ecclesiastical History*, Irenaeus, *Against Heresy*, and Westcott, *Canon of the New Testament*.

Topic 6
C S Lewis, the author of *Miracles* (Collins, 1947) is perhaps better known for his children's books including *The Lion, The Witch and the Wardrobe*, and his *Screwtape Letters*.

'Tell out, my soul . . .' was written some 30 years ago by Bishop Timothy Dudley-Smith on first seeing the *New English Bible*'s translation of the Magnificat. It now appears in many modern hymn books.

Topic 7
The translation by Professor E M Blaiklock of a papyrus in the British Museum was published in *Out of the Earth* (Paternoster Press, 1957).
The extract from 'In Search of Christ', an article written by Tom Davies, appeared in *The Observer*, 23 December, 1979.
The Eastern Star newspaper was published in 1964 by the Religious Education Press and is now out of print.
The Alternative Service Book 1980 is the service book used in many Anglican churches today.

Topic 9
The two verses from the hymn 'Praise to the Holiest in the height . . .' are part of Cardinal John Henry Newman's poem 'The Dream of Gerontius'. The hymn is in many hymn books.

Topic 10
Alec McCowen's *Personal Mark* is published by Hamish Hamilton, 1984.
Professor William Barclay wrote commentaries on all the books of the New Testament in the series *The Daily Study Bible*. This extract is from *The Gospel of Mark* (The Saint Andrew Press, 1964).

Topic 11
The quotation from the interview with Len Murray, a Christian and former Trades Union leader, was published in *Viewpoint* 1980, the magazine of the Inter-Schools Christian Fellowship.

Topic 12
The Dead Sea Scrolls in English was translated by G Vermes and is published by Penguin Books.
'What is Leprosy?' is from *New Day*, the magazine of The Leprosy Mission.

Topic 13

The article concerning Jesus' belief in demons was written by John and Eileen Trevenna and appeared in the *Methodist Recorder*, 25 August 1988.

There is a further extract from Professor Barclay's *The Gospel of Mark* (see notes for Topic 10).

'Begone unbelief . . .', written by John Newton, is in many hymn books. As well as 'Amazing grace . . .', the many other hymns he wrote include 'Glorious things of thee are spoken . . .' and 'How sweet the name of Jesus sounds . . .'

Topic 14

The quotation from the *Mishnah* is given in R T France's *The Man They Crucified* (Inter Varsity Press, 1975, republished in 1989 under the title *Jesus The Radical*). Chapter 7 of that book gives a very good background to the controversies of Jesus' ministry.

Topic 15

The comment of T W Manson is in *The Sayings of Jesus* (SCM Press, 1949).

The quotations about the Beatitudes are from *The Man They Crucified* (see notes to Topic 14).

David Field's *Christianity in the Modern World* (Hulton, 1983) is a useful book for the Contemporary Issues syllabuses of GCSE.

There is a quotation from Professor Barclay's *The Gospel of Matthew* (The Saint Andrew Press, 1965). See also notes for Topic 10.

The well-known quotation from St Francis of Assisi is quoted in *In Every Corner Sing* (Nelson, 1972) and in a number of books of prayers. It has also been set to music and is in a number of modern hymn books.

The quotation from Confucius is in *The Bible of the World*, edited by R O Ballou, published by Kegan Paul in 1940 but now out of print.

Topic 16

The 'newspaper' article is from the *Eastern Star* (see notes for Topic 7).

The comment from C S Lewis is in *Mere Christianity* (Fontana Books, 1955).

The extract from a preface to the Mass is from *The Roman Missal*, published by Goodliffe Neale Ltd, 1974.

Topic 17

The extract from the covenant service is from the *Methodist Service Book*, published by the Methodist Conference Office, 1975.

The prayer is from Susan Williams' *Lord of our World*, a collection of modern collects, published by Falcon in 1973.

Topic 19

'Two Went Up Into The Temple To Pray' by Richard Crashaw is included in *English Religious Verse*, compiled by G L May (Everyman's Library, J M Dent, 1937).

Topic 20

The extract from the Roman papyrus is quoted in Professor E M Blaiklock's *Out of the Earth* (see notes for Topic 7).

Topic 23

'The Declaration on the Relation of the Church to Non-Christian Religions' appeared in the Catholic magazine *The Universe*.

Topic 24

'Out of Reach', the brief poem by John Dutton, is included in *100 Contemporary Christian Poets*, edited by Gordon Bailey (Lion, 1983).

Topic 25

The extracts from the Nazareth Decree are included in *Out of the Earth* (see notes for Topic 7).

The quotation from Tertullian from *The Flesh of Christ* is quoted in the *Lion Concise Book of Christian Thought*, 1984.

The outline of the *Kerygma* is from Professor A M Hunter's *The Gospel According to St Paul*, published by SCM Press in 1966.

Biblical Index

Mark's Gospel

Reference	Topic	Reference	Topic	Reference	Topic	Reference	Topic	Reference	Topic
1:1–8	9 a)	4:1–20	11 a)	7:24–30	13 c)	10:35–45	18 f)	14:10–11	22 c)
1:9–11	9 b)	4:21–5	11 b)	7:31–7	12 g)	10:46–52	12 k)	14:12–21	22 d)
1:12–13	9	4:26–9	11 c)					14:22–6	22 e)
1:14–20	10 a)	4:30–4	11 d)	8:1–21	13 i)	11:1–11	21 b)	14:27–31	22 g)
1:21–8	13 a)	4:35–41	13 f)	8:22–6	12 h)	11:12–25	21 d)	14:32–42	23 a)
1:29–34	12 a)			8:27–30	16 c)	11:27–33	21 e)	14:43–52	23 b)
1:35–9	12 b)	5:1–20	13 b)	8:31 – 9:1	16 d)			14:53–64	23 c)
1:40–5	12 c)	5:21–4	12 l)			12:1–12	21 f)	14:65	23 d)
		5:25–34	12 f)	9:2–13	16 e)	12:13–17	21 g)	14:66–72	23 e)
2:1–12	12 d)	5:35–43	12 l)	9:14–29	13 d)	12:18–27	21 h)		
2:13–17	10 b)			9:30–2	18 a)	12:28–34	21 i)	15:1–5	23 f)
2:18–22	14 a)	6:1–6	14 g)	9:33–7	18 b)	12:35–7	21 j)	15:6–20	23 h)
2:23–8	14 b)	6:7–13	17 a)	9:38–41	18 c)	12:38–40	21 k)	15:21–32	24 a)
		6:14–29	16 b)	9:42–50	18 d)	12:41–4	21 l)	15:33–41	24 b)
3:1–6	14 c)	6:30–44	13 g)					15:42–7	24 c)
3:7–12	14 d)	6:45–56	13 h)	10:1–12	19 d)	13:1–37	19 g)		
3:13–19	10 c)			10:13–16	19 e)			16:1–8	25 a)
3:20–30	14 e)	7:1–13	14 h)	10:17–31	17 f)	14:1–2	22 a)	16:9–20	25 b) – e)
3:31–5	14 f)	7:14–23	14 i)	10:32–4	18 e)	14:3–9	22 b)		

Matthew's Gospel

Reference	Topic	Reference	Topic	Reference	Topic	Reference	Topic	Reference	Topic
1:1–17	8 a)	8:14–17	12 a)	13:1–23	11 a)	18:21–35	11 j)	26:14–16	22 c)
1:18–25	8 b)	8:23–7	13 f)	13:24–30	11 f)			26:17–25	22 d)
				13:31–2	11 d)	20:1–16	11 k)	26:26–30	22 e)
2:1–12	8 c)	9:1–8	12 d)	13:33–43	11 e), f)	20:20–8	18 f)	26:31–5	22 g)
2:13–23	8 d)	9:9–13	10 b)	13:44	11 g)			26:36–46	23 a)
		9:18–26	12 l)	13:45–6	11 h)	21:1–11	21 b)	26:47–56	23 b)
3:1–12	9 a)	9:20–2	12 f)	13:47–52	11 i)	21:12–17	21 d)	26:57–66	23 c)
3:13–17	9 b)					21:23–7	21 e)	26:67–8	23 d)
		10:1–4	10 c)	14:13–21	13 g)	21:33–46	21 f)	26:69–75	23 e)
4:1–11	9	10:5–15	17 a)	14:22–33	13 h)				
4:18–22	10 a)	10:16–25	19 g)			22:15–22	21 g)	27:1–14	23 f)
		10:26–7	18 j)	15:1–9	14 h)	22:23–33	21 h)	27:15–31	23 h)
5 – 7	15	10:28–31	18 k)	15:21–8	13 c)			27:32–44	24 a)
		10:32–3	18 l)	15:32–9	13 i)	25:1–13	11 l)	27:45–56	24 b)
[6:5–15	19 a)]	10:34–6	18 m)			25:14–30	11 m)	27:57–66	24 c)
				16:13–20	16 c)	25:31–46	11 n)		
[7:7–11	19 a)]	11:2–6	16 a)	16:21–8	16 d)			28:1–15	25 a)
		12:9–14	14 c)			26:1–5	22 a)	28:16–20	25 d)
8:1–4	12 c)	12:46–50	14 f)	17:1–13	16 e)	26:6–13	22 b)		
8:5–13	12 e)								

Luke's Gospel

Index